T0361560

Diary of a Crisis

Diary of a Crisis

Israel in Turmoil

Saul Friedländer

VERSO

London • New York

First published by Verso 2024
© Saul Friedländer 2024

All rights reserved

The moral rights of the author have been asserted

1 3 5 7 9 10 8 6 4 2

Verso
UK: 6 Meard Street, London W1F 0EG
US: 388 Atlantic Avenue, Brooklyn, NY 11217
versobooks.com

Verso is the imprint of New Left Books

ISBN-13: 978-1-80429-678-3
ISBN-13: 978-1-80429-680-6 (UK EBK)
ISBN-13: 978-1-80429-681-3 (US EBK)

British Library Cataloguing in Publication Data
A catalogue record for this book is available from the British Library

Library of Congress Cataloging-in-Publication Data

Names: Friedländer, Saul, 1932- author.
Title: Diary of a crisis : Israel in turmoil / Saul Friedländer.
Other titles: Israel in turmoil
Description: London ; New York : Verso, 2024.
Identifiers: LCCN 2024006951 (print) | LCCN 2024006952 (ebook) | ISBN
  9781804296783 | ISBN 9781804296813 (US ebk)
Subjects: LCSH: Friedländer, Saul, 1932——Diaries. | Netanyahu, Binyamin.
  | Arab-Israeli conflict—1993- | Palestinian Arabs—Politics and
  government—21st century. | Israel—Politics and government—21st
  century.
Classification: LCC DS128.2 .F75 2024 (print) | LCC DS128.2 (ebook) | DDC
  956.9405/5092 [B] —dc23/eng/20240315
LC record available at https://lccn.loc.gov/2024006951
LC ebook record available at https://lccn.loc.gov/2024006952

Typeset in Fournier by MJ & N Gavan, Truro, Cornwall
Printed and bound by CPI Group (UK) Ltd, Croydon CR0 4YY

To Orna

Contents

In the Guise of an Introduction

As my editor called it, this text is a *cri de coeur*. In December 2022, I had no intention of writing anything new beyond what had already been written and almost forgotten. But in January 2023, here I was, busy inscribing daily a kind of a journal of Israeli political events, quite instinctively adding, by association, comments that came to mind and various reminiscences. All this was done on the spur of the moment. Indeed, *un cri de coeur*. Why?

It took me a few days to understand that the political coalition Netanyahu had set up following the election was a monster, a monster with teeth that could devour the country. It took me a few more days to realize that each Israeli—those who lived in the country first and foremost, but also those who lived elsewhere and were attached to it, as I was—had to contribute what they could to stop the monster. I couldn't do more, because of age and health, but a diary seemed better than nothing.

Of course, I could have relied on the assurances given by our prime minister, that the liberal, democratic regime enjoyed by Israel would in no case be erased, that he was completely in charge in deciding what was allowed and what was not. It was possibly his intention when he promised this, but two elements of the situation made me wary. I knew what political fanaticism was, and I knew that Netanyahu was desperately attempting to get rid of the indictments which could land him in jail. His new alliances would allow him to subvert the judicial system to a point that would make it subservient to the political majority in power and thus allow him to dodge the sword hanging over his head.

Over the spring and summer, Israelis became increasingly aware of what the stakes were. They protested in the face of a minority of messianic fanatics and political autocrats, setting up an opposition that promised to bring a new unity and energy, beyond sheer politics, to a society that had seemed asleep for many years. However, as I note in these pages, the pro-democracy movement was silent on the Palestinian question, which is at the root of Israeli's deeper problems.

Then the Hamas attack of October 7 occurred. For Israel, totally unprepared, it was an earthquake. A war started that I describe in the second part of this diary. Nobody knows, as these lines are written, how it will end.

I

On the Brink

Tuesday, January 17, 2023

It's easy to shout "enough!" when ensconced in California. But it has become impossible for me, at ninety plus, to fly safely from here to Tel Aviv (fifteen hours there and sixteen hours back). Yet Orna and I cannot think of anything else. We scrutinize the daily news in Hebrew, we dissect it, we chew it, we swallow it, and we vomit. It reminds me of the German film with Curd Jürgens (*Des Teufels General*) about the disenchanted Nazi pilot Ernst Udet in which, at some point, Udet declares that one cannot eat as much as one would like to throw up. Somehow the sentence stayed with me over the years and here it is, handy again. Udet apparently committed suicide in 1941.

Well, we aren't so far along yet, but how will this end? Last week Netanyahu's docile justice minister, Yariv Levin, unveiled bills that would allow the government to control the appointment of judges and restrict the Supreme Court's ability to strike down legislation. Who could have imagined that in Israel in 2023, a prime minister would try to overturn the whole legal system with the help of a tenuous ultra-right-wing and ultrareligious coalition, to escape three indictments for fraud, bribery, and breach of trust? Mass demonstrations have started against the government and its plans, but will they be enough to compel

Netanyahu to backtrack? And if the coalition does not give in, and no new elections are in sight, what then?

This diary is open-ended. For the time being, it is just my private chronicle of an ongoing drama that will either lead to a celebration of the victory of democracy or an admission that the vibrant country I lived and worked in for decades is dead; that something else, something unacceptable, has taken its place.

Friday, January 20

Two days ago the Israeli Supreme Court voted by a majority of 10 to 1 that Aryeh Deri—the leader of the Shas party and Netanyahu's main ally, whom he appointed interior minister —could not serve due to two previous sentences for tax fraud and his own promise, in 2022, not to seek further public office in order to avoid a felony sentence. Instead he scrambled into a place in the present coalition. We do not know yet how Netanyahu will react to the Supreme Court's decision.

In many ways the new Israeli coalition is similar to other ultra-right governments in Hungary, Poland, Italy, and Turkey, and to the political program of the ultra-right-wing Republicans in the US (Trumpists). But it also has its specific characteristics. Thus, for example, in Europe, this kind of government is in the hands of a wealthy upper crust, supported by established religion, the army, and a majority of bamboozled "white trash" (intensely nationalist, xenophobic, and, more often than not, antisemitic). In the case of Trumpists, it is not supported by people of color. In Israel, however, Deri's party is essentially a party belonging to people of color, whose families immigrated in the 1950s from North Africa and the Middle East, who lived for years in dilap-idated transit camps and occupied the lowest strata of the labor market. These Sephardim (historically, Jews coming from Spain) were looked down upon by the Ashkenazim (Jews coming from Germany, and mainly from Eastern Europe).

I arrived in Israel from France, having earlier fled from Prague in 1939. It didn't help my parents. I was hidden, they were caught and murdered. The Israeli village in which my uncles lived and where I arrived in June 1948 was populated by German-speaking Czech Jews, the most Ashkenazi Ashkenazim you could imagine: no religion, little Hebrew, and all the habits of yesteryear, even as they were putting down new roots. Israel was not a refuge, it was a country that one called home, or "Heimat" if that was easier for you. But, unfortunately, racism existed in the new Heimat.

Let me be clear about this: soon after its creation, Israel, consciously or not, became a racist society. For all of us Ashkenazim, it was obvious that the newcomers from North Africa were somehow inferior types, not officially of course, not legally—we were not South Africa—but implicitly, practically.

We were not only almost unconscious of our racism toward the immigrants from North Africa, but totally oblivious of the existence among us of a small Arab minority living on the margins of the State, at its eastern border, and subjected to military administration by Ben-Gurion's socialist government.

At that time, I was working as Nahum Goldmann's political secretary. Goldmann was the president of the World Jewish Congress and the World Zionist Organization. Politically, he was on the center-left and helped finance various left-wing organizations and publications, such as Simha Flapan's *New Outlook*. He decided to make a trip to some of the Arab villages and visit some of the mayors to learn more about the situation. We were warmly received by one mayor, about whom I remember: but what submissiveness, what humiliation! On one side of the mayor's desk was a large photograph of Ben-Gurion; on the other side, a large photograph . . . of the founder of Zionism: Theodor Herzl.

The Israeli demographic majority shifted over time from the Ashkenazim to the Sephardim or Mizrahim (easterners, meaning Middle-Easterners), but the latter's social status did not change drastically. What changed was their political representation when, in 1977, the right-wing Menachem Begin and his Likud party won the elections. Begin had vociferously adopted the Mizrahim, while he himself was a Polish Jew and most of the members of his government remained Ashkenazim. But the Mizrahim felt that Begin had restored their dignity and they voted heavily for him. A few years later, in 1984, the Sephardi Chief Rabbi, Ovadia Yosef, founded the party that was to represent this Mizrahi electorate: "Shas" (Shomerei Sephardim, the guardians of Sephardim); his anointed disciple and successor was Aryeh Deri. Shas is strictly religious and right-wing, and it still somehow thinks in terms of the traditional hostility against Ashkenazim (although Netanyahu is as Ashkenazi as can be). Nonetheless, Deri and Bibi (Netanyahu's common nickname) have one major trait in common: both have been or are being indicted, the first for tax evasion, the second on three counts of corruption.

And Shas isn't the worst by any means. The new coalition includes truly abhorrent specimens: Bezalel Smotrich and his Religious Zionist Party; and Itamar Ben-Gvir, a former Rabbi Kahane disciple, and his Jewish Power contingent. I am sure that they will be quite prominent in the following pages.

A major difference between the Israeli right-wing coalition and run-of-the-mill authoritarian governments in power nowadays is the role of the army. Usually, the army supports a national authoritarian government. In present-day Israel, the army—including its boss, the Likud defense minister Yoav Gallant—have clearly indicated that all matters pertaining to the occupied Palestinian territories will remain its exclusive domain. Smotrich, the extreme right-wing ideologist whom Netanyahu appointed as finance minister and minister in the Defense Department in charge of civilian matters in Judea and Samaria—in other words, responsible for settlements and settlers in the Occupied Territories—was blocked by Gallant from interfering in the first case he instigated: the establishment of the new settlement Or Haim. Netanyahu had no choice but to support Gallant, probably nudged by his own Likud party and, some contend, by the White House . . . In his protest to the prime minister, Smotrich was joined by Ben-Gvir, but to no avail.

All of this does not turn the Israeli army into a fortress of legality; it is the melting pot of a multiethnic society, with the exception of its ultrareligious segment (to which I shall return presently). In that sense it is a people's army, but its handling of the Palestinian population is often brutal, particularly in the almost daily antiterrorist operations. It may be contributing to the noticeable brutalization of Israeli society. Yet in its firm stance against Smotrich and Ben-Gvir, it has created a further difficulty for Netanyahu's coalition, which is all to the good.

What I just wrote about the army is incorrect, if left at that: in an army that is among the most modern in the world, some of the infantry units ("Netzah Yehuda," among others) have, on occasion, brutalized the Palestinian population, sounding the alarm among Israeli and international human rights organizations. There is no doubt that this happens, but, do not let us forget, it happens in the context of heightened terrorist militancy instigated by Hamas and Islamic Jihad in the West Bank, and by Hezbollah in the north. Under such conditions, maintaining a thoroughly correct attitude is nearly impossible. Israel's problem is not the army as such but the decades-long occupation of the conquered territories.

As for the Israeli religious parties of today, they are both nationalist and ultra-Orthodox. Liberal Judaism never thrived in Israel. From the outset, Ben-Gurion, quite agnostic himself, accepted an arrangement whereby the religious aspects of private life (circumcision, bar mitzvah, marriage, divorce, funeral) would be enacted according to the rules of Orthodox Judaism. And, most importantly, at some later stage, the Knesset (the Israeli parliament) decided that the definition of who was a Jew would also depend on strict orthodoxy: a Jew who was born of a Jewish mother. This was essential for deciding who was entitled to citizenship and the benefits of the Law of Return. Conversions were considered valid only if performed by Orthodox rabbis. Over the decades, Conservative and Reform Judaism made some inroads, but only marginally so. In the meantime, relatively moderate Orthodox Jews (Mafdal, or National Religious Party) slowly dwindled. As for the ultra-Orthodox, also called Haredim, they are in a bizarre situation, as they do not recognize the State of Israel but have their own party (Agudath Israel, now merged with Degel HaTorah to become United Torah Judaism) and compete in elections—not because they have become more accommodating, but because they need financing for their schools (yeshivot) and other activities, and for their growing, impoverished, population.

As a result of these various changes, Netanyahu's administration comprises four religious parties: Torah Judaism, combining Degel HaTorah with Agudath Israel (ultra-Orthodox, but a regular fixture in Israeli coalitions, pursuing its own financial interests); Shas (an ultra-Orthodox Mizrahi offshoot of Agudath Israel); Religious Zionist (extreme nationalist, led by Smotrich);

and Jewish Power (also extreme nationalist, led by Ben-Gvir). There are still Haredim who do not recognize the state at all and do not cooperate, but they have become a small minority (Neturei Karta). The situation on the ground is actually most confusing, with rabbinical councils lording over Torah Judaism and Shas, and members of Torah Judaism belonging both to various Hasidic groups and the anti-Hasidic Litayim (Lithuanians), some voting for Ben-Gvir, etc. The religious map of Israel is a maze, but one fact is clear for the time being: the demographic balance is shifting rapidly in favor of the religious parties due to the extremely high birth rate of Orthodox families (at the beginning of 2023, 30 percent of the children in first grade were Orthodox).

The mysterious aspect of this situation is the weak presence of liberal Judaism in Israel. I have met quite a few deeply religious Israeli Jews who were the most accommodating, most understanding, and most liberal of people: my first father-in-law, Ben-Zion Meiry, who never said a word about the total absence of any religious observance in our growing family, or my very close friend and colleague, Uriel Tal, who, as I will show further on, wrote the most damning pieces about the Jewish religious fanatics. Where did all the liberals disappear to? Why couldn't their brand of humane Judaism thrive in the Jewish state? Why the accelerating rush toward fanaticism?

Saturday, January 21

Much has happened today. Smotrich announced that he would not participate in the weekly government meeting tomorrow, which may indicate he is thinking of bolting from the coalition and triggering new elections. This is, of course, the most optimistic scenario. On the other side of the political spectrum, Esther Hayut, the president of the Supreme Court and the first to take a public stand against justice minister Yariv Levin's "judicial reform," let it be known that if the Knesset approved the overhaul, she would not resign but would continue fighting. Among the opposition figures, Hayut is the most admirable, while the politicians who headed the previous government, such as Yair Lapid and Benny Gantz, have lost much of their authority.

Some 130,000 anti-Netanyahu demonstrators took to the streets in Israeli cities, 100,000 of them in Tel Aviv.

Sunday, January 22

Netanyahu "regretfully" fired Deri. The judicial reforms will possibly bring him back.

"Hi, elephant, you have become quite visible."

"Yes, everybody in the room knows me and, guess what, everybody loves me. I was everybody's pet for decades, but not as openly as today. Now, I mean everything for all those in power and for many other Israelis." As the reader will have guessed, this pet is none other than Israeli settling in the Occupied Territories. This is a very long story. I will only just begin it today.

Let's remember: the ideological and political father of Revisionist Zionism, Ze'ev Jabotinsky, pleaded for including "both sides of the Jordan" within his dreamed-for Jewish State. His successors became rather more modest and demanded Eretz Israel, that is, the whole of Palestine between the Jordan River and the Mediterranean Sea (as, on the morrow of World War I, the British government had separated Palestine from Trans-Jordan). All of these expectations remained rather theoretical, as between 1919 and May 1948 Palestine was turned into a British mandate by the League of Nations. After they had given contradictory secret assurances to both the Jews and the Arabs, and after promising a homeland to the Jews in Palestine in 1917 (the Balfour Declaration), the British became successively favorable to Jewish or Arab interests according to their immediate political aims.

Every colonial power was duplicitous in its day, but it seems to me that, in the Middle East in particular, British duplicity reached an apex. And, for good measure, the Colonial Office added a huge portion of antisemitism.

In November 1947, two years after the end of World War II and the Holocaust, and after a series of commissions of inquiry and vociferous debates, the United Nations voted the partition of Palestine between a Jewish state and a Palestinian state. The United States and the Soviet Union supported the decision; it was opposed by the Palestinians and the Arab states. I remember attending a huge celebration of the event at the Vel d'Hiv, the same cavernous hall in which the Jews of Paris had been held, in July 1942, before being sent to transit camps for deportation. The platform for dignitaries was so overcrowded that it crashed; some were injured. A bad omen.

The Palestinians launched an increasingly fierce guerrilla war against the Jewish population of the country; it turned into a generalized war involving Palestinian militias and the armies of the neighboring Arab states, plus Iraq, after the Israeli declaration of independence in May 1948. By 1949, Israel had won what became its War of Independence, and the Nakba ("catastrophe") for the Palestinians.

The 1948–49 war ended, among other things, with Israel controlling somewhat more than half the territory allocated to it in the 1947 partition plan and with hundreds of thousands of

Palestinian refugees, who had fled in terror after a string of massacres or after being driven away by the Israeli army on orders
from above. An uneasy armistice took hold with, over time,
incursions by Palestinian infiltrators and growing Israeli reprisals.
In October 1956 a brief war took place between Israel, France,
and Great Britain against Gamal Abdel Nasser's Egypt. The
obvious victory of these three strange bedfellows was annulled
by threats from the Soviet Union and an angry reaction from the
US president, Dwight Eisenhower.

Monday, January 23

A fundamental and dramatic change occurred in June 1967 with
the stunning Israeli victory in the Six-Day War and the occupation of the Gaza Strip, the Sinai Peninsula, the whole of the West
Bank of the Jordan, the Golan Heights, and, of course, the whole
of Jerusalem. Most Israelis considered this a miracle, and some
heard the "steps of the Messiah" (*paamei hamashiach*). Some,
very few, were wary of the consequences, and Zalman Aran,
the minister of education in Levi Eshkol's cabinet, famously
asked: "Wie kriecht man heraus?" (How does one crawl out?).
President Lyndon Johnson didn't demand the evacuation of the
Occupied Territories. In the Khartoum Resolution of September 1,1967, the Arab states proclaimed that there would be no
negotiations and no peace with Israel. Thus, the existing situation solidified and the first settlements followed: Gush Etzion
and several so-called military outposts. Even Eshkol, a socialist
prime minister, could not resist the pressure coming from the
right. Or, did he welcome it?

The Occupied Territories became a cancer in the Israeli body
politic and, even more so, in Israeli society. As my friend Jacob

Fried recently wrote to me: "Israel did not annex the territories; the territories annexed Israel."

Tuesday, January 24

Could all this end up in some kind of half-baked compromise whereby Netanyahu, in order to avoid international difficulties and too much internal turmoil, will rein in his most extreme and unreliable allies? Yesterday he traveled to Amman to promise King Abdullah that the status quo on Temple Mount would remain unchanged. It seems that he also refused to order the evacuation of a Bedouin village in the south of Jerusalem, Khan al-Ahmar, which for some time now has been a demand of the right. Such a compromise would be a logical endgame if our Houdini wasn't under three indictments and ready to take every political risk to avoid the probable outcome.

The governor of the Bank of Israel, Amir Yaron, warns Netanyahu of the dangerous international consequences for the country's economy if the judicial reform is implemented. According to the news, the PM dismissed the warning.

In the meantime, the ultrareligious Knesset members of Torah Judaism proceed with an initiative of their own: they introduce a bill preventing hospitals from bringing in hametz food (produced by leavened grains) during this coming Passover. And the whole coalition tries to insert new clauses into the Law of Return: for Jews only, not, for example, for grandchildren of mixed marriages, quarter Jews. It reminds them of nothing? Half Jewish, Quarter Jews, *Mischlinge ersten Grades, Mischlinge zweiten Grades*. What a shame!

Wednesday, January 25

Hundreds of senior economists and figures from the academic world, joined by thousands of students, have sent warning letters or joined the protests. All of this, according to Netanyahu, is but "a tsunami of lies." A previous head of the Shin Bet (the Israeli equivalent of the FBI) calls for a general strike to paralyze the country. Maybe nothing else will help.

Thursday, January 26

The major question regarding the post-1967 craziness and the standing occupation of the Palestinian territories is whether a messianic impulse is embedded in Zionism as such, or whether it mainly characterizes a segment, particularly a religious segment, of the population.

Zionism, during the period stretching from Theodor Herzl in the late nineteenth century to Begin's electoral victory in 1977, was essentially a secular movement, starting as such with Herzl himself, Zabotinsky, Chaim Weizmann, Ben-Gurion, and the major political parties (some of them originally Marxist) that dominated the political landscape. Until the Six-Day War the religious parties that actively participated in successive governments were moderate and accommodating (Yosef Burg's Mafdal, for example). But after that victory, they split and one wing became "messianic," seeing in the conquest of the whole of Eretz Israel the onset of redemption. As for Agudath Israel, it had no noticeable influence on political decisions and cared about its own interests only. As previously mentioned, private life in Israel was governed by religious rules, if and when a person needed to resort to them, but otherwise the religious presence was disregarded by an important part of the population. Now the newfangled demands of the religious parties have become one of the main dynamics in the internal conflict, and they may have a political majority supporting them in the Knesset.

The messianic settler movement, Gush Emunim ("the bloc of the faithful"), was founded after the Yom Kippur War of October 1973, in a meeting at Rabbi Zvi Yehuda Kook's Yeshivat Harav ("the rabbi's yeshiva"). The meeting brought together extreme right-wing and extreme Orthodox figures, all of them believing that messianic redemption had started with the conquest of the whole land of Israel in June 1967.

My friend Uriel Tal, whom I already mentioned, a prominent scholar of Jewish Studies at Tel Aviv University, presented a close analysis of Gush Emunim's publications, particularly of their magazine *Nekuda* (Point), and concluded that they were an Israeli version of fascism. They were. Uri did not hesitate, moreover, to compare the policy of settlements in the Occupied Territories to the Nazi colonization policy in the conquered East. Another late friend and colleague of mine, Amos Funkenstein, a polymath if there ever was one, compared Israeli policies toward the Palestinians to Nazi policies in the first years of the regime. I admit to not following Uri and Amos in these comparisons, because I feared that readers, when they read "Nazi," read "extermination," and that certainly was not what my friends meant.

Friday, January 27

Yesterday, a major operation in the Jenin refugee camp: ten Palestinians killed (including an elderly woman). Exchange of fire with the Gaza Strip. In the evening, a Palestinian from East Jerusalem ambushes people at the Neve Yaakov synagogue, north of Jerusalem: seven dead. Later, a thirteen-year-old Palestinian kid shoots and wounds two people. This is a terrible phase in an endless vicious circle. The ultras urge a fiercer clampdown; in my opinion, popular anti-Israeli violence can only be kept at a low level by the easing of restrictions on the Palestinian population and negotiations for a two-state solution.

The diehards on our side have a strong counter-argument: whereas at the beginning of the occupation, in the late 1960s and early 1970s, the Palestinian population did not cause major problems, this changed with the birth of Fatah and, more radically so, with the creation of Hamas (by Israel! in order to create a religious opposition to Fatah), with its lethal mixture of Palestinian nationalism and intense Islamic faith. The demonstration of this dangerous escalation came with Ariel Sharon's decision in 2004 to evacuate the Gaza Strip. Gaza first came under Fatah rule but, following local elections, Hamas took over, swept Fatah away, and has since instigated three wars with Israel, plus endless incidents. The obvious argument of our diehards is that any evacuation of the West Bank would be a repeat of the Gaza situation, with Hamas taking over the territory and their armed militias soon shooting at close range from their newly acquired Palestinian state at the most populous areas of Israel.

The answer to this is that peace means taking risks, probably with outside help: a demilitarized Palestinian state for years with some American presence on its territory, if necessary, and other pre-emptive measures of the same kind. If the Palestinians reject this kind of solution, then tension-lowering steps are the only way forward, for as long as it takes.

Nothing good can come out of Moshe Dayan's famous exhortation of 1953, on the tomb of a friend killed by a Palestinian infiltrator from the Gaza Strip ("Do not fear, brother Yaakov . . ."), and his vision of Israelis constantly living by the sword.

Sunday, January 29

Yesterday, Avihu Zakai, a former professor of history at Hebrew University, sent me the following quote from Jacob Talmon, the well-known, long-deceased Israeli historian of *The Origins of Totalitarian Democracy*:

> I began as a member of "Hashomer Hatzair" ["the young guardian," a Zionist Marxist political movement], in that atmosphere filled with emotions, under a crossfire from both sides: a messianic longing stemming from Eastern Europe and a Zionist fire from Eretz Israel. The messianic longing was born in me, the obsession, the *dibbuk* of the idea of salvation entered into me. [Talmon, "Socialism and Liberalism," *From the foundations* [Hebrew], 1962]

What Talmon meant by messianic fire from Eastern Europe is not entirely clear; he was probably alluding to Marxism, mixed with those vague longings for salvation that suffused the small and oppressed Jewish communities of Poland. This was not representative of the urban Jews of Warsaw or Krakow, and even less so of Jews from Germany or Western Europe of the pre-Nazi years. But because East European Jews of Talmon's generation were dominant among immigrants to Eretz Israel, the question of a messianic urge among those Zionists demands some more attention.

It may be remembered that I wondered whether the kind of messianic urge that erupted in Israel with victory in the Six-Day War had suffused Zionism from its very beginning. I still do not believe that religious talk of hearing the "steps of the Messiah" had anything to do with the kind of messianic longing mentioned by Talmon. I knew Talmon well and, as far as I could tell, he did not show the least sign of religiosity. There was an urge for salvation among the masses of East European Jews, but for a salvation from oppression, from life in the Golah, for Eretz Israel as the longed-for site of such salvation. Among the majority, there was no need for the whole land of Israel; a state was their maximum demand.

Incidentally, Talmon was one of the most courageous polemicists against the triumphalism in Israeli society following the Six-Day War and the early moves to settle the West Bank. In my view, his articles of those days in *Haaretz* were unmatched in their sharp analysis of the dire consequences of Israel's policies.

I didn't hold it against Talmon that, in 1961, when I resigned from my job at the Ministry of Defense and wished to resume my doctoral studies, he refused to find me a lowly teaching assistant's job in the Department of History at Hebrew University. (Following my two years with Goldmann, I could not continue moving from New York to Jerusalem and back, because I had gotten married and we had a child; thus I found a position in the Defense Ministry, where I worked as an assistant to Shimon Peres). I enjoyed the irony when in 1967 I was called from Geneva to Jerusalem to fill in for Talmon, who was leaving for a year at Princeton. Moshe Dayan, the much-acclaimed defense minister at the time, hated Talmon, and used a quote from Isaiah 41 calling him *tolaat Yaakov* (thou worm Jacob). Of course, Talmon was right, and today we face the consequences.

Monday, January 30

US Secretary of State Antony Blinken is in Israel, talking to Netanyahu. Let's hope that American warnings, if warnings there are, are not too half-hearted and that they address both the Palestinian issue and the anti-democratic policies of the coalition.

Some fifty law professors from American universities—among them Alan Dershowitz, in the past quite close to Netanyahu—have signed an open letter against the judicial reform project of our PM and his stooge Levin. I doubt that this will help; only US political pressure can. But will there be pressure?

Tuesday, January 31

It seems that there isn't a chance that Biden will press Netanyahu regarding the country's internal policies or even about the two-state solution. The US declarations are supposedly empty words; there are simply too many international problems that dominate American–Israeli relations (Iran, Ukraine, extending the Abraham agreements to additional Arab states, etc.). Moreover, with the upcoming presidential elections, Biden will not risk antagonizing part of the Jewish community. Realpolitik is what it is. It is also true, regarding the Palestinian issue, that Mahmoud Abbas, the elderly Fatah leader, is far from helpful when it comes to negotiations: he seems to have chosen confrontation by referring every problem to the UN, where the Palestinians are assured of an automatic majority but where decisions are mostly rhetorical.

Israeli drone attacks inside Iran (Ispahan) and in Northern Syria are even more frequent than usual. Does it mean that a generalized war is on the horizon? In flat landscapes the horizon may be far away, so shall we say "nearby"?

Wednesday, February 1

Khan al-Ahmar, the Bedouin hamlet in the south of Jerusalem, is a good reality test when it comes to distinguishing between declarations and policies. As I mentioned, some years ago the Supreme Court ordered the dismantlement of the village. Since then, it became a right-wing mantra that Khan al-Ahmar had to be pulled down, but international pressure led to postponements. Of course, Ben-Gvir and Smotrich demanded quick action but, lo and behold, for the ninth time, the government, in which they are ministers, has asked the Supreme Court to allow the postponement of its decision.

From the serious to the ridiculous: Lapid and Gantz, the two main figures of the previous government, have lost all credibility as leaders of the opposition, not least because of their acute rivalry. In the meantime, somebody unknown to the public up to now, the chairman of the Israel Bar Association, Avi Himi, has drawn increasing admiration and was mentioned as a potential head of the opposition, thanks to his cogent and energetic speeches against the judicial reform and other anti-democratic moves of the Netanyahu government.

Recently though, Himi announced that he would not enter the political fray. Why? What happened? Just when he had reached the necessary visibility and enjoyed growing support? Well, it all became clear some three days ago, when a scandal that was brewing for some time exploded: our hero had apparently exposed himself and masturbated in front of a female lawyer who had come to ask for a recommendation for being appointed to the judiciary. She told it to somebody who told it to somebody else, who told it to a journalist. It became the main item of all news programs; Himi stepped down from his position in the Bar Association, and the police are probably going to open an investigation. At least, Himi has now become well known to every Israeli. Alas.

Khan al-Ahmar is symbolic of the general situation in the West

Bank. Slowly but surely Israeli settlements grow in number, notwithstanding Palestinian and international opposition. The Israeli
left tries to slow down the settlers' progress but cannot stop it,
because part of the population that moves to the territories moves
there to get cheaper housing in a scenic environment: messianic
ideology incites, cheap real estate entices.

Thursday, February 2

Increasingly one finds allusions in the news to a semi-hidden
foundation financing the right-wing onslaught on Israeli
democracy: Kohelet (Ecclesiastes), supposedly financed—at
least in part—by rich American Jews. Whatever the case with
Kohelet may be, there is clearly a general anti-liberal offensive
on all fronts: judicial, religious, educational, in the media, and,
of course, the Occupied Territories. Nonetheless, two steps
forward, one step back. Thus, for the time being only, the new
plan to dismantle the Israeli Public Broadcasting Corporation
has been postponed. This certainly does not hinder one of the
most visible television journalists, Ayala Hasson, from spewing
her weekly Friday night pro-Netanyahu propaganda. Incidentally, it was the same journalist who came out with the story that
destroyed Avi Himi.

A few days ago I reported that, after the Supreme Court's
massive majority decision (ten to one), Netanyahu had to dismiss
Aryeh Deri. Apparently, Deri, impervious to all of this, continues
to work as interior minister and health minister, either from his
office or from his home. Didn't he famously declare in a Shas
party meeting: "If they oust us through the door, we will come
back through the window; if they oust us after that, we will come
back through the roof"? The PM will certainly not send the

police to arrest him for crass flouting of court decisions. Israel has become a jungle with some very dangerous predators.

Take Ben-Gvir. Where there is an opening for misdeeds, there he is. For example, he looks for any way of imposing harsher conditions on Palestinian prison inmates. He wants to reintroduce the death sentence for terror attacks. In the meantime he has managed to inflame the atmosphere by ordering all sorts of sanctions, including against women prisoners. This has heightened tension with Hamas and may lead to a generalized explosion. Ben-Gvir is the most objectionable and disgusting figure amid this entire gallery of freaks.

The trouble is that although I know all of this, I remain viscerally attached to the country where I arrived of my own volition, as a fifteen-year-old, post-Shoah orphan. At first I brooked no criticism, then things changed—but whatever my growing reservations may have been, the deep attachment to Israel as such, to its unconditional survival, remains. It would not occur to me that for Jews everywhere such an attachment is imperative. Not at all. And I am well aware of the fact that young American Jewish liberals had become disenchanted with the country well before the present government emerged. Israel is not an answer to antisemitism; in some cases, it reinforces antisemitism. But, for many of my vanishing generation, the attachment remains irrational and unshakable. This very attachment pushes those who still can to fight for the survival of what possibly was an illusion, a dream, but a dream that gave a meaning to their (our) entire lives.

The attachment wasn't entirely irrational until now. Orna and I have not lived in Israel since my retirement, for a set of purely practical reasons (health coverage, etc.). But we know how vibrant and friendly Israeli society still can be (particularly in Tel Aviv . . .), and on more than one occasion we considered moving back. Until now. And, from what I read and hear, not a few Israelis think of moving out.

Friday, February 3

Yesterday, during their meeting in Paris, the French president Emmanuel Macron warned Netanyahu that if the judicial reform was voted on and imposed, Israel would not be considered a democracy anymore. What could it mean? Hungary, a typical European authoritarian regime, doesn't seem to be suffering in any way . . . Should Netanyahu be more worried than Orbán? At least Macron's body language expressed his feelings: Netanyahu tried repeatedly to hug him to prove their close friendship; Macron did not respond even once.

More importantly for the immediate future: Roni Alsheich, the former chief of the national police, will speak tomorrow in Tel Aviv at the protest demonstration against the judicial reform. From what we know, he will warn, as all others have done, that the reform means a regime change granting unlimited power to the government. But beyond this, he will probably point out that he is speaking as a religious Jew, thereby addressing the vast group of progovernment religious Jews. Will he mention also that he speaks as a Sephardi Jew, a matter of considerable importance that could counteract the constant efforts of Ben-Gvir to get full control, as minister of internal security, of a police force that is traditionally Sephardi? Of course, it would also be meaningful for all ordinary Shas members.

Are we, the liberal-left, just pretending that all of this will help? That Biden, Macron, and all the Alsheichs will help? Or are we merely whistling past the graveyard? The fact is that in Israel's short history there have been surprising moves in both political directions: from left to right and from right to left.

From left to right? The most unexpected and grotesque example is the sudden commitment of some of the best-known Israeli writers, all of them traditional leftists, to the "whole of Eretz Israel" (Eretz Israel Hashlema) movement advocating the annexation of the conquered Palestinian territories in the aftermath of the Six-Day War. Adherents included the national poet, Nathan Alterman, and other well-known writers such as Haim Gouri and Moshe Shamir.

From right to left? The best example is the architect of the Likud and main promoter of the settlement policy, Ariel Sharon, who, as defense minister under Begin, led the First Lebanon War and was an accomplice to the Sabra and Shatila massacres. After becoming prime minister in 2001, Sharon accepted the need to get rid of the Gaza Strip; following the Likud's violent opposition, "Arik" left the party and created a new one, Kadima (Forward); he had apparently decided to get out of major parts of the West Bank, too, had he not suffered a stroke that put an end to his political career and ultimately his life.

Who could be the next Arik? Back to earth: stop dreaming!

Saturday, February 4

Much depends on tonight's protests: if the numbers grow, there is a slight chance that the regime change can be blocked. Otherwise, I do not know what else can help. The former attorney general, Avichai Mandelblit, put it exactly right: "All these disasters stem from Netanyahu's indictments." He, Mandelblit, is the man who started the process of indicting the sitting prime minister, which demanded a lot of courage. Little did he foresee that he was dealing with a wily mafia type ready to burn down his own house to save his skin.

The number of protestors in Tel Aviv (40,000) was not up to that of previous weeks but there were many more demonstrations all over the country. In Tel Aviv, Roni Alsheich said what he was expected to say and, hopefully, it will sink in. Ron Huldai, the long-serving and excellent mayor of Tel Aviv-Jaffa, warned that words would be followed by action. This is what should happen, but what could such action be? Only a general strike could be effective and that depends on the Histadrut (the general labor union). Will the Histadrut move? For some reason, I doubt it: the Histadrut has long since stopped being political. Actually, it is dominated by the Likud.

Sunday, February 5

The current attorney general, Gali Baharav-Miara, shows a lot of courage and steadfastness. It isn't clear though how far she can delay the oncoming legislation. Thus, the judicial committee of the Knesset started discussing the bill sponsored by the coalition that would establish the authority of Ben-Gvir, as minister of internal security, over the police force. The chief of police would get his orders from the minister, also regarding criminal investigations. In fact, the legislation would turn the minister into the de facto commander of the police: a political commander of the police. A highly dangerous situation.

The president of the State of Israel, Isaac Herzog, a rather wishy-washy politician, appears to understand nonetheless how dangerous the judicial reform is for Israeli democracy. Today he suggested a pause in the process to allow time for reconsideration. Levin, the justice minister, answered immediately: the reform will not be stopped for a minute, it will be pushed ahead. It is not clear whether Levin is merely Netanyahu's mouthpiece or the quasi-autonomous fanatic he seems to be, one of course working in unison with Netanyahu.

Monday, February 6

Levin has suggested introducing the judicial overhaul in several successive steps, leaving some of the most controversial propositions for later months, but accelerating others. His main acolyte is possibly more dangerous than he is: Religious Zionist Party's Simcha Rotman, head of the judiciary committee of the Knesset. His most urgent aim seems to be the reinstating of Aryeh Deri. Most probably, the postponed propositions are not yet ready. Those that are submitted should get voted on before the Knesset adjourns in April.

As for Ben-Gvir, he has abstained, notwithstanding his fiery declarations, from destroying the large building in East Jerusalem he promised to bring down. Two steps ahead, one step backward.

Three things are quite bothersome regarding the protest movement: the lack of leadership, the quasi-total exclusion of the Palestinian issue, and the danger of again having a majority of Ashkenazim facing the great mass of Sephardim. Nobody wants that, but the fact is that the Likud has a majority of Sephardi voters. Avoiding this trap should be an important aim of those who organize the demonstrations. There should be many more Alsheichs. Those who remember the Peace Now days will remember that the movement was soon tagged as Ashkenazi and elitist—which harmed and probably put an end to a movement that indeed did not represent the wider population.

As for dealing more seriously with the Palestinian issue, it is tricky due to the overall situation: today, the father of a child in a Palestinian school in East Jerusalem published the letter he sent to the Education Ministry, asking it to accept his son in a bilingual Hebrew-Arabic school, because in the present one the kids were systematically indoctrinated to kill Jews and become terrorists and *shahids* (martyrs) if need be. Apparently, this is not uncommon. A few days ago, a thirteen-year-old child from East Jerusalem shot a soldier and his father. These are the results of such indoctrination.

Tuesday, February 7

For some time now, I have wanted to say a word about the constant bandying of "antisemitism." There is a French expression: *le ton fait la musique*. It is quite apposite. You immediately recognize antisemitism when you sense hatred. Otherwise you have to be quite careful before hurling the accusation. It can be a matter of unexamined tradition, like for a Catholic, prior to Vatican II, repeating the traditional prayer on Good Friday: "Let us pray for the perfidious Jews." Many such Catholics hardly paid any attention to the words, as offensive as they were. Today, of course, people aren't so naive about anti-Jewish slurs and some seem to enjoy the immunity of free speech to make a splash and get publicity, particularly if they are in the media or in radical-left or radical-right politics. In the States, it's not only hateful but becoming dangerous. Yet, notwithstanding all this, level-headed criticism of Israeli policies has generally little to do with antisemitism.

Due to the onrush of measures, demonstrations, speeches, and insults, I almost forgot to mention two rather striking characteristics of our new coalition: the rarity of women in its upper echelons and its hostility to LGTBQ issues, aimed at the school curriculum. Why there are so few women not only in the cabinet but also among general directors of ministries is probably due to religious reluctance. As for homophobia, despite the seriousness of the issue, one could not keep a straight face after Netanyahu appointed the gay Likudnik Amir Ohana as chairman of the Knesset: each time he arose to speak, the Orthodox members turned their heads in an opposite direction and covered their eyes . . . that's the Israeli parliament in 2023.

Today Smotrich announced that the building of new settlements would be hastened. Given American and French warnings, this is quite a test for the boss.

Biden's State of the Union speech can be read in two ways regarding the Israeli situation. On the one hand, the president barely touched on foreign policy and the situation in the Middle East was not mentioned. On the other hand, he did not cease to sing the praises of democracy. Israel was probably not on his mind, but the subject may come up if and when he invites Netanyahu to meet him. In any case, Blinken and others will not forget.

Wednesday, February 8

There is a basic problem that I have postponed addressing, partly because it is so complex: Israel aims at being Jewish and democratic. Let me deal with it in very simplistic terms. Even at first glance, the conjunction is impossible, a contradiction in terms: the Arab citizens of Israel do not have the same rights as Jewish ones. De jure, they do not have a "Law of Return"; de facto, they do not have conditions identical to those of the Jewish population in many domains of daily life. Of course, this could be improved, but tacit solidarity with the Palestinians from the Occupied Territories will remain a dominant emotion for a majority of the Arab population and thus, the argument goes, full de facto rights would be dangerous. Thus, for as long as the conflict persists, Israel has to be Jewish and only very partially democratic. And, if the present government fulfills its aims, the democratic part of the equation will tend to zero. The joke is that after the massive immigration from Russia and the Ukraine, the Jewish dimension of the state is itself getting somewhat slenderer.

At least we enjoy reading about Sara Netanyahu's demands from the Shin Bet to ensure their personal security. The husband is the sad face of the situation, Sara'le is our involuntary comic relief.

Some encouraging pieces of news: today, in heavy rain, some 1,000 officers and soldiers of the reserve (in Israel, reserve duty is compulsory up to one's forties) started a 50 km march from Latrun to Jerusalem. It has been organized by reserve general and former chief of staff Moshe "Bogie" Ya'alon, and includes members of the most prestigious commando units, as well as a ninety-three-year-old veteran of the 1948 Independence War. A major demonstration is planned in Jerusalem, next Monday, in front of the Supreme Court. As we have seen over the last few weeks, many Israelis won't take what is happening lying down.

Thursday, February 9

Deri wanted to push a Shas-sponsored law about the Kotel (the Western Wall): half a year in jail for people coming to the Wall in inappropriate dress or with music. Netanyahu has shelved it, for the time being. Deri has acquiesced. It indicates nonetheless where the coalition is moving. The ayatollahs should be ashamed: they will soon be out-ayatolled. But don't worry too much: a spate of less visible measures are getting through: thus, in forthcoming courses for paramedics, boys and girls will be trained separately.

Today the marchers to Jerusalem are already 2,000-strong.

Finally there was a clash between Ben-Gvir and Yaakov "Kobi" Shabtai, the chief of police. After demonstrations against the reform in Jerusalem, Ben-Gvir went after the head of the Jerusalem police for not having stopped "the anarchists"; Shabtai praised his Jerusalem colleague for showing common sense. Will Ben-Gvir attempt to dismiss him?

Friday, February 10

Another terror assault in Jerusalem: two children dead, a six-year-old and an eight-year-old (who died three days later), and five people wounded. The terrorist, a Palestinian from East Jerusalem, rammed his car into a group waiting at a bus station. He apparently is a psychiatric patient. Of course, Ben-Gvir has been calling for the wildest retaliation measures, all of these completely pointless against a single offender, according to counter-terror specialists. Such crazy steps can only inflame the situation.

An unnamed senior member of the coalition strongly criticizes Ben-Gvir: "One cannot announce retaliation measures from the sidewalk." Fine, but he is wrong: Ben-Gvir loves sidewalk announcements, the more incendiary the better; it adds to his visibility and will garner him votes when elections come. People forget who Ben-Gvir is. Do you remember who was a master of outrageous proclamations that drew increasing masses of voters? We dislike some historical comparisons, but we cannot remain completely blind to lessons from the past.

This being said, one cannot skip the fact that Hamas and Islamic Jihad celebrated the attack and that there was quite some militant excitement in several West Bank towns. All this is possibly a preparation for the Ramadan which, this year, starts on March 22.

Saturday, February 11

The Tel Aviv municipality building hung a banner over its front with the full text of the Independence Declaration of May 1948, a model of democratic principles.

Monday may prove an important day. Rotman will try to ram the first reading of some of the judicial reforms through the Knesset judiciary committee. The opposition will use all possible delaying tactics. But the real drama will take place outside of the Knesset: a mass demonstration against the reform should fill the streets of Jerusalem and a day of widespread strikes is supposed to paralyze much of the country. Let's hope that it all takes place as planned.

In the meantime, Ben-Gvir is expected to summon the chief of the Jerusalem police, Doron Turgeman, to a disciplinary talk.

Today, the sixth weekly demonstrations took place in Tel Aviv and other cities. In Tel Aviv, according to the organizers, some 150,000 people participated; tens of thousands more marched in other cities.

Sunday, February 12

At today's meeting of the government, ministers resolved to introduce a law that would limit the authority of the Supreme Court to intervene in government appointments. This would allow the reappointment of Aryeh Deri as minister of the interior and minister of health. Informally, the law is known as "Deri law 2." The proposal has to be voted by a majority of the Knesset and accepted by the Supreme Court. For once, members of the opposition have issued a joint warning against the initiative. And, exceptionally, President Herzog will speak to the country in a few hours from now. One cannot expect much from somebody like Herzog, but let's wait and see.

In the meantime, Ben-Gvir continues to announce that he ordered the police, etc., etc. Former police chiefs have compared him to an irresponsible mischief-maker, a small child, or a stand-up comedian. Netanyahu cannot dismiss him, because doing that would be the end of his Knesset majority.

The minister of education says that teachers who strike tomorrow will forfeit their salary, while students skipping school will receive a "missing" mark in their file. The principal of one of the major Tel Aviv high schools has encouraged the students to be in Jerusalem tomorrow. Private donors declare that civil servants who lose salary will be reimbursed.

Herzog spoke well and offered some principles that would allow for negotiations between the coalition and its opponents. He had hardly finished when the coalition announced that votes in favor of various aspects of the judicial reform will take place tomorrow morning, as planned. If so, the strike and the Jerusalem demonstrations will also take place, as planned.

The government has authorized nine new outposts and the construction of thousands of new homes within existing settlements in the West Bank. This may increase the tension with the US. Is it a sheer Likud provocation to keep the coalition afloat? Of course, there could be a long interval between the authorization and anything actually happening.

Monday, February 13

Levin and Rotman didn't postpone the first round of votes on the reform laws, but announced their willingness to meet with Lapid and Gantz in Herzog's presence as early as tonight to find a compromise. On the face of it, this looks like a retreat. Is it merely clever window-dressing, sheer pretense, or are the two hooligans, and Netanyahu in the background, ready for some concrete talks? The 90,000 demonstrators who marched yesterday in Jerusalem may have incited this untypical readiness for negotiations. Some say that members of the Likud are demanding dialogue. A poll taken yesterday showed that over 60 percent of Israelis are against the judicial reforms.

Knesset member David "Dudi" Amsalem from the Likud, who, after pestering Netanyahu, is supposed to become minister in the Justice Department, went all out against any compromise: "The reform will be voted in full if you want it or not." He vowed to put an end to the domination of the "elite," those who participated in the Monday demonstration, with "their Rolexes and their Mercedes." Amsalem, who is Mizrahi, pretends to fight against the Ashkenazi elite that, according to him, rules over the country and his brethren, those who work "as gardeners for the elite." Amsalem is playing his usual vote-getting card, but it appears that a growing number of Likud Knesset members want a compromise.

Tuesday, February 14

A stormy meeting between Smotrich and the heads of the main Israeli banks. They tried to explain to the new minister of finance that the judicial reform is a danger to the economy. He apparently got angry and the encounter did not end well. The fact is that money is being transfered daily from Israeli banks to foreign ones.

In my opinion, Netanyahu's decision to disregard foreign warnings and go for more settlements is clever: part of the protest movement is on the nationalist side and may become supportive of the coalition because of the settlements push. Let's hope I am wrong.

From the beginning, the Zionist enterprise as perceived and supported by the majority of East European Jews—with the exception of "cultural Zionists" like Asher Ginsberg, known as Ahad Ha'am, "one of the people"—was intent on settling Eretz Israel by force, if necessary. The Arab population of Palestine was determined to resist this foreign invasion, also by force. As trouble started from the early years of Jewish colonization, some German Zionists like the sociologist Arthur Ruppin dreamed of cooperation with the local population in establishing a Jewish presence in the country and founded a movement to that effect: Brit Shalom, or "a covenant for peace." Ruppin abandoned his peace project on the morrow of the Arab massacre of the Jewish population in Hebron, in 1929, where some sixty-seven Jews were killed and scores injured and maimed. The Arab attack was triggered by rumors that the Jews would take over the Temple Mount. The same rumors are periodically spread to this day.

Some other German Jews took up the coexistence dream (Hans Kohn, Martin Buber, Gershom Scholem, Ernst Simon) and established Ihud (Unity), a peace party that advocated a binational state. They represented the most prestigious names of the newly established Hebrew University and were strongly backed by its American-born rector, Judah Magnes. But it was a dream without a chance in the absence of any significant Palestinian response, the urge of the immense majority of the Yishuv (the

Jewish community of Palestine) to fight, and Ben-Gurion's hard-knuckled realpolitik.

Not that I would have opposed militant politics when I boarded the *Altalena*, a ship belonging to Begin's Irgun, in June 1948. I was fifteen and wanted to fight. I did not fight on arrival, because my age—which I had hidden—was discovered, but my attitude stayed mainstream and hardline for many years. I did not particularly enjoy my three years in the army but my attitude did not shift leftward until the late 1960s or early 1970s. It is only then that I realized how determined the successive "socialist" governments were to push settlements and Israeli control over the Palestinians.

During the years spanning the creation of the State of Israel to the Six-Day War, only the extreme Israeli left went on promoting the idea of a binational state, a stand that, after 1967, became the more widely accepted—but still supported only by a minority—advocacy of the two-state solution. Today, this is fast turning into another empty dream: on the one hand, the relentless Israeli settlement policy, and on the other, the fierce "no compromise with the Jews" stand of Hamas, Islamic Jihad, and, behind them, Iran. Tragically, the "no compromise" stand is dominating social media and flooding Palestinian education and youth more generally. In the last few days, Palestinian shooters from East Jerusalem have been, successively, thirteen and fourteen years old. The leader of the West Bank Palestinians (the Palestinian Authority), Mahmoud Abbas, although moderate in principle, is elderly, corrupt, inefficient, and increasingly confrontational.

Today, a new incident between Smotrich and Defense Minister Gallant regarding the evacuation of a Jewish settler's farm illegally established on Palestinian land. On the defense minister's orders and with Netanyahu's reluctant agreement, border police units started evacuating the farm. Youth from yeshivot and a female Knesset member from Jewish Power tried to block the action. Just before the end of the evacuation, Netanyahu gave the order to stop it. Gallant is outraged. Smotrich: "If Gallant has a problem, he can leave his keys . . ." As for Ben-Gvir, he is accusing the border police unit of brutality, which drew a strong response from the commander of the force. Let us hope that, with clash after clash, this coalition will disintegrate.

Some $4 billion has already left Israeli banks for foreign ones as a result of the judicial reform.

Wednesday, February 15

The guerrilla war between Ben-Gvir and the chief of police, Kobi Shabtai, continues. Moreover, some commentators believe that Netanyahu has lost control over the events and that he is finished. Hopefully.

President Herzog asks Attorney-General Gali Baharav-Miara to allow Netanyahu to launch a dialogue between the coalition and opposition—not to participate in it, but just to launch it. She refused; it is precluded by a previous court decision that forbids him to deal with judicial issues that could touch on his own indictments. She is formally right, and such decisions are her domain. It may be regrettable under the circumstances.

Thursday, February 16

Today *Haaretz* gave an overview of what they know about Kohelet, the ultra-right libertarian organization that for some ten years now has been promoting a regime change in Israel in favor of extreme religious nationalism. Apparently they utilize some 150 researchers, coordinated by one Moshe Koppel, to feed their ideas to various ministers, Knesset members, and high officials. According to the article, Yariv Levin shared their ideas for years. In the past, Netanyahu blocked Levin; now, as it became convenient due to his own legal troubles, he supports him. Kohelet is apparently financed by some Jewish-American billionaires.

Kohelet, as described in that article, sounds a bit like Dan Brown's Opus Dei, in slightly less mysterious garb. It is hard to see, however, how the present Israeli government's push to destroy the freedom of the courts and promote a religiously controlled society fits with the quasi-anarchist doctrines of libertarians. In short, we haven't yet deciphered the ultimate secret codes of the message hidden behind our national catastrophe. Maybe it is merely wrapped inside Netanyahu's indictments. What a letdown!

Friday, February 17

It is a strange comfort, yet it is true: Israel has been on the brink of catastrophe several times and each time it pulled itself together and overcame the crisis. In 1948, when the Egyptian army advanced in the South, the Jordanian Arab Legion in the East, the Syrians in the North . . . or, on Yom Kippur 1973, when the Egyptians overwhelmed the Israeli defenses in the Sinai and the Syrians managed the same on the Golan. This time, though, the threat of catastrophe is internal: a political confrontation that could lead to civil war—unimaginable, and yet this is not pure fiction. One cannot believe that this is not pure fiction.

The only event I remember as something slightly similar happened in June 1948, when "my" ship, the *Altalena*, a "liberty ship" of World War II vintage, docked off the shores of Kfar Vitkin with its 900 passengers (most would-be soldiers, but also some real soldiers, Americans and others). It carried tons of weapons and ammunition. The ship had been chartered by American Revisionists (led by Peter Bergson) and those who gave it the order to sail were French Revisionists, in both cases political allies of Menachem Begin, the chief of the Irgun in Palestine, a terrorist right-wing underground movement during the British Mandate, that was fiercely fought against by the mandatory power and by the mainstream left-wing parties of the Jewish community, mainly Ben-Gurion's Mapai ("the workers party of Eretz Israel"). The names have changed between then and now but, basically, the opposite camps are not entirely dissimilar, unfortunately with reversed roles.

Notwithstanding his impassioned calls for support, Begin did not have a chance against Zahal (the Israeli defense forces). The *Altalena* sailed to the shore at Tel Aviv, as Begin hoped to raise the city's population to its defense. To no avail. The ship was set on fire by what Ben-Gurion called "the blessed gun." Sixteen men were killed, some while swimming ashore. The blackened hull remained in full view from the coast for several months, before being sold for scrap.

Saturday, February 18

I read in the news that several veterans of the fighting on the Golan during the Yom Kippur War were about to transport an armored car, sent there in commemoration, to the coming demonstration in Tel Aviv; the police stopped them. It would have reminded people of the awesome threat of those days and the terrible price in lives. It reminded me of something else. At that time, I was a member of the Israeli Pugwash group, a branch of an international organization (named after a small Canadian town) established in the 1950s by Bertrand Russell and Albert Einstein, at the height of the Cold War, to allow for informal contacts between American and Soviet academics in the search for dialogue openings, with the tacit knowledge of their respective governments.

In May 1973, Bill Polk, a member of the US Pugwash group and director of the Adlai Stevenson Institute in Chicago, phoned me in Jerusalem and invited me to a very confidential meeting with a Palestinian delegate, plus the usual American, Soviet, and Egyptian members of the group. The participation of a Palestinian was a first. Of course I agreed, but mentioned that I had to inform the prime minister's office and receive authorization. I called Mordechai Gazit, the director of Golda Meir's office. In my mind, this was a great opportunity to meet a Palestinian representative. Within minutes Gazit called me back: "The prime minister wants to see you." When? "Now."

I had never met the "old lady," a chain-smoking, Milwaukee-raised Zionist of a generation that knew no nuances and no compromises, "the only man in the Cabinet," Ben-Gurion said about her when she was labor minister. She became prime minister at Levi Eshkol's death in 1969 and led the Alignment (Mapai and Mapam) to its greatest electoral victory later that same year. She was tough on the Israeli "Black Panthers" (Mizrahi activists) and on everybody else.

"Shaul," she addressed me, although we had never met, "I forbid you to participate in that meeting in Chicago if a Palestinian is present. There is no Palestinian people. We were all Palestinians under the British mandate; I had a Palestinian passport. The so-called Palestinians are Arabs from Syria who came here during the mandate. You understand me?" I left, rather dazed; there was no point in arguing. I called Polk. The meeting took place, without the Palestinian participant.

A few months later, in October 1973, in spite of accepting in principle Kissinger's idea of having Egyptian sovereignty over the Sinai while allowing Israel to be in control of its security in this region, Golda Meir's narrow-mindedness and stubbornness greatly contributed to what could have turned into an unredeemable military catastrophe for Israel. Over 2,200 soldiers paid with their lives. Two students of my small graduate seminar at Hebrew University, Shaul Shalev and Avi Shmueli, were among those killed.

Today, over 100,000 people demonstrated against the judicial reform in Tel Aviv and all over the country.

Sunday, February 19

The government is supposed to vote on the establishment of the Ministry of Settlement and National Projects under Minister Orit Strook of the Religious Zionist Party, Smotrich's party. Minister of Defense Gallant opposed it, but the cabinet will supposedly vote its establishment nonetheless. This comes as the American Ambassador to Israel announced that President Biden had advised Netanyahu "to pump the brakes" on the legal reform. Not sure at all that it will help; the prime minister may well have lost control of the situation.

The US has managed to convince Israel to postpone its plans for new settlements and the Palestinians to drop any attempts at condemning Israel in international forums until August. Thus the Palestinian-sponsored complaint to the Security Council is postponed. This is quite an American achievement; the Smotriches and Ben-Gvirs are furious but they will not dare to act against the agreement. At least, let's hope so.

The most unexpected demonstration took place yesterday evening in one of the oldest settlements, Gush Etzion: right-wingers, many of them belonging to the Religious Zionist Party, came out against the judicial reform. They do not deny the need for some changes, but they see the danger in attempting to ram a radical reform down the throats of most of the population. They demonstrate in favor of dialogue, somewhat in line with Herzog's proposal. Among the demonstrators, a few Netanyahu relatives.

Monday, February 20

The first reading of some of the laws for the judiciary overhaul will take place in the Knesset during the night. Violent demonstrations against it outside the building and inside. Demonstrators were forcefully expelled from the Parliament's balcony.

The head of Shin Bet (the Israeli security service) warns that the country stands on the brink of a catastrophic explosion. Likud veteran Dan Meridor calls on Netanyahu to stop the legal overhaul for the sake of the country. Many Likud members wonder if the boss is still in charge.

The president of the Security Council expresses profound concern at Israeli plans to build up the nine temporary settlements (*maahazim*) authorized earlier in the month. The US does not criticize the declaration.

Those whom he wants to ruin, Jupiter maddens (*dementat*).

Tuesday, February 21

The coalition is attempting to install a political majority on the nominating committee for Supreme Court justices, so that it can control forthcoming appointments—including the replacement for Chief Justice Hayut, who is about to retire in the fall. This would ensure that the next Supreme Court would be ready to exonerate Netanyahu and, all in all, to accept a system of nomination of judges and various laws that would limit the independence of the judiciary in the future. Apart from their immediate political aim, the supporters of the reform aim at changing the supposedly "old boy" method of Ashkenazi judges "adopting" Ashkenazi colleagues to the court, to the exclusion of any "Moroccan" justice.

Some supporters of the judicial legislation also give the US as an example of a democracy in which justices are politically nominated. This is forgetting that the US Supreme Court takes its decisions within a highly elaborate constitution which the court can interpret but not amend.

At 1:00 a.m., the coalition voted in a first reading in favor of two main pieces of legislation. The Knesset majority within the judicial selection committee will be able to control the appointment of Supreme Court judges, and the Supreme Court will henceforth not be allowed to amend any of the Basic Laws (in Israel, a series of Basic Laws, unlike " regular" laws, deal with the individual liberties of its citizens as they were outlined in Israel's Declaration of Independence).

Ben-Gvir threatens: if his office does not receive the supplementary budget he is asking for in order to appoint additional police personnel, raise police salaries, and set up a national guard, he will leave the government. If only he could keep his word for once!

Some four years ago Avi Maoz's ultrareligious Noam, which is part of the government (albeit a tiny one) established a confidential list of fifty gay personalities whom it accuses of undue influence in media and entertainment. A journalist just revealed its existence. Maoz has been given a position in the Ministry of Education, but Netanyahu promised that the status of the LGBTQ community would not change. Let us see. In any case, the religious parties suddenly besiege the country from all sides.

The latest joke making the rounds: don't forget to set your clock back 2,000 years.

Wednesday, February 22

According to some news outlets, Israel is about to attack Iran's nuclear installations. It could explain Netanyahu's rather passive behavior in the face of growing internal chaos: keep the coalition going until this crucial operation is over. A very dangerous but probably necessary gamble.

Three more bills passed first readings. The override law nullifies the Supreme Court's ability to declare laws unconstitutional. Another eliminates the court's ability to review political appointments. A third forbids hospitals to introduce hametz during Passover.

Whereas the third proposal simply demonstrates the power of ultrareligious parties in the coalition, the second would allow Deri's reinstatement. As for the first law, it puts an end to the influence of the Supreme Court in any controversy touching on fundamental issues, the guarantee of democratic rule.

In short, the coalition is rushing through this regime-changing overhaul, without showing any real readiness for compromise.

In a raid into Nablus and the firefight that followed, the army killed ten Palestinians and wounded about a hundred. These raids will not put an end to terror attacks; they only add to the violence.

Thursday, February 23

In the Knesset, a tempest of insults from all sides. Never have our so-called parliamentary debates been so violent and so disgusting! In the comments online, somebody wrote: "The face of the Knesset is like the face of the country." Unfortunately, this is correct, but the racist and anti-Arab insults come from one side only: the present coalition.

You won't believe it but, in the meantime, Netanyahu, and mainly Sara'le, his wife, have obtained state financing for two houses, a huge budget for clothes, and an unlimited budget for traveling. Sara'le has an enormous, and some would say catastrophic, influence on him. She apparently takes part in crucial nominations.

According to sources, the government approved today the construction of over 7,000 new houses in the West Bank. A spokesman for "Peace Now" called it "spitting in the face of the United States" after Netanyahu promised the Americans to abstain from new constructions until August. Also today, Smotrich has been put in charge of civilian development in the West Bank, notwithstanding Defense Minister Gallant's previous opposition.

These extraordinary steps may stem from the coalition's difficulties in agreeing on the budget for next year, which has to be voted by tomorrow. Ben-Gvir, it will be remembered, threatened to leave the coalition if his demands for financing the police are not satisfied. Expansion of settlements is probably the only promise that can convince him to compromise and stay.

Friday, February 24

The budget has been approved: Ben-Gvir received 9 billion out of the 14 billion shekels he asked for. He will stay; he possibly never thought of leaving.

A former US ambassador to Israel got it right in his speech to a Democratic constituency: the Israeli government is acting cleverly in pushing its measures at a time when the US is facing a convergence of global problems: Ukraine-Russia, China, inflation, and forthcoming elections. Unfortunately, very cleverly.

Interesting article by Yuval Harari, the globally renowned professor of history at the Hebrew University in Jerusalem, in the newspaper *Yedioth Ahronoth*: his analysis of the situation is not different from the one generally heard, but when asked what he would do if the government succeeds in its plans, now or later, he declared that he would leave the country. Fine, and what about the hundreds of thousands who cannot leave?

One of my uncles was already a Zionist (Blau-Weiss, a German Jewish youth movement) before World War II, and so was my mother. She could not convince my father but visited Palestine with another of her brothers sometime in the mid-1930s. This brother did not like the nationalism of the Jewish community there. Instead he turned to anthroposophy and emigrated to Sweden. Zionists were right in the context of the times, of course, but their nationalism became a curse that exploded after 1967 and 1977 (Begin's accession to power). Poor Begin: compared to Netanyahu and his acolytes, he was a Polish gentleman.

A law allowing for the dismissal of the National Library director was voted when the attorney-general left the committee room for a few minutes. Gangster methods. It is called the "Law for the Transparency of the National Library."

Former prime minister Ehud Barak declares that soldiers confronted with an illegal order should refuse to obey it . . . I wonder when Netanyahu will give the order to arrest Barak. You think that I am joking: Knesset member Tally Gotliv demanded Barak's arrest in a television interview. Incidentally, Barak was Netanyahu's commander in Sayeret Matkal, the most elite special forces unit of the army.

Netanyahu is reportedly closing the day in a confidential meeting offering ministers arguments to better "hit" the opposition with. The man is truly poisonous (I just read that "poisonous" has become a word for all occasions in our idyllic country).

In the meantime, air force pilots are threatening to refuse to fly. They will possibly be followed by Intelligence reserve officers. More than high-tech people moving out, turmoil in the army will create the deepest of reactions. The army is the idealized self-image of the country.

Saturday, February 25

Political religions of the extreme left or extreme right—and even more so, religious-messianic regimes—function according to dynamics of their own, dynamics that know only the impact of increasing speed, until they destroy themselves or are destroyed by superior force.

In Israel, the regime set up by Netanyahu and his allies is a typical messianic one, a mixture of extreme nationalism and extreme religiosity, with added clannish and personal interests. Both tendencies were present from the very beginnings of Zionism, overshadowed for decades by the battle to establish the state, external threats, ordinary politics, and a struggling economy. The fanatics were well known and active on the scene (the rabbis Kook—Abraham Isaac Kook and his son Zvi Yehuda Kook—and their disciples on the religious side: Geulah Cohen, Yuval Ne'eman, Rehavam Zeevi, and multifaceted Sharon on the nationalist one), but their impact seemed minimal, as strong personalities and seemingly strong political parties were in the saddle.

Then came 1967, followed by 1977 and 1995. Prime Minister Yitzhak Rabin's murder by the religious-nationalist Yigal Amir after the two Oslo Accords between Israel and Arafat's Palestinian Liberation Organization brought forth a strong reaction, but a subterranean fire of fanaticism was burning, cleverly stirred up by politicians such as Netanyahu (for his own interests). Now the results are in.

The Israeli fanatics will not slow down on their own. What could be the outside agent bringing them to an unexpected stop? You might have expected some forceful intervention by President Biden, but that will not happen. As for the Israeli opposition, it is too polite, too civilized. Thus, nobody can see the end of this avalanche, except through the intervention of an act of God . . . Isn't it grotesque that an atheist like me should ask for an act of God against our army of religious fanatics?

The trouble is that the Palestinians also have their irreducible fanatics. They probably will not accept any agreement and strive instead for Israel's disappearance. Edward Said, one of the most prominent of Palestinian voices, was also a diehard of the "refusal front" on the morrow of the Oslo Accords. Oslo, for Said, was "a Palestinian Versailles." Intifada 1 and 2 were the most recent large-scale murderous expressions of Palestinian refusal. On various scales, such murderous initiatives were an integral part of the Palestinian response from the beginning of Zionism. Of course, this says nothing about Palestinian frustration, humiliation, and suffering before, and mainly since, 1967.

Saturday evening (this evening), some 160,000 demonstrators in Tel Aviv, tens of thousands in Haifa, and more than ever in various towns all over the country. And in Tel Aviv they are getting less polite. Good!

Ehud Barak's speech to the crowd in Tel Aviv was particularly important. It expressed again, more forcefully, what he had already ventured beforehand and what led Knesset member Gotliv to demand his arrest: if Netanyahu manages to overturn Israeli democracy, if Israel turns into a full-fledged nationalist-religious dictatorship, the duty of officers, state employees, and others will be to refuse to obey orders. During the last few days, former heads of the Mossad have said the same thing. Unheard of in Israel!

Sunday, February 26

Two youngsters from a settlement shot and killed by a Palestinian terrorist in Huwara, a small town near Nablus, as they were driving through. In response, the cabinet voted the death sentence for terrorists. A Ben-Gvir demand. There was no death sentence in Israel, except for "Nazis and their collaborators." It was applied only once, on Adolf Eichmann.

The cabinet also voted for the cancelation of the Incapacitation Law, which allows the attorney general to recommend that the prime minister or any other minister be declared unfit to fulfill his or her functions, if dealing with matters touching on subjects related to his or her current indictments. The first Knesset vote on its revocation will take place in a few days.

Two days ago, *Haaret{* published a cartoon showing Netanyahu, with Sara'le and son Yair, as Nero singing while Rome is burning; Herzog is holding a tiny bucket of water . . .

In response to the dismissal of the director of the Israeli National Library, considered too liberal by the new education minister, people whose manuscripts and other papers are deposited at the library (including me) have decided to retrieve them and find other archives.

The de-escalation summit that took place in Aqaba, Jordan, with the participation of officials from Israel, Jordan, the Palestinian Authority, Egypt, and the United States, led to some positive decisions, such as the stop on discussion of new settlement units for four months and on authorization of outposts for six months. It has little chance of success, however: Hamas called it "worthless," while Smotrich declared immediately that the settlements were under his authority and new initiatives would not stop for a minute. As for Ben-Gvir, he put it simply: what took place in Jordan, remains in Jordan.

After the shooting in Huwara, a savage rampage by hundreds of settlers: torching of Palestinian cars and of tens of homes, one Palestinian killed, dozens wounded, general destruction. About 400 settlers were involved in this unparalleled mayhem. During the assault, which lasted some three hours, neither police nor army appeared on the scene. Where were they? Everybody on Twitter knew; they did not? Nobody informed them of what was happening? Or maybe they were ordered not to intervene? Six people were arrested at first, but all were released. Ultimately some two settlers are under arrest . . . for having attacked police and IDF officers, not for harming Palestinians, God forbid.

Monday, February 27

On March 22, I have to briefly address colleagues and students at Tel Aviv University (via Zoom), on the occasion of an evening event to celebrate, with a few months delay, my ninetieth birthday. I asked whether, given the situation, I could speak about the political situation and was told: as much as you wish.

I will use the introduction to this diary and quote Curd Jürgens as Udet (in fact, the first to say that line was Max Liebermann on the day of the *Machtergreifung*).

The timing for this event will have depended on the availability of space on a given evening, but it occurred to me that it could also have been determined by the date as such: March 22 is the eve of the day on which, exactly ninety years ago, the Weimar Republic was overthrown by a majority vote of the Reichstag granting full powers to Adolf Hitler. This, of course, should not be considered as a direct allusion to present events, but nonetheless it is helpful to remember how a parliamentary majority can shatter a democratic regime.

Let us return to the present. The settlers' riot in Huwara—or, as it is rightly called, the pogrom in Huwara—should remind us once again of the heart of the problem, that essential aspect many of us refuse to confront directly: the Palestinian issue. It is at the core of our overall conundrum, our political sickness, our long-term social malaise. For tactical reasons, in order not to push away the more right-wing-oriented demonstrators—willing to fight against the judicial reform, but who oppose any common political action with Palestinians—the Palestinian question has been set aside by the opposition. The Palestinians themselves are abstaining from participation. For both them and us, it is a mistake. At this moment of truth for the country, tactical considerations should not stand in the way of basic moral principles and, mainly, for those who do not want to hear about moral principles, such considerations should not hide catastrophic practical consequences.

I do not know whether the conflict with the Palestinians can still find a peaceful solution; nobody knows. Maybe it never could, from the very beginning of Zionism. But there is no doubt that the continuing domination of the Occupied Territories and constant expansion of settlements fans the flames of conflict. And the brutality of our operations in the territories not only exacerbates Palestinian violence, but increasingly brutalizes our own society. Very few of us are ready to recognize that the fight for democracy is inseparable from the recognition of equality of treatment for Arab and Jewish citizens in Israel and an end to the domination over Palestinians beyond our borders. And, in immediate and concrete terms, there is much more.

If the judicial overhaul gets through, a Knesset majority will be capable not only of cleansing Netanyahu and Deri of all wrong-doing but of resolving on the annexation of the West Bank. I know that this is not said aloud these days, and seems to have been forgotten out of fear of international, particularly American, reactions. But didn't the Aqaba decisions mention a moratorium on settlements of only six months? Do you think that, once the six months have elapsed, Ben-Gvir and Smotrich will let it go? As with all nationalist-religious zealots, they will never abandon one of their major goals. Once they have their way, there will be many more Elon Morehs, to paraphrase Menachem Begin, but also many more Huwaras, and, why not, many more Deir Yassins. And, all at once, Israel, as everybody here knows it and loves it, will have disappeared, to be replaced by an authentic and criminal apartheid state.

All this looks dreary, and our democracy clock is close to midnight, but in fact all the polls show that more than half the population is against the policy being pushed through the Knesset, and probably against the present parliamentary majority, as well. The weekly demonstrations are immensely encouraging: they are saving the country's honor. But they cannot in and of themselves stop the self-interested politicians and crazy fanatics. Civil disobedience is the most powerful democratic way of influencing the course of politics, and thank God that it is spreading. Such resolve of some of the best among us should give hope to all and restore our confidence in the coming of better days.

Some of you may have seen, in a recent article in *Haaretz,* a quote from Victor Klemperer's diary, written shortly after the Nazis came to power: "Naked violence and horrible hypocrisy find their expression in official ordinances . . . Nobody breathes freely anymore . . . More than fear, I feel shame . . . For the first time, I feel political hatred against a whole group." And Klemperer added "deadly hatred," words that, I hope, we will never have to use here.

I will end with that.

However, let me pursue this trend of thoughts for a while. If, over a period of years, it becomes obvious that Israel cannot be peacefully accepted by a Palestinian independent entity or state, notwithstanding external guarantees, then defense measures will become unavoidable. But legitimate self-defense is fundamentally different from a divine right of domination over the whole of Eretz Israel. One may argue, of course, that from the outset Zionism laid claim to the whole of Eretz Israel—a divine promise for some, historical rights for others. But let us admit it: from the outset, the sacred formula "Jewish and democratic" was an illusion, only defensible by dint of twisted logic.

Let's get back to the present. Nahum Barnea, a veteran Israeli political commentator, wrote in today's *Yedioth Ahronoth*: "The government needs to decide what it is. Is it resolved to enforce law and order on Arabs and Jews alike? Or is it a fig leaf for the hilltop youth, who do as they please in the territories? That same question also applies to the army which has thus far failed to deal effectively with either Palestinian terrorism or Jewish terrorism." Barnea's words are courageous, but this government is a settler government and its decisions will be settler decisions. The only good decision it can take is to resign and call for new elections!

Could Avi Maoz's resignation today be the first swallow announcing the spring? Probably not, as he musters one voice only and will go on supporting the coalition in the Knesset. But if Netanyahu respects the Aqaba decisions, then Smotrich and Ben-Gvir will go. That would be the end of the coalition. But our Houdini may well convince the US that he is all in favor of the de-escalation decisions, while proving to his two acolytes that he is actively pushing new settlements.

In 1928, Arthur Ruppin, the most pacific of peaceful German Zionists, the founder of Brit Shalom, which I already mentioned, wrote to the like-minded Hans Kohn:

> There is no parallel in history to the aim of Zionism to settle the Jews peaceably in a country which is already inhabited. Such an entry by one nation into the country of another is known in history only by means of conquest; so far, no nation has ever been willing to tolerate another nation settling beside it and claiming complete equality and national autonomy . . . The Brit Shalom was to become the forum to consider and discuss the problem.

As I mentioned, Ruppin abandoned the dream of such a peaceable coexistence after the massacre of tens of Jews in Hebron and other places by Palestinians, in 1929.

Tuesday, February 28

Today, Likud Defense Minister Gallant declared that he opposed the calls for disobedience in the army: one should not use the army for one side or the other. He is wrong, the dispute is not between one political opinion and another, but between dictatorship and democracy. The fact that he did not react to Barak's first statement and waited for several days after the second spate of declarations shows, in my opinion, that he has been compelled to say what he said.

The turmoil of the last few weeks has compelled me to rethink some basic assumptions and to go back to much earlier times. My father, the least interested in Zionism that anyone could be, wrote to a friend in London, shortly after we fled from Prague and arrived in Paris:

> Although the news coming from Palestine is not very favorable . . . everybody agrees that one has the feeling of being at home there, as a free citizen. We can all appreciate what that means today. I don't want to begin the same comedy all over again in another state or in another country and would rather remain a *schnorrer* all my life, or wage war on the Arabs. But it will be a year at best before our turn for an immigration certificate comes up, and for people like us there is no way to decide things so far ahead.

My parents' turn for immigration certificates never came. They were murdered in Auschwitz.

Whatever other moral justifications there may be for Zionism

—and there are—the only incontrovertible one, although *a posteriori*, of the immigration to Palestine up to 1945, is that without anybody having foreseen it or having been able to foresee it, this immigration not only was a last refuge for some, but also saved the lives of about half a million European Jews. The children of those immigrants were born in Palestine and, later, in Israel; the evolution thereafter was what it was.

Former attorney general Mandelblit calls for the abandonment of the judicial overhaul, which he named a "judicial horror" (*toeva hakikatit*).

Knesset members from Torah Judaism complain that Netanyahu is not fulfilling his promises and that budget appropriations they should have received have not been paid. Ben-Gvir complains about exclusion from important meetings of the Security Cabinet and, generally speaking, about promises regarding new outposts not being kept. In short, one hears some cracks in the coalition structure on top of Avi Maoz's resignation. These are but early cracks at this stage. No death rattle yet.

Tomorrow the Knesset will vote for the first time for the cancelation of the Incapacitation Law.

An Israeli-American was shot near Jericho while on his way to a wedding.

Wednesday, March 1

On March 22, the month-long Muslim festival of Ramadan will start. It has usually been a month of heightened tension, particularly in Jerusalem.

The cancelation of the Incapacitation Law received initial approval (*hatsba'ah tromit*) in the Knesset along with a death sentence law for terrorists.

Huge demonstrations in Tel Aviv and other towns in "a day of disruption." Thirty-seven demonstrators arrested in Tel Aviv. Eleven demonstrators evacuated to Ichilov hospital. Police used stun grenades; Ben-Gvir exhorts it to action against the "anarchists."

Two Palestinians suspected of involvement in the shooting near Jericho have been arrested.

President Herzog called again for urgent talks. Former defense minister Gantz to Netanyahu and to Knesset chair Ohana: "Let's go to Herzog!" In the speech that followed, Netanyahu didn't say a word about the possibility of such talks; he compared the demonstrators for democracy to the settlers who torched Huwara: both groups were acting against the law . . . In the meantime, Smotrich declared with utmost earnestness, without batting an eyelid, that the State should eradicate Huwara . . . I don't think that anything like this has ever been heard in Israel. American officials expressed their disgust. Smotrich should not be allowed entry into the United States. Neither should Netanyahu.

As usual, in the midst of this unprecedented turmoil, Sara'le is offering some comic relief. She found the perfect day to visit her Tel Aviv hairdresser. People found out and soon hundreds were demonstrating in front of the hair salon. The police had to rescue the careless wife in an armored car as the demonstrators chanted: "The country is burning and Sara is getting a haircut." In Hebrew it rhymes: *Hamedina boeret veSarah mistaperet*. The joke is that Sara'le was not intimidated in the least; she insisted on having a full three hours of hairdressing and documented on selfies the stages of her beautification, while tens of horse-mounted policemen were blocking demonstrators from approaching the salon, helicopters hovered overhead, an armored car was standing at the ready, the Shin Bet was mobilized . . . Some conspiracy specialists assume that her wily husband managed the whole opera from afar and then staged, for the TV channels and the reporters, the highly moving reunion with his beloved Sara'le, who appeared to suffer from post-traumatic stress.

Thursday, March 2

Will Netanyahu give the order to attack Iran ahead of schedule, to save himself and his coalition? The man's egotistic madness is so monumental that any such step is possible, notwithstanding the overall risks. The trouble is that very few people in the country are knowledgeable enough to weigh responsibly on the decision. And is the US kept informed of all our Napoleon's decisions? It is doubtful.

I have told elsewhere of my work with Shimon Peres in 1960–61. I was a very small cog in a huge machine, although I carried an impressive title: head of the Scientific Office of the Vice-Minister of Defense. I had inherited the job of a truly impressive person, Shalhevet Freier, who left after quarreling with Shimon and returned later as head of the Israeli Atomic Energy Commission. I went under the name of Shaul Eldar (Hebraization of names in public service was compulsory at the time), and I was privy to one of the most secret domains in the country. I had probably been hired because of my fluent knowledge of French, as France and French companies were massively involved in the construction of the Israeli nuclear installations.

I am telling this because, at the time, this extremely daring and complex enterprise was in the hands of extremely daring but very responsible people: Ben-Gurion, as prime minister and minister of defense, and Peres, as vice-minister of defense, and particularly in charge of the nuclear effort. In years past, Netanyahu was generally considered as a cautious person as far as military decisions were concerned (Gaza, etc.). Now, however, since his judicial travails and with this coalition in hand, he seems to have thrown caution to the wind and is ready to risk everything to save his own hide.

Sara'le declared today that yesterday's vaudeville could have ended in murder . . .

Ben-Gvir is threatening Gallant because Gallant ordered the arrest of Huwara incendiaries who threatened army personnel. Levin apparently threatened Netanyahu because he planned to suggest compromise regarding the judicial reform in his address to the nation. The prime minister changed the address and dropped the compromise. What a shame!

Friday, March 3

Gallant saved himself: the army used force to stop left-wing demonstrators from entering Huwara to express their solidarity with the Palestinian population. As I said at the outset of this diary, one would like to eat as much as one wants to puke.

From widespread comments, it becomes obvious that thousands of Israelis will not report for reserve duty when called up, if the judicial reform gets through. They will refuse to serve under a dictatorship. Such civilian disobedience took place in Israel, on a small scale, during the Second Lebanon War. This time, refusal may be more important by far—and it may be dangerous.

Yaya Fink, an observant Jew, repelled by the Huwara rampage and the fact that many religious Jews were among the arsonists, launched a fundraising campaign for those Palestinians who suffered damages. Within twelve hours, some $465,000 was collected. Of course, Fink was called a traitor by the opposite side and received death threats.

This evening, 120 former and present leaders of American Jewry called on Jewish organizations not to give a public platform to Smotrich during his planned visit to the States later this month. Unfortunately, the "Bonds" which invited him—as they have every Israeli finance minister in the past, to energize the sale of Israel state bonds—have not rescinded their invitation. In any case, no US official will meet with the minister. As for Netanyahu, he has not yet been invited to meet Biden, a very unusual situation for a newly elected Israeli prime minister and, supposedly, a "friend" of the president.

Saturday, March 4

A group of senior congressional Democrats has addressed a letter to the president asking him to use all his influence to stop the judicial reform in Israel. They foresee quite correctly that if the reform is voted, the ultras will be able to push through the annexation of the West Bank with unforeseeable and catastrophic consequences for Israel, the Palestinians, and the whole region. They are circulating the letter to add many more signatories (a copy of it reached the Israeli news outlets).

In the meantime, Jewish organizations are asking the State Department to cancel Smotrich's visa to the US.

A record number of demonstrators. In Tel Aviv, there are about 160,000, and across the country, an estimated 250,000. It is the ninth week of demonstrations. Israel has never seen such mass popular mobilization for such an extended period.

Eli Ben-Elissar was one of my friends during my student years in Paris. We studied at Sciences Po and worked together at the

Israeli Embassy. This was in the 1950s. I was not aware of the fact that he was a member of Herut and close to Begin. In the late 1970s, after Begin's electoral victory and Sadat's historic visit, Eli participated in the Cairo negotiations. He later became chairman of the Foreign Affairs and Defense Committee of the Knesset, then ambassador to France. He died during his stay in Paris. I am telling all of this because we met quite often at my house in Jerusalem when Eli had to be in town for Knesset meetings. By then I had moved to the left and was a member of Meretz (at some stage, the party chairperson, Shulamit Aloni, asked me to be the person closing the list), so that Eli and I did not see eye-to-eye regarding the main political issues, particularly the occupied West Bank. Eli's—and his party's—position was that Israelis and Palestinians could live and interact peacefully in an Israeli-controlled West Bank, notwithstanding the settlements. Israeli control was necessary for security reasons.

It may be that some of Begin's acolytes believed this, but the argument became increasingly threadbare as the years went by, and my meetings with Eli tailed off. The trouble is that, as I have already mentioned, the settlements started immediately after the Six-Day War under Mapai (socialist) governments; that socialist prime ministers did not believe in the reality of a Palestinian nation (remember my meeting with Golda Meir?); and that the present situation has deep historical roots. In short, I dare say that there is a kind of unconscious drive to occupy the whole of Eretz Israel among many Israelis.

The commander of the air force held an exceptional meeting with reserve pilots who are considering refusing to serve if the judiciary reform and its enabling laws are passed. This is an unheard-of threat in Israel. The commander seemed to fully understand the motivation of this elite group, although of course he tried to dissuade them.

The Chief of Staff Unit officers who, in July 1976, liberated the Entebbe hostages detained by Palestinian and German hijackers in the Ugandan capital, have declared their opposition to the reform. The extraordinary Entebbe operation was under the command of Netanyahu's brother Yoni, who was killed in the fighting.

Sunday, March 5

Netanyahu and Sara'le have to leave on an official visit to Italy in four days from now. The El Al company cannot find a copilot and a cabin crew for the trip . . .

It is probably in order to strengthen his credentials before this visit to a neofascist government that Netanyahu is backing Smotrich's attempts to clear himself from the general revulsion caused by his call for eradicating Huwara. In his comments in Hebrew (not in English) the prime minister added criticism of the US ambassador to Israel, who had expressed himself against Smotrich's remarks: "Nobody is immune from mistakes, not even diplomats."

Tomorrow, the Knesset is supposed to vote on a law allowing Likud Knesset members and their families to collect contributions to cover the prime minister's legal and medical expenses. As for Sara'le and her two sons, their security will be ensured from now on by the Shin Bet. In the meantime, El Al announced with pride that they found a pilot ready to fly the couple to Italy.

Thirty-seven out of forty reserve pilots of an elite air force unit will not report for training in protest against the judicial initiative. This kind of abstention is rapidly spreading to other units. Minister of Defense Gallant is worried enough to call for immediate talks. Netanyahu, Levin, and Rotman are supposedly in favor of dialogue with the opposition, yet they are still pushing their legislation forward at top speed. A poll held in the last few days shows that the coalition would lose seven seats if elections were held now.

The Knesset voted in a first reading for the law authorizing hospitals to prevent the bringing in of unleavened food during Passover. Lapid called it "religious coercion."

An internet campaign initiated by Arab personalities, which already had a million views among Israeli Arabs, is calling on them to participate in the protests against the judicial overhaul. It points out that the Arab population would be the first to feel the consequences of the proposed legislation. Massive Arab participation, although not welcome by some Jewish demonstrators, is urgent and would be a significant boost.

Monday, March 6

President Herzog announced that a compromise regarding the judicial overhaul was extremely close and that now was the time for political leaders to take over. In a response, unusually drafted in common, Lapid and Gantz praised the president for his efforts and declared their readiness for talks, but set as a precondition the pausing by Netanyahu of the legislation in the Knesset. Netanyahu has not yet reacted.

Two hundred physicians declared that they will not report for reserve duty. All former commanders of the air force to Netanyahu: stop the reform!

Instead of saying a word about stopping the overhaul, Netanyahu lashed out against those reserve officers who will not report for reserve duty. Ben-Gvir stood at his side and added some nonsense of his own. Is this the running amok of desperation or the brazen self-assurance of two hardened hoodlums who believe that they can topple the justice system? As for Herzog, he is possibly full of goodwill, but he also may be either just naive or basking in the limelight during his own fifteen minutes. The only benefit of this whole episode is the proof, once again, of Netanyahu's resolve to get the new judiciary laws through to save his skin, and, mainly, the proof that Lapid and Gantz can stand together.

About a week after the pogrom in Huwara, settlers returned to the town and celebrated Purim with dances. Some soldiers danced with them and that is the real shame. Where are the officers, where is discipline, what is the position of the army command? Will there be any sanctions?

Michael Bloomberg, Jewish former mayor of New York, a billionaire, and a great friend and benefactor of Israel, came out in the *New York Times* with a very strong op-ed piece against the Netanyahu government's policies. In his view, if it pushes on, "Israel is courting disaster."

Ben-Gvir, who cannot stand being out of the news even for an hour, announced that information has reached the police that indicates growing incitement to murder him. When a police spokesman indicated that no such information had reached them, the publicity-crazy minister ordered him to report for a clarification, which means a dressing-down.

Tuesday, March 7

Last night, an operation took place in Jenin. The Palestinian suspected of shooting the two Israeli youths in Huwara was killed, as were five other Palestinians. Nine more were wounded. The vicious circle doesn't stop.

Herzog's compromise proposal doesn't seem to get anywhere; many consider it insufficiently clear. In any case, Netanyahu did not answer; Levin and Rotman are determined to push ahead.

The pilots who were supposed to stay away from reserve duty tomorrow will report to their base, but instead of flying they will hold a conversation with their crews about the political situation. They call the debate a "fighters' conversation" (*siah lohamim*), the name given to a famous soldiers' conversation on the morrow of the Six-Day War; it was organized by Amos Oz, among others, (translated into English under the title "The Seventh Day") and it expressed, already in 1967, some of the same doubts surfacing now and comparing the suffering of the Arabs forced to flee to the fate of Jews fleeing not so long before. It was impressive, given the overall atmosphere of quasi-hysterical nationalist jubilation engulfing Israel in those postwar days.

I quoted extensively from the "fighters' conversation" in a book I published in French in 1969 under the title *Reflexions sur l'avenir d'Israel* (Reflections on the future of Israel) in which I foresaw, if I may say, that a prolonged occupation of Palestinian conquered territories would destroy the values that Israel was supposedly built upon. I do not feel proud about my foresight of what the occupation would do to Israel, for the simple reason that I did not think, at the time, of what it would do to the Palestinians . . . It took me two to three more years to understand that.

The organizers of the demonstrations have announced a huge "protest against dictatorship day" for Thursday. Even if only part of the program they are planning gets accomplished, it will be quite impressive. The demonstrations seem to be growing in scale and impact.

In one of the dispatches from the Holy Land, I read that some interviewees envisaged a return to the biblical situation whereby the Kingdom of David and Solomon split into two separate kingdoms: Judea and Samaria. One state that would be more traditionalist, more religious, etc., and a state that would be essentially liberal and secular. *Grosso modo*, the first one for the Mizrahim, the second one for the Ashkenazim . . . This is, of course, not very serious, but it is probably the first time that such an extravagant idea has been aired. Unfortunately, a not-so-hidden racism suffuses it. It is the unmentioned plague of this whole situation.

A group of specialists came up with compromise suggestions that Levin calls a breakthrough. But, as far as all such news is reliable, the fanatic justice minister is not ready to stop the overhaul process during negotiations. I assume that if he insists on continuing his blitz campaign, there will be no compromise acceptable to the opposition.

Settlers attempted again to create chaos in Huwara before being stopped at the last moment.

Moody's Investors Service, one of the companies that sets the international credit rating of countries, warned of a potential downgrading of Israel if the judicial overhaul is voted. It seems that Netanyahu is getting worried by the dire consequences in a vast number of domains and is trying to slow Levin down, without success up to now.

Wednesday, March 8

The translator from Hebrew to Italian refuses to translate the speech Netanyahu is supposed to deliver at a Rome synagogue on Friday: it is a speech that is dangerous for democracy in Israel, she declared. About the visit, some have written that Netanyahu is joining Giorgia Meloni in "international isolation." The opposition will attempt to prevent Bibi's and Sara'le's departure by blocking access to the airport; Ben-Gvir swore to keep it open. The police will use force.

My friend Kobi is calling Rotman a "Savanarola with *tzitzes*" (tassles). Good, but Rotman is not the problem. The problem is Netanyahu and, possibly, Levin.

Netanyahu is something of a puzzle. He is dogged by corruption scandals and full to the brim of himself, but far from dumb. Moreover, he doesn't care about ideology, only about power and the good life. Could it be that in order to escape indictments that would have probably turned into minor plea deals, he is ready to become the destroyer of Israel?

American Jewry may be splitting along the same fault lines as Israeli society. The biggest supporters of Netanyahu and his zealots are the Trumpists and, particularly, the Evangelicals, who align their politics with their theological convictions. Hidden from view are the billionaires of Forum Kohelet. A dangerous coalition. It so happens, though, that the chief economist of Kohelet has doubts about the Israeli judicial overhaul because of its negative economic consequences.

Israeli women form human chains to protest the judicial overhaul.

Thursday, March 9

Many of the demonstrations are led by high-ranking reserve officers. Six were arrested for preventing access to the Kohelet offices in Jerusalem, more arrests than for the hooligans in Huwara . . . The Ayalon Highway to and from Tel Aviv was blocked for several hours. Now the seashore road is barred. The voice of protest is heard clear and loud. Netanyahu, who arrived at the airport in a police helicopter, declared to the Italian media that the protests show the strength of democracy in Israel. The man is a shameless stand-up comedian.

On Ben-Gvir's orders, Amihai Eshed, commander of the Tel Aviv police, has been moved to another position. Ben-Gvir targeted Eshed because of his lenient attitude toward the demonstrators.

In an unprecedented show of resolve, President Herzog, in a speech to the nation, came out against the judicial overhaul. He told Knesset members that they were responsible for the spreading chaos. He is calling for an immediate coming together of both sides around an agreed-upon project. That part looks like his past demands; it will not work if Levin and Rotman do not stop rushing through with the legislation.

Terror attack in Tel Aviv: three people badly wounded. The attacker, who was found hiding in the staircase of one of the surrounding buildings, fled into an alley and was shot there. Now the police are looking for whoever brought him.

The chief of staff admitted that the army failed in Huwara.

Friday, March 10

The commander of the air force reinstated the colonel who was dismissed yesterday for his involvement in the reserve pilots' threat not to report for call-ups if the judicial overhaul was passed.

The dismissal of the Tel Aviv police chief Amihai Eshed, on Ben-Gvir's orders to Commander of Police Shabtai, was put on ice by the attorney-general when it became clear that Shabtai acted under pressure from the minister. A number of police chiefs demand Shabtai's resignation.

In today's article in the *New York Times*, "The Social Rifts That Led to Israel's Judicial Crisis," Patrick Kingsley, the Jerusalem bureau chief of the paper, points to the origins of the present confrontation in the 1990s, when Chief Justice Aharon Barak established the authority of the Supreme Court over political constituencies such as the settlers' movement and the ultra-Orthodox community. In other words, the court represented the position of liberal-minded, secular Israelis against the extreme-nationalist and extreme-religious communities. The court did occasionally protect Palestinians against settler encroachments (it was not excessively liberal regarding Palestinian rights) and limited the attempts of the Haredim to escape military service. It supported the evacuation of the Gaza Strip and the demolition of its settlements. Thus the court became a focus of hatred for the extremists of both the settler and Haredi camps. At the time, the justice minister who supported Aharon Barak was Likud member Dan Meridor, and, a few years later, Netanyahu also expressed himself in favor of such liberal legislation.

Netanyahu's personal troubles with the Justice Ministry and the growth of the settler movement and the ultrareligious community changed the picture and led a politician desperately attempting to escape condemnation for a series of alleged misdeeds to link up with the only constituencies that shared an interest in overcoming the court's authority. This strategy brought about the present coalition and its program for judicial overhaul.

If one takes into account the wider state of Israeli society, beyond the structure of the judiciary and its powers, then a far deeper rift has to be taken into account: the rift between Mizrahim and Ashkenazim, mentioned here on several occasions. The dismissal of Aryeh Deri from his ministerial appointments and the specific overhaul measures aiming at his reinstatement are partly an expression of this. Let's remember: Shas, of which Deri is the uncontested leader, is altogether nationalist, ultra-Orthodox, and Mizrahi (Sephardi) by definition. Moreover, some of its most vocal Knesset members, such as David Amsalem, nurse a violent anti-Ashkenazi resentment; it is a widespread undercurrent that influenced the electoral results.

As I previously mentioned, the expenses of the Netanyahu family, including two private homes and all hosting expenses, are covered by public funds, without any transparency obligation. There is nothing like this among major Western democracies, according to an Israeli research center.

Saturday, March 11

The terror attack in Tel Aviv and the deepening crisis did not deter the Netanyahus from spending the weekend in Rome. Sara'le probably wants to go shopping. Public protests have followed them to Italy.

Hopefully, Netanyahu enjoys his Roman holiday, notwithstanding a serious diplomatic defeat: the agreement between Saudi Arabia and Iran to restore relations, after seven years of rupture. Our PM, dead set on isolating Iran internationally and constantly hinting at a forthcoming rapprochement with the

Saudis, got exactly the opposite. Under its new government, Israel has no foreign policy anymore and is facing growing isolation; the Iran–Saudi agreement is one more failure, and a dangerous one.

This evening, the tenth week of demonstrations. Somewhat before 8:00 p.m., about 50,000 demonstrators in Haifa, the largest protest the city has ever seen. In every city and town in the country, even in very small locations, thousands take part. The movement is getting much stronger by the week.

Some 180,000 demonstrators in Tel Aviv.

Police commander Yakov Shabtai declared tonight, regarding his submission to Ben-Gvir's order for the dismissal of the Tel Aviv police chief : "I was wrong regarding the time and the way; it will happen after Ramadan." But he did not cancel the dismissal. He is probably too afraid of being himself dismissed by Ben-Gvir.

Sunday, March 12

Did you notice? Netanyahu was away in Rome for the last three days; at the end of this week, he will be in Berlin, and on the following week in London . . . It seems that he is keen on being away from his country at the time of its worst crisis. In fact, he will not be at the only place where he would love to be seen: at the White House.

The PM came out against the attorney general on the police issue: the government alone has authority over the police. Also regarding dismissals and nominations within the force? Yesterday, on the television evening news, Ben-Gvir was beside himself regarding the police issue. It looked as if we were about to witness an act of God. But no, not this time. The man is probably planning the attorney general's dismissal.

The same Ben-Gvir has apparently also decided to cause as much damage as possible to the Bedouins. Without any order having been publicized, a sudden surge of house destructions is taking place in the Negev. Some of the houses had been built decades ago.

Yesterday, in the online news, some idiotic commentator congratulated Levin and Rotman as the DJs of a new party in which even Netanyahu belongs already to the past. Without mentioning Amsalem, but using his arguments, he welcomed the new party guests, the new elite that is throwing out yesterday's oligarchy, in particular the Rehavia judges, who in the opinion of this dumbass form a small group of self-appointed masters opposed to the nation's elected representatives. (Rehavia is a Jerusalem area mostly inhabited by German Jews and a well-educated bourgeoisie.) Those elected representatives, he forgot to add, are rushing to eradicate democracy and, according to the polls, are opposed by a majority of Israelis.

Levin and Rotman do not plan to pause, even for a day: during the week, they will present the "override law," which permits a Knesset majority to reverse a Supreme Court decision. It is at the core of the entire overhaul.

My former university, Tel Aviv University, organized a week of debates about the judicial reform during which some speakers defended the overhaul and were sharply criticized by militant students from the opposition. The rector, Professor Mark Steif, wrote a strongly worded letter attacking the students and got an even sharper response. The question is how far, in a fight for democracy, opinions of the opponents of democracy should be given free expression in an academic debate, in a liberal university, under the guise of even-handedness.

Ehud Barak declared on CNN that Israelis should opt for

civil disobedience if the Knesset passes the judicial overhaul that would paralyze the Supreme Court and turn the country into a dictatorship. It should include army reservists. He added that if the country was in danger, everybody would report for duty.

The Israeli Air Force is participating in a large exercise over Nevada. Is Iran on or off?

The United Arab Emirates, which established relations with Israel in the framework of the Abraham Accords, and were becoming major clients of its defense industries, canceled a very important order in view of the ongoing legal turmoil.

Monday, March 13

In the small town of Netivot, a group of religious schoolteachers took girl students of Ethiopian origin for a three-day trip. Along the way the schoolteachers exchanged comments making fun of the students because of their looks, etc. Some of the girls managed to take pictures of what the teachers were sending: pure racism of the most extreme kind. It is now all over the news. These are teachers in a religious Israeli school, under the new dispensation. You may be sure that they will not be dismissed.

Smotrich arrived in New York. No official wants to meet him, except for the demonstrators protesting against his visit. Nonetheless, yesterday evening he spoke to the "Bonds" that had invited him and stressed the "common values" shared by the US and Israel. No doubt, the man has a sense of humor . . . He also plans to speak to meeting of the Zionist Organization of America (ZOA), a right-wing organization close to the Republicans. Next week, he plans to be in Paris. These people have incredibly thick hides, like their puppet master, Netanyahu. The Curd Jürgens/Udet quote that I used at the beginning of this diary is much too weak.

Today, the Knesset is about to vote on three major laws at the heart of the overhaul. Amsalem, the clown we have already met several times, will introduce a further law: a prime minister in office cannot be indicted for a whole series of misdemeanors or felonies. This should trigger a strong response from the Supreme Court, if it is approved.

At the end of the week, Netanyahu will be on his way to Berlin. There, thousands of demonstrators will hopefully be waiting for him.

Police Commander Shabtai told his district chiefs that he is the only one authorized to speak with Ben-Gvir on any operational matter. In other words, if Ben-Gvir gives operational instructions to a district chief during a demonstration, he should be referred back to Shabtai. Ben-Gvir's entourage explains the commander's instructions as stemming from pressure coming from the attorney general. The police should be proud of one major achievement: all in all, there have been no demonstrators seriously injured during the last ten weeks. That is probably not what Ben-Gvir is proud of.

Israel is on its way to become an authoritarian, apartheid theocracy, something like a mixture of the old South Africa and contemporary Iran. Two constituencies are competing to achieve this as fast as possible: the settlers and the ultra-Orthodox. An unholy alliance, if there ever was one. It appears that even Orthodox women are worried by the upcoming tightening of religious laws. Apparently, the religious legislation will also spread to areas that have been in the secular domain up till now. Among the Orthodox Knesset members, Moshe Gafni is the one pushing their legislation. Demonstrations are planned in front of his house in Bnei Brak (a town of ultrareligious inhabitants).

President Herzog, on receiving the honorary citizenship of Tel Aviv, announced that he was about to propose an ultimate compromise, after having heard from people on all sides. The problem is that, even if Herzog's compromise is acceptable, it remains unlikely that the coalition will be ready to stop the rush toward finalizing the overhaul, and the opposition will be unwilling to talk while the rush goes on.

Ben-Gvir did not wait to react to Shabtai's instructions to police district chiefs not to speak directly with the minister: he is holding a conference with them.

The Saudis did not allow the Israeli minister of tourism to attend the international tourism conference, organized by the United Nations, which is taking place in their country.

The Knesset majority voted in a first reading for the cancelation of the exclusion law, called in semi-slang "the fortification law." After the final vote, it will protect the prime minister from being excluded from matters connected with his own indictments. The same for Deri.

In the early morning hours, the Knesset voted for the "override law" (*How hahitgabrut*). This law, if it is enacted (after three votes), will essentially eliminate the judiciary's political influence.

Tuesday, March 14

On Wednesday, Netanyahu will be on his way to Berlin. According to a senior commentator on security matters, the PM's weekly trips to Europe aim to prod European leaders to convince Washington—which doesn't hasten to invite him—to impose, together with them, the "snap back" clause of the prior agreement with Iran on the Islamic Republic; this clause would allow a weapons embargo, among other sanctions. Iran's weapons exports to Russia, helping Putin in his aggression against Ukraine, amply justify such a "snap back." According to the same commentator, up to now the Europeans have listened politely but have not promised anything. It seems doubtful that they will go along with a man of so tarnished a reputation as today's Netanyahu. But at least this maneuver allows him and Sara'le their weekly escapades.

One thousand Israeli personalities from all fields have addressed a letter to Scholz and to Sunak, asking them not to meet with Netanyahu, in view of the regime change he is overseeing.

The overall picture is as weird as can be: a modern and highly successful country rushing toward its demise, under the stewardship of a politician who doesn't care a damn for the ideological goals of his acolytes. More than half the population appears to be opposed to this collective craziness but, up to now, that fact doesn't halt the rush to national suicide.

Strangely enough, from its inception seventy-five years ago, Israel has survived and prospered with the same apparently incompatible groups within its body politic: a liberal, secular, majority; the ultra-Orthodox religious; and the messianic ultranationalists. The growth of the two groups of ultras was noticed, but not considered a serious danger until Netanyahu, at the helm of the traditional right, managed to cobble together the coalition that is now in the hands of its most extreme elements. The extremes dictate policies and, when thwarted, even slightly, threaten to leave the coalition and bring about new elections. Coming now, with a majority of the population turning against them, such elections would be a catastrophe for the traditional right, the Likud; for the ultras, who would lose the benefits they can achieve at this moment; and for Netanyahu personally. They all know it. But they rush on like a herd of lemmings toward collective demise, the demise of the country as such.

Tomorrow, there will be attempts to disrupt Netanyahu's departure for Berlin. Today, a demonstration took place in front of Moshe Gafni's house in Bnei Brak, a town of ultrareligious inhabitants. The demonstrators were pelted with tomatoes and eggs. In the Likud there is a simmering discontent regarding the direction in which things are moving.

Once the laws included in the overhaul are voted and somebody appeals against them (there will be many such appeals), the Supreme Court will have to vote on their constitutionality. There is little doubt that the court will reject the whole package, if no major changes are introduced. Then what?

After the pogrom in Huwara, two of the alleged ringleaders were arrested and put on trial. The court let them go due to lack of proof. Gallant, the defense minister, sent them to administrative detention. Today, fifty Knesset members of the coalition signed a petition to Gallant to free them.

Wednesday, March 15

In Merom Hagalil, a little girl of twelve prepared for weeks to sing at some celebration. Today, her performance was canceled because of the presence of some ultra-Orthodox men in the audience. In Ramat Gan, a thoroughly secular city, the municipal swimming pool was compelled to impose separate bathing hours for men and women . . .

Not to be left behind, Moshe Gafni introduced legislation for a massive increase in job openings for Haredim (the ultra-Orthodox). The question is: what kind of jobs can people fill, who never went through a regular school curriculum, who never learned the most basic English or mathematics, not to speak of anything else, except for Torah and Talmud?

After two days in the States, Smotrich is hastening back to "follow the overhaul." Maybe, it's because nobody wants to see him in Washington? The media in Israel are full with jokes about our finance minister's English.

He wasn't even able to read correctly what had been prepared for him in writing. It doesn't seem to bother him; after all, instead of going to school, he spent his time pushing the Palestinians out of the redeemed land of greater Israel.

Netanyahu's trip to Berlin will be very short: he is leaving tonight and coming back tomorrow, officially due to a security issue kept strictly under wraps for the last few days. There are also internal debates within the coalition about a potential compromise regarding the overhaul. A bad compromise would be bad as such, and, moreover, could deflate the opposition.

Information has been released regarding the security issue: the suspected terrorist who hid a bomb near the Meggido crossroads, in Galilee (a bomb that seriously wounded a motorist) entered the country from Lebanon and was shot before he managed to slip back. This indicates that Hezbollah, aware of the growing rift within Israeli society and possibly in coordination with Hamas, plans to incite trouble, in the context of heightened terror activities in the West Bank, probably also in view of Ramadan, which starts on March 22. The Shiite group, a proxy for Iran, has tens of thousands of missiles aiming at Israel's major cities and other strategic targets.

Herzog came up with a very reasonable and acceptable compromise: the coalition would not have a majority in the parliamentary committee that appoints Supreme Court justices; for voting Basic Laws, the Knesset would need eighty members and four readings; to cancel Basic Laws, the Supreme Court would need two-thirds of the justices from a total of eleven members. These are some of the proposals. The coalition immediately rejected Herzog's compromise. The opposition fully accepted it. I hope that Herzog will choose the only dignified and courageous next step: resignation.

According to several news outlets, Netanyahu apparently agreed to negotiations on the basis of Herzog's compromise, but is supposed to have told him: "Convince Levin." Either he knew or guessed that Levin would reject the proposal and wished to keep up the image of the wise statesman, able to rise above partisan squabbles, or else he—the man who brought all of this about—is a hostage of the extremists in his coalition, from the Likud and, of course, from beyond.

Thursday, March 16

It became clear: Levin threatened to resign if Herzog's compromise was accepted, and threatened, moreover, to take Smotrich and Ben-Gvir with him. Netanyahu gave in. The PM is most probably in the hands of the worst of our fanatics. Ben-Gvir demands the attorney general's dismissal.

Demonstrations in Tel Aviv and scuffles with the police and some ultras. In Jerusalem, demonstrators, disguised as municipal workers, marked out a red line from the central police compound through city streets to the Supreme Court, with an inscription in Hebrew, Arabic, and English: "Drawing the Line." The police arrested five of the "workers."

Army operation in Jenin. Four Palestinians killed.

Former Israeli prime minister Ehud Olmert asks world leaders to shun Netanyahu.

Friday, March 17

Shabtai to Ben-Gvir: "The police will remain apolitical and act only according to the law." Ben-Gvir will throw one of his usual tantrums and threaten the police commander. Shabtai should find full support among his officers.

Inscription on Justice Minister Levin's house, while he sits *shiva* (mourning) for his father: "Levin is an enemy of the people." The inscription has been denounced by both the coalition and the opposition.

From Sunday on, about 750 reserve officers from the air force, intelligence, and special forces will not report for call-ups.

First Arab demonstration in Israel, in Kafr Manda, an Arab village in the Galilee. The organizer, at the head of some 250 participants, declared: "The ratification of the overhaul will cause irreversible damage to the Arabs in the country."

In Israel, the present situation is often compared to the Yom Kippur crisis of October 1973, the surprise attack of the Egyptians and Syrians against a dangerously unprepared country. It looks as ominous in many ways. But in 1973, Israel seized the initiative again after about one week. Now the situation has been moving from bad to worse for more than ten weeks, and no resolution is in sight.

A recent poll among US Democrats indicates that their traditional sympathy for Israel, as opposed to the Palestinians, has been reversed: a majority now sympathizes with the Palestinians. Most Republicans keep supporting Israel. Both results may add to Biden's reticence to invite Netanyahu.

The last two entries can be pushed further. In October 1973, it was Nixon who decided on an airlift of supplies to a badly depleted Israel, since the Soviets had started an airlift to Syria. In case the simmering conflict between Israel and Iran were to turn into full-scale war, with the addition of Iran's proxies and its new ally, Putin's Russia, would Biden come to Israel's assistance, if it were needed? He once promised to do so—but now?

According to news reports, it is inexact to say that Netanyahu accepted Herzog's compromise while Levin opposed it and compelled Netanyahu to backtrack. Netanyahu apparently himself rejected the compromise from the outset. If this is true, Machiavelli would have been proud of our PM: a trickster if there ever was one.

Saturday, March 18

Ramadan starts four days from now: dozens of warnings about attacks. It seems that there is coordination between the various Palestinian organizations; they are aware of Israel's deep internal divisions, that's to say, Israel's weakness.

This afternoon, the eleventh week of demonstrations. Next Thursday, a day of national paralysis. In the meantime, the coalition rushes ahead with the overhaul.

Today, Smotrich's plan for the West Bank was disclosed in the news. It was written in 2017. Our minister starts from the axiom that no Palestinian state should be allowed west of the Jordan. This being the starting point, he offers three options to the Palestinians. Option one: stay in a Jewish state that will include the Occupied Territories (Judea and Samaria) as an integrated minority that, over time, will acquire Israeli citizenship and share all the benefits and obligations of the Jewish citizens, including service in the army. Option two: be relocated to a neighboring Arab country. Option three: for those who would refuse to move and who remain Palestinian nationalists, to suffer all the hardship of facing the Israeli police and army. Now I understand better what my friend Eli Ben-Elissar (remember him?) meant by peaceful coexistence.

Does Smotrich, who is supposedly an intelligent zealot, imagine that the world will quietly let Israel enact such a plan; that the US, in particular, will help? His recent foray to Washington has hopefully taught him a few things. But, intelligent or not, he has remained a zealot. A plague on him, if his plans haven't changed!

In Tel Aviv, hundreds of women joined the demonstration in the red dress of the TV series *A Handmaid's Tale* to express their opposition to the male dictatorship that the ultra-Orthodox would impose.

Sunday, March 19

Netanyahu ordered the chief of staff to clamp down upon the reservists' refusal to report for call-ups; he also ordered the police commander to take stern action against the demonstrators. The chief arsonist warning against volunteers fighting the flames. Is the man unhinged? In the Likud, people are more polite: they say that Netanyahu is not himself anymore.

An Israeli car shot at in Huwara: two people wounded. Palestinian and Israeli delegations are meeting in Sharm el-Sheikh (in Egypt) to defuse the situation on the eve of Ramadan. Israel apparently promised not to build in the territories during the coming four months. And what happens after that?

Israeli TV news Channel 14, always a source of right-wing news and conspiracy theories, somewhat like Fox News in the States, is becoming the most popular channel in the country. Recently, they informed their viewers that the CIA was behind the demonstrations against the judicial overhaul . . . This is a dangerous development, and only determined court action can put an end to it.

Rotman (chairman of the judiciary committee) came up with some ideas of his own about how to soften the judicial overhaul. Netanyahu is supposedly considering Rotman's proposal to allow the Judicial Appointments Committee with its coalition majority to replace two liberal justices of the Supreme Court, including its president, Hayut, with more conservative ones. After two years, the committee will consider a widening of the committee's membership. The other laws of the overhaul package would be delayed in the meantime. It would be very strange if the opposition was ready to discuss a proposal manifestly aimed to get Netanyahu and Deri onto safe ground.

Biden spoke to Netanyahu, for the first time in three months. It seems clear that the PM will not get the prized invitation to the White House while the judicial overhaul is a source of internal discord, and as long as efforts to de-escalate tension with the Palestinians are not seriously implemented. Good for Biden.

The main strategist of the Islamic Jihad was killed in Damascus, probably by Israeli operatives.

Monday, March 20

The opposition rejected the compromise engineered by Rotman and accepted by Netanyahu. It was foreseeable from the beginning. The coalition is facing a bad dilemma: the PM told his acolytes that Defense Minister Gallant would resign if no acceptable compromise was found, given the situation in the army. Avi Maoz announced that he would not vote automatically with the coalition, but would decide his vote case by case. A number of Likud Knesset members denounced Rotman's compromise as surrender. It's hard to see how Netanyahu will get out of this without a real compromise, at least along the lines of Herzog's proposal.

In a speech to former members of Betar (the youth movement of Begin's Irgun) in Paris, Smotrich, on a private visit, reportedly declared: There is no Palestinian people. The Palestinians are an invention of less than a hundred years. My grandparents were the true Palestinians, etc. Unfortunately, as will be remembered, this was an opinion also shared by Israeli socialists like Golda Meir.

Betar was already strong in Paris in the immediate post–World War II years. After the socialist Habonim ("the builders") refused to send me to Eretz Israel, during the prestate months of early 1948, because I was too young to fight, I changed the date of birth on my ID and, on the advice of a friend, presented myself at the headquarters of Betar, Hotel des Deux Mondes, Avenue de l'Opéra. They quizzed me: "What do we want?" My friend had prepared me and I shot back: "Both banks of the Jordan!"—exactly Smotrich's map of greater Israel that stood next to the podium during his speech, and which incensed the Jordanians. In 1948, I had but a very fuzzy idea of what both banks of the Jordan meant.

The Paris Betar leaders were hotheads then and later, and when Menachem Begin, the commander of the Irgun, indicated his readiness to cancel the sailing of the *Altalena*—by then docked in Port-de-Bouc, with 900 passengers aboard and tons of weapons —because of Ben-Gurion's warning to desist, the heads of the Paris Betar, in mid-June 1948, gave the ship the order to sail.

Likud accepted Rotman's "compromise" on the overhaul, particularly regarding the nomination of the next two justices. The Knesset vote will start tomorrow. Of course, it will pass.

Netanyahu will do anything to escape condemnation. The Supreme Court will probably oppose the law. Justice Minister Levin declared today that the Knesset will not allow opposition from the court.

Today, the Knesset will vote, in a first round, for "Deri law 2." The law, to be adopted, must get through a second and third vote. It will get through. It remains probable, however, that, again, the Supreme Court will declare the law unconstitutional. Will the Knesset not allow this either? Supposedly, all this should take place in the next two weeks, before Passover.

The tension between Ben-Gvir and Police commander Shabtai is worsening: the commander wanted to name a senior officer to an important position; Ben-Gvir refused to confirm the nomination. Shabtai then appointed the officer as his personal assistant, but the minister avoids signing off on the appointment. In the meantime, Knesset member Amsalem is threatening Shabtai: people will be arrested, don't be among them.

Tuesday, March 21

Yesterday the Knesset reversed the decision taken under Arik Sharon's premiership, in 2005, to evacuate a few settlements near Nablus. The Knesset calls this the "cancelation of the separation law." Settlers had already infiltrated one of the abandoned settlements, Homesh, which became a symbol of their defiance. Now, the settlers have won. As Peace Now declared: "A Messianic Revolution is taking place . . . This government will inevitably destroy our country." That is correct, but what are you doing to stop the Revolution? Unfortunately, the General Federation of Labour, the Histadrut, remains passive.

In Washington, the US State Department called the cancelation of the separation law a provocation that hampers de-escalation efforts.

The organization of reserve officers that initiated the march to Jerusalem and other demonstrations has warned that if the overhaul is confirmed by the Knesset, thousands will refuse to answer call-ups. In a message to Gallant they said: "The army for which you are responsible is going to pieces in front of your eyes."

The Likud minister of the economy, Barkat, declared that were the Supreme Court to oppose Rotman's compromise, he would obey the court's decision. Unusual and interesting. In the Likud, people say that Barkat did not declare this on his own. Did Netanyahu find the ladder that would allow him to climb down from the tree? Does it mean that Levin and Rotman will have to be replaced? Could it lead to a rebellion of the hardliners of the Likud? Fascinating and, possibly, promising.

Wednesday, March 22

After an American rebuke, Netanyahu insisted that the cancelation of the separation law was the cancelation of a humiliating law, but added that settlers would not return to the five vacated sites. How will Smotrich react?

A *Haaretz* article uncovered fake information disseminated by the IDF during the 2021 Guardian of the Walls operation in Gaza, directed at Israeli citizens. This is a shameful attempt to mobilize one's own public opinion for a bombing and destruction campaign. It was possibly a first—but who knows?—and, from what we can tell, it didn't influence anybody. What else shall we discover in the coming months and years?

At the outset of this Knesset session, Moshe Gafni of Torah Judaism introduced a law threatening jail terms for Christian missionary activity among Jews in Israel. Christians saw this as persecution. Netanyahu reassured them today: no measures will be taken against Christian activity. Our political and religious zealots do not stop for a moment: they attack from all sides, without respite. They are aware of their unique opportunity and do not want to miss it.

Thursday, March 23

The Knesset voted for the "incapacity law" limiting the conditions upon which a sitting prime minister can be declared unfit for office. This protects Netanyahu from being compelled to leave office as a result of the indictments against him.

Massive demonstrations all over the country, particularly in Bnei Brak, the Haredi area.

Defense Minister Gallant said in the morning that he would make an announcement. Netanyahu is expected to speak in the evening. Now, at 9:00 p.m., Gallant has decided not to speak, after conferring with the PM. Everybody is waiting for Netanyahu's announcement.

Netanyahu spoke. He announced that he is getting involved in the judicial overhaul (now that the Knesset has amended the incapacity law that precluded his intervening in judicial matters). According to all interpretations (and also according to me), he did not say anything new, except for his personal involvement in the overhaul, and announced: "Rely on me." That isn't enough. The crisis will get worse. Lapid, paraphrasing the Bible, commented: "The voice is Netanyahu's, the hands are Levin's."

The attorney general to Netanyahu: you are not allowed to intervene in legal issues; you are acting against the law.

Friday, March 24

Gallant will probably speak out quite soon. Tens of reserve pilots will not report for call-ups in the coming week. Netanyahu is in London and has met Sunak. Against all tradition, there was no common declaration after the talks. A crowd of Israelis demonstrated against Netanyahu, all along the route from the airport to the front of 10 Downing Street. But, as usual, the N's enjoy their European holiday (the third within a month). Maybe, in fact, they don't enjoy it so much. Sara'le hoped to leave their hotel through a back door, but demonstrators had it covered so she had to get back. Poor N's.

A courageous speech by the president of my university, Tel Aviv University, against the judicial overhaul. He spoke about the possibility of the university going on strike. Will other universities follow? I wonder whether there won't be budgetary reprisals.

The only thing that could explain Netanyahu's weird behavior is that he plans an attack on Iran in the very near future. It would put an end to the protests, restore national unity, and save his skin. It could mean heavy retaliation from Iran and its allies, particularly Hezbollah, and a very difficult moment for Israel.

According to rather precise and detailed information, on the Palestinian side there is an ongoing debate between two strategies: either try to hasten Israel's demise, or leave it to stew in its own juices.

The army, responsible for the security situation in the West Bank, is using all possible means of de-escalation, particularly with the start of Ramadan. In direct opposition to this policy, Ben-Gvir and the police accelerate the destruction of houses built without permits in East Jerusalem and cancel any partial easing for Palestinian security prisoners, even for women—an easing usually permitted for Ramadan.

If the attorney general sends Netanyahu to the Supreme Court for meddling in the judicial overhaul, because of a conflict of interest given his existing legal troubles, and if the Supreme Court condemns Netanyahu for a breach of the law and he doesn't react according to whatever the court enjoins, the country will have officially reached a full-fledged regime crisis.

According to today's poll, a majority of Israelis were unconvinced by Netanyahu's speech and a majority thinks that Gallant should resign. Apropos a resignation, one doesn't hear a word from Herzog anymore. What astonishing courage.

Tomorrow, the twelfth week of demonstrations. Next week, as I have said, will be a week of "national paralysis."

Saturday, March 25

The protests against the judicial overhaul are spreading to the army conscripts. Thousands of demonstrators in front of Defense Minister Gallant's house. The only time protesters have harassed a defense minister in Israel were the protests against Dayan, after the Yom Kippur War. He was considered responsible for the initial catastrophe; Gallant is held responsible for the coming one.

Gallant will speak this evening.

Massive protests all over the country.

At the beginning of the week, a huge package of 141 laws will be introduced for final readings and votes before Passover and the Knesset recess. Among them, the "hametz" law and some others demanded by the ultra-Orthodox. In the meantime, the Netanyahus have been filmed having dinner at the Savoy; there is a lobster on the table nearest the camera, a non-Kosher dish if there ever was one. The two faces of Netanyahu. The ridiculous side of the drama.

Two Israelis wounded in a drive-by shooting in Huwara.

Gallant has asked for the overhaul to be paused. According to him, the rift has penetrated the army and there is an immediate and tangible threat to Israel's security. Coming from a Likud minister, the most important in the cabinet after Netanyahu, this may be a turning point. Three other Likud Knesset members, Avi Dichter, David Biton, and Yuli Edelstein demand the same: postponement until after Independence Day, that is, until May, which may lead to major changes. Huge applause from the demonstrators all over the country. Let's see how Netanyahu will react. It seems that he has no choice but to postpone. That could be the end of his coalition, but I am not sure.

Of course, Ben-Gvir calls for the dismissal of Gallant and all those who demand a postponement of the overhaul. The apocalyptic but not unrealistic view could be that the crazies will accept the postponement, wait patiently until after Independence Day, and then resume the overhaul to its bitter end. It would be difficult to restart the protests again after such a break.

Sunday, March 26

The chief of staff, the head of the Mossad, and the head of the Shin Bet are reported to share Gallant's concerns about the legislative blitz. Israel's enemies are aware of the internal rift and are ready to exploit it. That couldn't be clearer. But nothing seems to slow down our crazies or impress Netanyahu. How weird.

Former chiefs of staff, dozens of retired generals, and so on, declared that Gallant's warning demanded an immediate meeting of the security cabinet to discuss the situation. By refusing to call such a meeting, Netanyahu becomes personally responsible for whatever dire developments that may take place. Again, no reaction from Netanyahu. The man should be declared unfit and removed from office.

Another Netanyahu trick: the law on judicial appointments will be voted on, probably today, but the appointment committee will not be set up before negotiations with the opposition have taken place. Netanyahu to Herzog and Gantz. Herzog answered with a flat "no." Gantz seems ready to talk. How naive can he be! Or, how desperate to be in the good graces of the godfather?

Defense Minister Gallant has been dismissed.

A tsunami of protests in the middle of the night. Hundreds of thousands on the streets. The police cannot handle the situation. Fires lit on the Ayalon Highway. Incredible. Heads of towns and localities will start hunger strikes from tomorrow. The trade unions (the Histadrut) are joining the protests. From tomorrow, the universities are on strike. Israel's consul general in New York has resigned.

Netanyahu convened a cabinet meeting in the middle of the night. A senior member of the Likud (Edelstein?) declared that Netanyahu and Levin are destroying the Likud. The ultra-Orthodox are in favor of stopping the overhaul, but they will accept what Netanyahu decides . . . Deri declared the same. Levin is against stopping. I am proud of Israel and Israelis. Hopefully, Netanyahu's end is approaching.

This time, Lapid and Gantz issued a declaration in common. They call on members of the Likud to refuse to replace Gallant (the two candidates are Dichter and Nir Barkat): "Whoever accepts to replace him brings shame upon itself." It's hard to see how anybody would be stupid enough to accept the job. Of course, Netanyahu may decide to take the ministry upon himself.

As I was looking at the huge demonstrations on the evening news, it occurred to me that even such angry protests, which in many other countries would have turned violent, remain "bon enfant" in Israel. Jews are used to violence against them, but not to intra-Jewish violence. I said some weeks ago that the demonstrators were too polite: it is true, but inherent to Israeli demonstrations and, I admit it, luckily so. Even the deep social resentments underlying the crisis do not change such "atavistic" norms.

This may be contradicted by the fact that Rabin was murdered and that individual violence is rife. I think that it remains true about mass demonstrations, but let us see how it goes.

Monday, March 27

Seventy thousand demonstrators this Monday morning in front of the Knesset. The Ayalon Highway to Tel Aviv is sporadically blocked. Most flights to and from Ben Gurion Airport are canceled. Histadrut joining the protests seems to have been very effective.

Gallant did not yet receive the letter that confirms his dismissal. He spoke to the Security and Foreign Affairs Committee of the Knesset headed by Edelstein and gave details about the country's precarious situation.

Students' committees in secondary and junior high schools have decided on a strike from tomorrow on.

Netanyahu will supposedly announce the stopping of the judicial overhaul, but has not yet done so. Levin said that he would accept any decision. Smotrich and Ben-Gvir are against stopping. Of course. But even Ben-Gvir has not decided to vote against the coalition and bring it down. It is an internal Likud secession of the extreme right that probably worries the PM. Moreover, a right-wing counter-demonstration has been announced. It seems that the overhaul will be postponed to the summer session of the Knesset. Netanyahu may be waiting to see how the counter-demonstration fares.

According to news outlets, the counter-demonstrators are on their way to Jerusalem, to the Supreme Court. Netanyahu and Ben-Gvir apparently decided not to cancel the overhaul, but to slow it down. It should be accomplished by July. They probably hope that if the opposition protests have to stop for two or three months, they will not have the energy to resume.

Ben-Gvir, according to news, will receive a new private army, parallel to the police, a "National Guard." That is his price for remaining in the coalition. Netanyahu is ready to sell his mother to stay in power! If Ben-Gvir gets this private police, he may attempt to fight opponents on the streets, in due time. Very dangerous.

Some 20,000 coalition supporters demonstrated in front of the Supreme Court and in other spots in Jerusalem. From the news photos, one gets the impression that these are essentially students from yeshivot, which doesn't make them less dangerous.

Netanyahu announced the postponement of the overhaul until the end of July, to allow time for conciliation talks. He welcomed Gantz's readiness to negotiate. The Histadrut boss immediately declared an end to the strikes. I'm not sure that the opposition will relent and wait patiently for the summer. It's probable that when the summer comes, the coalition majority, possibly after some minute changes, will push for the ratification of the overhaul package. For the time being, nobody wants to seem opposed to the time-out.

Ben-Gvir got his private army, but it will take a lot of legal work for it to become official, and beyond the legalese, there will be complicated negotiations with the police to delimit their respective domains. An official private army is a rare occurrence in a democracy.

In Tel Aviv, the demonstrations went on. To reopen Ayalon, the police used stun grenades and water cannons.

Gantz and Lapid announced their readiness to negotiate. Lapid was much more careful than Gantz: he mentioned the possibility of a trick, given his overall experience of dealing with such an inveterate trickster as Netanyahu. In any case, Herzog declared that the President's Residence was open for talks.

The coalition lost eleven mandates according to the latest polls. Gantz got twenty-two mandates, Lapid twenty-one. Likud went down from thirty-two to twenty-five. Likud Knesset members accuse Netanyahu and Levin of destroying the party.

Tuesday, March 28

The *New York Times* and *Time* magazine seem to understand better than our own (Israeli) news outlets that Netanyahu has completely lost it and is acting erratically. His juggling act has not a chance of success. He will probably end up a hostage of his extreme-right wing acolytes.

The conversation between representatives of both camps will start tonight in the President's Residence. In principle, this is how it should be, but I remain very skeptical about the coalition's intentions. It is hard to believe that Netanyahu has instructed his delegates to hold a bona fide negotiation with real compromise in mind. Their aim is probably to delay long enough to deflate the mass protests and then to renew the legislative blitz.

I am glad to see that my skepticism is shared by several

journalists of *Haaretz* and the leaders of the protest movement. It appears that the coalition went so far as to ask advice from Poland, where mass protests occurred against a judicial "reform" launched in 2015. At some stage the Polish opposition thought it had won, but the negotiations petered out, the opposition was demobilized, and the government renewed its onslaught.

A protest demonstration has been called for Saturday evening, as in all previous weeks. Let's see what happens. Incidentally, the so-called spontaneous counter-demonstration in favor of the overhaul was very well organized ahead of time and the participants were violent when they managed to get at opposition protestors. So much for my theories about Jewish violence. All this will become highly dangerous once Ben-Gvir's private army is set up.

Some new laws will have to wait, but not the law allowing Knesset members and families to contribute donations to Netanyahu. Otherwise, how could impoverished Sara'le pay for her hairdresser and Netanyahu pay for his lobster at the Savoy?

In his press conference, Biden was quite explicit: "Israel cannot go on that way." He added that he was very worried about the situation, like many supporters of Israel. Responding to a comment by the US ambassador in Israel that Netanyahu would be invited to the White House after Passover and Ramadan, a spokesman for the White House declared that no invitation was in the works. That should help a bit. To the opposition's amazement, the judicial appointments bill has been placed on the agenda and is ready for a second and third vote at a moment's notice. It is the main bill that has to be discussed at the president's. The coalition argues that formally submitting the law was just a procedural step.

Wednesday, March 29

In his press conference, Joe Biden may have said that Israel should drop the overhaul. Today, Netanyahu answered that Israel was a sovereign country and that even the best of friends should not meddle with its internal politics.

Lapid is quoting a twit from the Levin camp to one of Likud's MKs (members of Knesset) to show that the justice minister doesn't have the least intention to slow the legislative overhaul; Levin denies this. Most opposition politicians are skeptical regarding Netanyahu's intentions. They are right, and the submission of the judicial appointments bill is ample proof. Hopefully, the coming Saturday demonstration will show Netanyahu that his trick does not work.

It all reminds me of the following allegory about a driver at a crossroads who, instead of waiting his turn, accelerates. Of course, the other drivers let him through to avoid an accident. The trick works nine times out of ten, but on the tenth time, another driver decides to go by the rules when his turn comes around, and a collision takes place. The trickster doesn't survive.

It seems that a majority of coalition Knesset members are against voting now for the "contributions to Netanyahu law," a shameful law that reeks of corruption to the high heavens.

The difference in social origin (Mizrahim versus Ashkenazim) between the two opposing camps saw sad expression in the letter sent today by tens of Air Force mechanics to the defense minister, the chief of staff, and the commander of the Air Force. They declared that the refusal of thirty-seven fighter pilots to answer call-ups made them feel like second-class citizens and demanded that these pilots not be readmitted for service if they do not apologize for their initiative.

Thursday, March 30

It seems that Gallant will stay in office; though he may have to apologize for the public way he announced his concerns regarding the security of the country, while Netanyahu was in London.

On the other hand, a hardline religious-nationalist extremist, Avihai Boaron, will join Likud MKs, replacing Amsalem, who has been appointed to the Justice Department (how his domain will infringe upon Levin's remains to be seen). This new MK is a particularly fanatic representative of the "second-class citizens" and the organizer of the demonstration of supporters of the overhaul that took place in Jerusalem. Today they will march in Tel Aviv, from the Museum Place to the government district. Social resentment turns the political confrontation into a powder keg. It is this powder keg that Netanyahu exploits relentlessly to achieve his political-judicial goal.

If Netanyahu and his acolytes take seriously the counter-protest of the right that they organized, or if they just pretend to, they may parade it as an expression of a popular will to scuttle talks they didn't want in the first place. Only US pressure can stop them, and even this will not do much to ease internal tensions that have reached a boiling point.

A small sign of hope: some 2,000 young people from all social and political backgrounds were brought together in Hayarkon Park in Tel Aviv, by the most various organizations, in an effort to initiate conversations about how to preserve the unity of the country. If this effort grows, it may have a tiny chance.

It may look as if my paragraphs contradict one another, but this simply expresses my contradictory fears and hopes. Sorry, folks, but the situation is loaded with contradictions, and I feel battered by contradictory feelings.

Friday, March 31

Much depends on the strength of the coming demonstration on Saturday. Some 20,000 people participated in the counter-demonstration in favor of the judicial overhaul yesterday in Tel Aviv. Netanyahu claimed 100,000.

Netanyahu may possibly keep Gallant, but tries to make him pay. He wants the minister to resign from his MK seat; Gallant refuses. He wants Gallant to apologize not only for the way he publicized his concerns about the country's security, but also for his having called for a halt to the overhaul because of its consequences. Not clear how Gallant will react to these systematic humiliations. In the meantime, MK Biton, the Likud chairman of the Knesset Economy Committee, called for his Likud colleagues not to accept the replacement of Gallant as defense minister, as, in his opinion, Netanyahu made a mistake in attempting to fire him. Biton will be punished for this courageous step.

Saturday, April 1

A young Arab man peacefully walking in East Jerusalem was shot dead by Israeli police. He was a physician who had just completed his medical studies. The policemen declared that he had grabbed a gun and was aiming it at them; they felt in mortal danger and shot. Their body cameras didn't register the whole event; most unlikely, declared a high-ranking police officer. The internal investigations department of the police is looking into the shooting. Tomorrow, the Arabs of Israel will go on a general strike.

Police brutality against Israeli Arab citizens is well documented and reflects a much wider attitude. Now imagine what the behavior will be when Ben-Gvir gets his private army, thanks to

Netanyahu. He is a declared Arab-hater and wishes to see as many of them as possible transferred beyond the country's borders and, if possible, to have the West Bank Palestinians transferred as well. Incidentally, the transfer of Arabs living within the future borders of a Jewish State is an idea as old as Zionism itself.

Some 175,000 demonstrators in Tel Aviv, many thousands in other cities and towns. The attempt to demobilize the protest movement may be failing. The main question: is the conciliation attempt genuine, or one more Netanyahu trick? In the meantime, Gallant has still not received his dismissal letter and continues to participate in the activities of his office, including a meeting with Netanyahu on defense issues.

Sunday, April 2

Simcha Rotman, the infamous chair of the Knesset Constitution, Law, and Justice Committee who, with Levin, is pushing the overhaul, declared to the *New York Sun* that the demonstrations were the beginning of "a war of religion" and made it clear that the reform drive would be resumed in due course. Simultaneously, Minister Miri Regev announced that the overhaul would start up again after Independence Day. Even if Netanyahu is minded to tone down some aspects of the overhaul, it's hard to see how he will get it swallowed by a majority of the Likud. After all, there are no more private armies to be handed out. Possibly, Miri Regev will be appointed defense minister (she was one of the candidates to replace Gallant). What else?

In fact, Rotman's remark about "a war of religion" isn't as farfetched as it looks. The great scholar of Jewish mysticism Gershom Scholem repeatedly posed to his listeners and readers the following question: "Can Jewish history manage to re-enter concrete reality without being destroyed by the messianic claim which [that re-entry is bound to] bring up from the depths." The religious fanatics of our day are, of course, those who incite the sort of "war of religion" mentioned by Rotman, and it is a kind of debased messianic urge that pushes them on, and him among them.

As may be remembered, I have wondered several times whether there was something of this messianic urge in Zionism and my answer was negative regarding all the decades stretching from the Congress of Basel in 1897 to the beginning of Begin's premiership in 1977. I was right, on the face of it, but wrong regarding the undercurrents. Well, I know better now. The fascist-like dimension that surfaced in Gush Emunim after the Yom Kippur War—and that my friend Uri Tal grasped so well—should have opened my eyes, but it did not, for the simple reason that the superficial aspect of Israeli life did not look different, notwithstanding all the political crises.

It could be that my stemming from a totally assimilated family and my passage through Catholicism made me particularly blind to those religious undercurrents. My Swedish uncle Hans, the anthroposoph, was repelled by what he considered the militant nationalism of the Zionists during his visit to Palestine in the 1930s. This nationalism expressed itself in fierce anti-Arab policies, such as pushing Arabs out of the labor market and considering how to get rid of an excess of Arab population in the future Jewish state. This nationalist enthusiasm may have been necessary for the creation of the state and its immediate survival but became dangerous once it mixed with religious messianism. What may have been necessary for the creation of the State of Israel could be deadly for its survival. Will an attack from the outside save the Jewish state before internal turmoil destroys it?

Netanyahu declared that he was getting involved in the judicial impasse because it was his duty as PM, because the country was in a national crisis. His intervention, he said, had nothing to do with any personal indictment. This led to a censure from the attorney general. He forgets to mention that he is responsible for triggering the national crisis. Nobody takes him seriously anymore.

What I was saying about the danger of messianism, following Scholem and Aviezer Ravitsky, represents one more dramatic twist in the history of a people who would have had to abandon a thousand years of beliefs to be capable of entering modern history. The only way the dilemma could possibly have been avoided would have been a constitution with a firm separation of Synagogue and State. But would that have contained the currents in the underworld? Not according to Scholem, and not according to what we see. Moreover, let us remember that, under one form or another, religious nationalism broadly coincides with the social division in Israeli society. Nowadays, the Ashkenazis are generally the more liberal and secular, but their religious-nationalist leaders have from the outset been the most extreme and the initiators of this deadly synthesis (the Rabbis Kook, father and son).

According to the news, the leaders of the Israeli economy met with Herzog and told him what they thought of today's main coalition figures: the insults I may be using here and there are nothing compared to what they have to say. The least is that "Levin is ready to burn down the country" or that Barkat is "a rag." They are unanimous about one thing: "In one month, they have managed to destroy the country." As for Netanyahu: "He is out of it."

Monday, April 3

Netanyahu will not dismiss Gallant "for the time being," which means that he will not dismiss him at all. Officially, it is because of the security situation; in reality, to hide the fact that, under pressure, he changed his mind. Netanyahu and Gallant went together to visit the Tel Nof Airbase, where Netanyahu praised the air force chief for taking a tough attitude toward those reserve pilots who had refused to report for call-ups.

The chairman of the Bank of Israel announced that according to the bank's forecasts, in the best of cases, the financial losses due to the overhaul would be about 14 billion shekels per year for three years, in the worst of cases, 48 billion shekels. An official of the bank warned: "red light for the shekel."

It is time for a comic interlude. Ben-Gvir appeared at the Supreme Court to defend himself against a complaint that he, a notorious racist, had been appointed minister of national security. Ben-Gvir, who fends for himself, admitted that he had been a racist when he was fourteen and had made mistakes in the past; he argued that although he had not changed his opinions, he had become more sensitive since he joined the government. The judge then asked him whether he had reached the utmost point in sensitivity, or whether he still had a bit of a road to travel.

I must admit that I look less and less for the comic aspects of a situation that, notwithstanding the conciliation talks, does not bode well. The coalition will not give in and, in a few weeks or less, it will push the overhaul through the Knesset and then all hell will break loose, leading God knows where. I fear the explosive potential of social resentment among the Mizrahim. It is in Israel that this particular wound has festered, as a result of the conditions under which the immigration from North Africa took place.

I realized this, with particular clarity, in 1966, when I was invited to teach at the French University of Montreal and rented an apartment from a Jewish Moroccan family with whom I quickly became very friendly.

This family was quite well off and lived in Westmount (a wealthy part of Montreal). I realized that the rich Moroccan Jews, like all other middle-class or wealthier North African Jews, left in the 1950s either for North America or France, while the poor, the illiterate, and the sick were shipped to Israel to add to the Jewish population in the Promised Land. In Israel, as I said before, they were parked, often for years, in ramshackle transit camps near cities or in development towns on the periphery of the country. No wonder that in what was supposedly their Land, they stayed at the bottom of the social structure, while in North America and in France they soon mingled with the bourgeoisie and often reached some top intellectual, and even political, positions. In Israel, the situation has improved over the decades, but, as I mentioned, Begin came to power thanks to these Mizrahi battalions and Netanyahu exploited to the hilt the seething resentment of these supposedly "category B" citizens.

An Iranian drone was downed near Lake Tiberias; another one was downed over Gaza. Israel bombed Iranian or Hezbollah targets in Syria for the fourth successive time this week. Some Iranian advisors killed. Very unusual. Does Netanyahu try to provoke a large-scale Iranian response, which would represent a casus belli? In more standard actions, Israeli forces entered Nablus and killed two Palestinians suspected of aiding the gunman responsible for the Huwara double murder that ignited the mayhem. The vicious circle never stops.

Tuesday, April 4

A psychiatrist who deals with ultra-Orthodox patients in Israel told me that, as has always been the case, they are mainly interested in concrete (financial) advantages for themselves and their community, and indifferent to the other religious legislation pushed by their leaders through the Knesset.

Tomorrow is the eve of Pesach. In my uncle's village, where I stayed during the first years of my life in Israel (from 1948 to 1951), its German and Czech inhabitants did not particularly observe the traditional ritual of Haggadah reading and, if they did, they did it for the enjoyment of the children. In short, I do not remember any particular attachment to religion. In some kibbutzim, particularly of the Marxist Hashomer Hatzair, the Haggadah had been rewritten in the national-political spirit of the times. This was not the general picture of course, but the Israel of those years was in majority secular or, at most, moderately observant for the sake of tradition. All of this changed, as we saw, first in 1967, and more thoroughly in 1977. Yet it is only now that the membership of the radical ultrareligious parties in the coalition has created a dangerous situation because of their relentless activism.

For the opposition, the threat of religious compulsion, of Israel turning into a theocracy, may be as obnoxious as the possibility of dictatorship. It is hard to see how youth who for the most part grew up in total religious freedom will submit to religious laws and edicts.

In Poland (I do not know about Hungary) the population has remained fervently Catholic, so the above may not have been a major obstacle to Jarosław Kaczyński's regime change. Actually, the governing party uses the defense of Pope John Paul II (against allegations that he covered up pedophilia cases among Polish priests while archbishop of Krakow) as a major propaganda theme in this election year. Traditional Catholic piety is at the core of Polish identity.

Tension between Ben-Gvir and Shabtai about who will have authority over a National Guard remains unresolved.

Wednesday, April 5

As was to be expected, the tension in Jerusalem leads to scuffles. Hundreds of Palestinian youngsters entered Al-Aqsa Mosque late last night and started "fortifying" the sanctuary. After fruitless negotiations, the police entered the mosque and arrested some 350 youngsters. Most of them were released during the following hours. In the morning, calm had returned and prayers could be resumed. In the meantime, as a reaction, rockets were launched from Gaza on the surrounding settlements. The air force attacked twice. Gaza and Jerusalem are now relatively quiet. All in all, nothing dramatic yet.

The war between Ben-Gvir and Shabtai intensifies. Yesterday the minister apparently leaked a very problematic remark by the police commander, that it was in the Arab mentality to massacre each other. If this spreads—and according to the police, the quote is absolutely out of context—such a remark can do a lot of harm. The leak probably came in response to Shabtai's previous speech, stating that the national guard would stay under police control. It seems that in Ben-Gvir's entourage, people have recorded the conversations between the two, and other leaks can be expected.

I was asked to write something about Ben-Gvir's private army. I won't, not because the militia isn't dangerous; it is extremely dangerous. But I find it hard to believe that Ben-Gvir will be able to set it up. The man is a clown, good at issuing threatening declarations in all directions. He managed to threaten Netanyahu about wrecking the coalition, but such a step is hardly believable. Where would the man find such a chance to threaten once more? He managed to antagonize the police to a point that has turned them into his enemies. Where will he find the volunteers for his force, if not among policemen? The scuffles in Al-Aqsa started again. The police again used force to evacuate the mosque. Two rockets fired from Gaza during Seder evening. In Um el-Fahem, an Arab town in Israel, hundreds gathered in a solidarity protest with the Al-Aqsa demonstrators. Luckily, up till now, nobody has been killed on either side.

Thursday, April 6

A barrage of rockets was fired from Lebanon during the night; some thirty-four rockets, the heaviest attack since the Second Lebanon War. Iron Dome intercepted most of them. Two people were slightly wounded. Is this a Hezbollah initiative or a Palestinian one? Netanyahu is calling a cabinet meeting for tonight. The Israeli reaction will probably depend on which organization is behind the firing.

From first reports, Palestinian organizations in Lebanon are responsible for firing the rockets, probably with Iranian help. Also, a few mortar shells were fired on Metullah. There is a high probability of a strong Israeli response, both in the North and South. Netanyahu declared at the end of the cabinet meeting: "The internal discussion will not be an obstacle to our response. Our enemies will pay a price."

The Second Lebanon War was tough. It was initiated by Hezbollah which, in a raid over the Lebanese border, captured

7 Israeli soldiers. In the response that followed and lasted about a month, Israel lost 140 soldiers and Hezbollah about 500; Israeli cities in the North suffered a number of missile attacks; and the Hezbollah fighters, Iranians or trained by Iran, proved very resilient enemies. This time, Hezbollah denies involvement.

I dislike being a military correspondent, although I arrived intending to fight but was exempted when my age was found out. The three years I spent in the army excluded fighting units because of a heart murmur (bicuspid aortic valve) that had been discovered years before but was only identified and operated on forty years later. It shows you that one can live with heart murmurs . . . I served in the intelligence unit that became the famous Unit 8200 in later years. I feel proud telling about it, although I lack all the talents that today would point to a potential candidate.

Well, in those days my French was perfect.

An air force attack on Gaza during the cabinet meeting. Simultaneously, on the Palestinian side, a meeting of top leaders of Hamas and Islamic Jihad in Beirut to plan their response to the Zionist misdeeds in Al-Aqsa. Unfortunately, as in every year at Passover, several zealots tried to access the Temple Mount to offer a sacrifice. They were stopped by the police but this may have triggered the response of Palestinian youngsters who then started fortifying the mosque. This would explain the chain of events. Utterly stupid, except that, this year, the zealots have the clown Ben-Gvir to support them.

After the operation over Gaza, an attack on Palestinian bases in southern Lebanon. The assumption is that these operations will reassert Israeli deterrence and not lead to a war.

Friday, April 7

Until now, moderate Israeli reaction. Heavy criticism from Smotrich and Ben-Gvir regarding such moderation, but nothing beyond that. Netanyahu implies that this is just a first step. Two sisters were killed in a terror attack, their mother badly wounded. The family, West Bank settlers newly arrived from England, was on its way for a vacation. The father was driving ahead with two other children; he heard about the killing on the news. The two terrorists apparently came from Nablus or Jenin. More details on the brutality of police action at Al-Aqsa. Videos have spread all over the Muslim world, while Israel remains silent. No wonder that this inflames the Palestinian territories.

No idea how one gets out of this horrible situation. The only solution, in my opinion, is pulling out of the West Bank, as I already said several times. Of course, with international presence in the territories, demilitarization, etc. Two states, with economic links, possibly a federation. There is no doubt that the zealots, who consider mastery over the territories as a step in the divinely pre-scribed move toward messianic redemption, will fight a pull-out tooth and nail. The question is: how many people would support them? Today the majority of Israelis are apparently supporting the opposition, but will that stand when the rush toward the judicial overhaul resumes, once the holidays are over? And then what, after some cosmetic improvements? Moreover, while the majority may support changes to the judicial overhaul and may fight for the independence of the Supreme Court, no majority is guaranteed for a pull-out from the territories. Far from it.

This Friday evening, a terrorist car ramming in Tel Aviv: four people were wounded, the car overturned, and the driver is being held. The accumulation of over-the-border attacks and terror aggressions turn this into a particularly dire situation.

Actually, one person was killed and six wounded from the car ramming in Tel Aviv. The dead person is an Italian tourist, the wounded are British tourists. The killer is an Arab from Israel, from Kafr Kassem; he was shot. His family expresses disbelief. The Israeli-Arab parties condemn.

Saturday, April 8

Notwithstanding the disagreements between the two countries, the US has reasserted its support for Israel in the midst of the present tensions. With an eye on Iran, the US sends a nuclear submarine to the Red Sea.

Three rockets from Syria to the Golan. No damage.

In Tel Aviv, 140,000 demonstrators notwithstanding the holidays. Impressive.

Great tension in Jerusalem. Tomorrow, benediction of the Cohanim (the priests) and traditional access of Jews to the Temple Mount; hopefully without clashes, but police forces are reinforced to a maximum. Reinforcements in Tel Aviv as well. All in all, maximum readiness for possible further terror attempts.

In moments of maximum tension, Israel shows great resolve. Pity that such resolve takes place at such an awful internal conjuncture. This government should collapse as soon as possible. Not sure that it will. The steadfast demonstrators are our pride.

Sunday, April 9

In Jerusalem, last night and this morning elapsed quietly, although some thousand Jews were allowed to access the Temple Mount for prayers.

Netanyahu officially briefed Lapid, as head of the opposition, about the security situation. Upon leaving, Lapid declared that he came in worried and left even more worried. The government was dysfunctional, etc. In this case, it is indeed so. In such a serious situation, the defense minister is in limbo and a clown is in charge of internal security—a domain, according to Lapid, that should be left exclusively to the police. Of course, he is right.

I didn't yet speak of a relatively new group in our promised land: "La Familia." It started as a violent group of soccer fans of the Betar Jerusalem football team and is turning into a dangerous association of hooligans, ready to go after journalists, and particularly after demonstrators. They may become Ben-Gvir's militia. The police is supposed to intervene and make some arrests. They haven't yet.

According to a poll, the results of which will be published on this evening's news (Channel 13), if elections were held today, Netanyahu's coalition would fall from sixty-four mandates to forty-six, while the previous Bennett-Lapid coalition would get sixty-four mandates, even without the participation of the Arab parties. The Likud would go down from thirty-two mandates to twenty; Gantz's National Unity Party would more than double its numbers from twelve today to twenty-nine, and Lapid's "There Is a Future" would be slightly weaker, from twenty-four to twenty-one. These are extraordinary results that show ordinary electors understanding perfectly well whom they are dealing with. But how does one bring elections about? How does one bring this government down?

The results of the poll also indicate that the social resentment to which I attached much importance is less decisive than I thought. Shas would receive nine mandates and the combined list of the Religious Zionist Party and Jewish Power eleven mandates, which means that the messianic crazies are relatively marginal. Torah

Judaism with six mandates keeps its low numbers and, from its viewpoint, it is right to grab all the financial advantages that it can accumulate in the present context.

The situation on Temple Mount is the immediate problem. In the last ten days of Ramadan (which start in four days), many Muslims sleep in Al-Aqsa and, in past years—including under previous Netanyahu governments—the Mount has been closed to Jews. Now, opinions are divided and Netanyahu will have to decide.

Monday, April 10

The mother of the two sisters killed three days ago died today of her wounds. A Palestinian youngster was killed near Jericho.

Thousands of settlers, ministers Smotrich, Ben-Gvir, and the other ministers of their parties, plus their Knesset members, participated in a march to the evacuated settlement Eviatar. Ben-Gvir declared: "We are not blinking, we are getting home, to the Temple Mount and to Jerusalem." The march was heavily protected by the army; soldiers were seen using force against journalists. These settlers are true fanatics and they will not give up.

In the meantime, both sides met in Herzog's residence and agreed on various technical matters relating to the substantive discussions that will start immediately after Passover. The atmosphere is apparently positive.

Netanyahu held a press conference. Three main points: Gallant remains as defense minister; the previous government was responsible for the worsening security situation; Ben-Gvir's national guard will not be under his command, but under the command of one of the existing security forces (the army or the police).

Netanyahu was asked about yesterday's poll and brushed it off. Regarding the security situation, he promised that his government would repair all the damage caused by its predecessor. In fact, these were all merely general statements, except regarding Gallant. Netanyahu understood that dismissing Gallant would bring his coalition down.

The leaders of the opposition derided Netanyahu's declarations. Gantz: "whining." Lapid: "loss of control." Bennett: "no leadership." In Tel Aviv, thousands demonstrated against the PM, as they grasped that the government has tried to shift all responsibility for the current difficulties onto the opposition and the protest movement. What poor leadership!

In his rebuttal, Bennett proved that Netanyahu lied brazenly in his description of the security situation under his predecessor. Netanyahu is an inveterate liar, but now it works less and less. He should give it up, but he won't because of the indictments hanging over him.

The settlers, with Smotrich and Ben-Gvir at their head, are a real danger. Israel started on this path in the far-away past, but even if a leader like Begin was a true believer in the whole of Eretz Israel ideology, he remained a weird kind of liberal. In 1983, I received the Israel Prize for History from his religious education minister, Zevulun Hammer, although my opinions in favor of the two-state solution were well known. On the morning of the prize distribution, I joined a group of protesters against a new settlement at Har Bracha, in the West Bank; that did not stop Hammer from handing me the prize in the presence of President Yitzhak Navon a few hours later. This was another right, this was another time, and, let's admit it, this was another Israel—or, more exactly, another Israel in power.

Tuesday, April 11

Last week, Bogie Ya'alon, ex-chief of staff and defense minister, explained it most coherently: Dov Lior, Smotrich's and Ben-Gvir's rabbi, was also years ago the rabbi of those Jewish underground members who, among other glorious deeds, planned to murder Arab mayors and blow up Al-Aqsa, and were arrested at the last moment by the Shin Bet. Their plan was to precipitate the "final war" as the ultimate moment of the messianic process, the war that would bring about the coming of the messiah. Nice people. But now our two jokers are important ministers in Israel's government and, who knows? Dov Lior may still be their rabbi.

Incidentally, Dov Lior, the author of any number of racist statements and a steady inciter of violence against Arabs, dedicated a book of his to Baruch Goldstein, the murderer of twenty-nine Arabs at prayer in the Cave of the Patriarchs mosque. Ben-Gvir had a portrait of Goldstein hanging in his living room for years, until the recent elections. As I said, nice people.

Netanyahu decided to continue the policy of forbidding the access of Jews to the Temple Mount during the last ten days of Ramadan. Ben-Gvir objected strenuously, calling it "giving in to terror," "a security scandal," and "forsaking the lives of the worshippers at the Western Wall." For once, the crazy zealot didn't get the last word. For once. Netanyahu, please continue and, if you can, please throw him out. And Smotrich too.

Thursday, April 13

There was nothing much to write yesterday and there is nothing today, the last day of Pesach. How wonderful! But here the day has merely begun, and in Israel it is far from ended . . . Imagine closing this diary because all is quiet in the Holy Land: no police brutality, no military incursions into Palestinian strongholds, no terror attacks, and, especially, new elections on the horizon. In short, a dream.

But let's remember: everything should start again "after the holidays," that is, from Sunday on. In the meantime, the police are on high alert in Jerusalem, since tomorrow is the last Friday of Ramadan, potentially a very explosive day.

Friday, April 14

It seems that this last Friday of Ramadan will be peaceful, notwithstanding 130,000 Palestinian worshippers on Temple Mount. Only seventeen people were arrested for flying the Hamas flag; they will soon be released. This is quite an achievement for both sides.

If the weekend remains peaceful, Israelis will flock to the beaches and other nature spots. Don't forget that in its inhabited areas, the country is very densely populated, which, incidentally, is one more explanation for the move to the territories. Not only relatively cheap housing and great landscapes, but space. Never mind if that space belongs to others.

A few days ago, a very strange incident took place. In a Jerusalem yeshiva for girls called Horev, girls of the twelfth grade organized a Purim party, which they filmed. The film was soon all over the country and created a tempest. Its title: "If the Yeshiva Was Sephardi" or something like that. In a series of eight scenes, the girls juxtaposed their habitual, respectful Ashkenazi lives with imagined Sephardi behavior. The girls blackened their faces, introduced themselves with typical Sephardi names, hung portraits of Sephardi rabbis on the walls, and played their Sephardi roles, as obnoxious as those were in their imagination.

The fact that eighteen-year-old girls can be silly is nothing new, but that religious Israeli girls can play racist roles is somewhat more surprising, and within a strictly religious school at that. Where did they get their notions? From their families? From their teachers? Is it official yeshiva ideology? Everybody was up in arms, and rightly so, but it shows that even today, in a strictly nationalist-religious school, there is explicit anti-Sephardi racism. And, what nobody seems to have mentioned: has this religious Zionist school no Sephardi students? And don't forget: these religious Zionist parties, Smotrich's and Ben-Gvir's, display open, quasi-official racism against Arabs. But, who cares, for them Arabs are just Arabs.

Fiery anti-Israel speeches in Iran and by the Hezbollah chief from somewhere in Beirut, on the traditional day of solidarity with Palestinians. In a first, the Shiite Iranian president Ebrahim Raisi directly addressed a Gaza meeting of Suni Hamas and Islamic Jihad, promising support in their struggle for the liberation of Palestine (Iran apparently spends some $100 million per year financing Hamas's acquisition of weapons). Simultaneously, the Iranians launched cyberattacks against Israeli post-office services, banks, the electricity company, and the water company Mekorot. These attacks have been neutralized.

Hezbollah chief Hassan Nasrallah, the Iranian stooge, made fun of the Israeli rocket attacks of a few days ago; according to him they hit a banana plantation, and also killed a few sheep . . . Yet Israel is not taking lightly the coordinated threats from all sides: it stays on the highest alert for the coming days, at least to the end of Ramadan. As I mentioned, the Palestinians themselves are remaining peaceful.

Although Netanyahu and Herzog tried to dissuade it, Moody's downgraded Israel's rating from "positive" to "stable."

At least one troublemaker has been sent packing: Yair Netanyahu, the PM's son, who was broadcasting tens of inflammatory tweets per day, wildly accusing the CIA, the State Department, and anybody else, of being in league with the opposition to harm his father, was apparently told by the father himself to shut up; he chose to leave the country for a time.

Saturday, April 15

Demonstrations against the judicial overhaul remain strong: 140,000 protest in Tel Aviv, thousands more all over the country. In Netanya, demonstrators against the reform and demonstrators supporting it. The city is largely in the hands of Shas and other coalition parties.

Testimonies about the now notorious Jerusalem religious girls yeshiva (Horev) are coming out on the news: "racist and elitist." Actually, we all knew that the Lithuanian ultra-Orthodox yeshivot, and their communities more generally, avoided the inclusion of Sephardi Jews—one more reason for the creation of Shas. The truth is that in our daily life in Jerusalem, we kept to strictly Ashkenazi acquaintances, to a homogeneous Ashkenazi community, without ever thinking of it or discussing it. It was natural. But I think that it was also natural on the other side, the Sephardi one, not to mix socially with Ashkenazis. Perhaps so, but it was probably resented. In the schools, there was profiling. If you were Sephardi, you were not automatically directed to a secondary school, but rather to a professional one.

On the lighter side: one of my children had a Sephardi friend at school, who somehow managed to enter the Jerusalem Rehavia Gymnasium. This friend had to write an essay in history on the uprising of the Warsaw Ghetto. I wrote the essay and did my best. The teacher didn't like the result. The kid, probably then in eleventh or twelfth grade, got a bad mark. Did I write a poor essay or was this some late profiling?

Nowadays, the resentment finds unabashed political expression, cleverly manipulated by Netanyahu. Of course, he did not miss the chance to attend the traditional Mimouna feast (a North African–Jewish traditional celebration) after Passover, nor to give an interview that totally misrepresented the political situation in Israel to *Meet the Press*. What a trickster! The Mimouna is no big deal, but another concession to the Orthodox parties is. Military service for the students of yeshivot will either be completely scrapped or seriously cut short, in return for whatever financial payback to the army. Zahal (as the IDF is also known), which up to now aimed at being the whole people's army, will be the army of only one part of the population.

Monday, April 17

Tomorrow is Holocaust Remembrance Day in Israel, still a significant commemoration for a diminishing segment of the population. The elaborate ceremonies are mostly politicized and greatly overdone, yet they keep some relevance for that segment and it is good that they take place. The moment when in midmorning, at the sound of a siren, all cars stop and the drivers get out and stand at attention, together with all the pedestrians, remains extremely moving. On the other hand, the organized school trips to the camps in Poland have something brash and uncouth about them.

In the war years, the Yishuv (the Jewish residents in Palestine before the establishment of the State of Israel) did not attach much importance to what was happening in Europe, except, as Ben-Gurion put it, that nobody would remain to build the Jewish state. This was not a glorious page in the history of Ben-Gurion's leadership, nor of the mainly socialist political elites of Eretz Israel. This indifference was quite widespread.

After the end of the war, notwithstanding the Yishuv's efforts to bring survivors to the Land of Israel, those same leaders established a clear distinction between "ordinary survivors" who were just "dust" and the ghetto fighters who could be compared with the fighters in Eretz Israel. That view did not impress all ghetto fighters. In Claude Lanzmann's film *Shoah*, Antek Zuckerman, one of the surviving leaders of the Warsaw ghetto fighters and a "Ghetto Fighters" kibbutz member, put it unabashedly: "If you could lick my heart, you would be poisoned." He referred to the Yishuv's attitude during the war and later.

I did not suffer from discrimination when I met with the "sabra" kids in the Shaul Tchernichovsky High School I was admitted to in Netanya, in 1949, but I know that other youngsters who arrived from postwar Europe did, in the various institutions they joined. The sabras (the children born in Eretz Israel) considered themselves as the elite, of course, and the newcomers were often called "soap" (*sabonim*), according to the story that the corpses of Jews were turned into soap. This did not happen systematically, but it happened. Actually, speaking of discrimination, many of the young newcomers from postwar Europe were its earliest targets, maybe even before the immigrants from Yemen and certainly before those from North Africa. Israel remains an intricate caste-like society.

Wednesday, April 19

Political activity will remain less intensive until May 1, when the Knesset reconvenes. The negotiations go on at the President's Residence. It seems that they concentrate on the appointment of the Supreme Court justices, mainly that of the chief justice (appointment by seniority or not, for example).

Lapid declared that if the coalition makes the least move to push ahead with the overhaul, his party will leave the negotiations forthwith. It's hard to believe that the Levins and Rotmans won't try to resume the overhaul. It is also hard to believe that the negotiations will lead anywhere. The question is whether Gantz, by now at the head of the biggest opposition party according to the polls, will be tempted to abandon the opposition and join Netanyahu for some hefty reward (defense minister and vice prime minister?). Of course, this is merely wild speculation.

Let me return to yesterday's remark about Israel being a caste-like society. Don't think, for example, that the distinction between sabras and others was sufficient. Not at all. Among the sabras, there was a clear distinction between the children from kibbutzim and those from cities, the kibbutz being the perceived aristocracy (and within that category, there was a competition between the oldest kibbutzim, the Deganias, and some very old and famous village cooperatives, Nahalal). This turned into distinctions between the units in which you served in the army, etc. Nowadays, it is more a matter of tribes: the North Africans, the Russians, the Ethiopians, the Yemenites, the *yekes* (the Germans; the appellation dates from the 1930s and stems probably from the German word *Jacke*, "jacket"), the Israeli Arabs, and so on. There is intermarriage, of course, mainly among the Jewish tribes, but the distinctions are far from having been eliminated.

One may argue that these kinds of distinctions are pretty common in any Western nation created by, depending on, or dealing with immigration—and in many Eastern nations, too. Quite true, but for a nation under constant siege like Israel, relatively subdued social resentment may become an existential issue.

Thursday, April 20

Defense Minister Gallant warned today that Iran was extremely close to the production of nuclear material for military use. Moreover, for Israel, the next war will have to be fought simultaneously on all fronts. Not good news, but expected for some time. The big question: will the US stand with Israel in a major emergency? Biden's distaste for Netanyahu is quite obvious and the pressure from the "Progressives" in the Democratic Party against any pro-Israeli involvement will be fierce.

Moshe Koppel, the chairman of Forum Kohelet (the right-wing association standing behind the present Israeli coalition), made a strange declaration. He was not worried if the judicial overhaul didn't get through in the next two or three years; it would get through in any case in the more distant future for the good reason that the rate of reproduction of the Orthodox community in Israel was much higher than that of the secular population. A strange declaration indeed. It did not occur to Mr. Koppel that, at first contact with the modern, secular environment, a sizable segment of initially Orthodox young people will turn away from Orthodoxy and move over to the secular world, as happens with Orthodox Jews in the US, for example, and to a lesser degree in Israel itself, as well as in other religious communities. Or, alternatively, that a segment would remain Orthodox, but politically liberal enough to defend the judicial institutions that their brethren are attacking now.

It has been decided by whatever government authority that Minister Ben-Gvir would be the assigned speaker in Be'er Sheva, at the commemoration ceremony for the soldiers fallen in the wars of Israel, traditionally held on the eve of Independence Day. The Be'er Sheva population is up in arms: they don't want the clown Ben-Gvir, who never served in the army. They decided that they would sing the national anthem, "*Hatikvah*," with their backs turned on him, during his speech.

The police officer who, a few weeks ago, hurled a stun grenade on demonstrators in Tel Aviv, without any provocation, and badly wounded one of them, tearing off his ear, got the year's distinction award of the Tel Aviv police force. Nice, don't you think?

Friday, April 21

Yesterday, a very emotional speech by retired chief justice Aharon Barak, who, in his day, set the basic legal framework, akin to constitutional laws, for Israeli democracy. He expressed the hope that the protests would turn into demonstrations by millions of people, the hope we all share. As he was speaking to supporters in front of his house, hooligans mobilized by the government were yelling "Resign!" to a man who had resigned seventeen years ago. How sad and shameful.

Speaking of shame: Netanyahu wishes to send Knesset member May Golan as consul general to New York. The lady, who left school at age fifteen, is a declared and proud racist, known for her anti-African statements. Consul in New York? A spokesperson for the State Department made clear that Golan's language was unacceptable in the United States. How desperate can Netanyahu be?

When I come to think that in the 1950s, Arthur Lourie, to whom I was indirectly related through the marriage of one of my cousins to his brother, was Israeli consul general in New York, I cannot but wonder how far Israeli public service has come crashing down! Arthur, who over the years became director general of the Israeli Foreign Ministry, had been a law professor in South Africa before joining the prestate Jewish Agency and then the Israeli diplomatic service; he was a highly sophisticated individual, a friend, and an equal in many ways of another South African Jew and eventually Israel's foreign minister, Aubrey "Abba" Eban. But May Golan is a Knesset member of the Likud, had an appointment in Netanyahu's office, and knows some English.

A poll published on the evening news indicates that 60 percent of the population does not consider that this government represents them. Even more telling is the fact that on the eve of the seventy-fifth anniversary of the State of Israel, 48 percent of the population, instead of being cheered by the country's achievements and optimistic regarding its future, think that the coming years will be worse.

Analysts estimate that Netanyahu will not necessarily abandon the present course, but will try to cool things down until after the summer. It does not sound safe for the future of the coalition.

Saturday, April 22

For the sixteenth week in a row, about 165,000 demonstrators against the judicial overhaul protested in Tel Aviv, half a million all over the country. A major confrontation will take place two days from now, on the Commemoration Day for fallen soldiers.

Yuval Diskin, the former head of the Shin Bet, spoke at the Tel Aviv demonstration. The present coalition, he said, was legally elected, but is morally unacceptable; it was put together by a man who is himself under indictment and who acts only to further his own interests: "Netanyahu," Diskin exclaimed, "you are not the solution, you are the problem!" Strong words!

Justice Minister Levin insists on going on with the judicial overhaul: "That's what we have been elected for." According to senior government members, May Golan will not be appointed consul general in New York. That she was even a candidate is strange.

Sunday, April 23

A growing deficit in the state budget, as a result of various promises to the religious parties. According to the law, the budget has to be voted by the end of May—otherwise the Knesset must disband and new elections have to take place. Will the coalition obey the law? Hard to believe or to hope for in the present context.

A few ministers understood the feelings of the bereaved families and won't come to the cemeteries tomorrow, on Israel's Memorial Day. But the clown Ben-Gvir doesn't understand: he knows that he is not wanted in Be'er Sheva but he insists on going, because he must be in the news.

Yesterday, a meeting of delegates to the Zionist Congress took place in Tel Aviv. Herzog came and spoke. Netanyahu canceled his own participation, officially because of other obligations, in fact because he learned that thousands of hostile demonstrators were waiting for him. On that same day, negotiations between the two sides took place for seven hours at the President's Residence in Jerusalem: the atmosphere is supposedly positive, but the positions are still very far apart.

Monday, April 24

A terror attack in Jerusalem, near the Machane Yehuda market: eight people run over by a car, wounded to various degrees. The driver has been "neutralized," according to the police.

On the television program *Face the Nation*, Netanyahu was pushed quite hard by the tough interviewer Margaret Brennan. He had to admit that Golan would not be appointed as consul general in New York, that he had had to cancel his attendance at the meeting of Zionist Congress delegates in Tel Aviv because of demonstrations against him, and that he would rein in Smotrich and Ben-Gvir, etc. In short, not a very impressive performance by the PM on the seventy-fifth anniversary of the State of Israel. Incidentally, he tried to use an old trick of his, to create a sense of intimacy by calling the journalist "Margaret," but she did not reciprocate with "Bibi" . . .

This evening, the official commemoration ceremony for the fallen soldiers. Ben-Gvir seems to be the controversial politician to insist on speaking. We shall see what happens.

Over 10,000 participants in a joint Israeli-Palestinian commemoration ceremony organized by the "Forum of Bereaved Families for Peace" in Hayarkon Park in Tel Aviv. The ceremony was able to take place after some 150 Palestinians were authorized to cross over to Israel from the West Bank. Defense Minister Gallant had forbidden this, but the Supreme Court reversed the decision. On the street, outside the park, right-wing demonstrators yelled insults at the "leftist traitors" and shouted "Kahane is alive" (*Kahane hai*), Kahane being the extreme right-wing terrorist rabbi whose party was forbidden in Israel, but whose members were, among others, the murderer Baruch Goldstein and Ben-Gvir, our minister and evil clown.

Tuesday, April 25

This morning most other commemoration ceremonies took place. While the main one at Mount Herzl passed off almost undisturbed, insults and severe clashes among bereaved families took place in Be'er Sheva, during Ben-Gvir's speech, as foreseen. The evil clown insisted on coming and on speaking amid heavy security. Clashes occurred during other ceremonies, too. A sad reflection of the overall situation.

At the Tel Nof Airbase the commander spoke of an upcoming challenge that the pilots have not experienced since 1973 (the Yom Kippur War). Is this what gives Netanyahu the confidence he displays?

Transportation Minister Miri Regev, who is in charge of the commemoration ceremonies and the official celebration of the seventy-fifth anniversary of the State of Israel, reportedly gave instructions to television channels to cut any signs of disturbances. This dumbo doesn't understand that this is precisely the kind of censorship that people do not want.

Tens of thousands came to the demonstration in Tel Aviv, where the text of the Declaration of Independence will be read. Some 2,500 demonstrated in silence in front of the place of the official ceremony, at Mount Herzl, in Jerusalem.

Wednesday, April 26

Tomorrow, the "protest of a million" is to take place in front of the Knesset. It is a protest that has been worked on for several weeks by supporters of the judicial overhaul. Levin, Rotman, and Smotrich are scheduled to participate; their main slogan: "They won't steal the results of the elections from us." Netanyahu has been invited but will not attend "for security reasons." It is reported, however, that he actively participated in the preparations. From the news, it is not clear whether Shas will also be there. The Orthodox parties will abstain. It all means that part of the coalition will push for the passage of the judicial overhaul when the Knesset reconvenes.

A Knesset member of Ben-Gvir's Jewish Power is proposing a law aimed at applying the criteria of the Law of Return to employment in all government offices. Outright discrimination against non-Jews.

Thursday, April 27

About 100,000 participants in the demonstration in Jerusalem in support of the judicial overhaul. Officially, the Likud financed some 5 percent of it, which means that it actually financed somewhat more. But never mind, they organized their thing quite well, even having a corner for Orthodox participants. They, however, didn't come.

Levin showed that he would be quite at ease in Ben-Gvir's party: he gave a speech that was nothing less than pure hatred against the Supreme Court and the worst demagogic poison that can be imagined. I don't know whether Jerusalem has heard anything that foul for a long time. What a shame! The goal is obvious: to put an end to the conciliation talks that continue in the meantime at the President's Residence.

The more I think about it, the more it becomes obvious: the goal of Levin is not only to put an end to the conciliation talks, but to become the next leader of the Likud, to push Netanyahu out of the way. If nobody stops him, he may bring disaster on the country.

There is more and more talk of attempting to create a new structure for the country, a federal one, something like Switzerland. One canton for the Orthodox, one for the secular Jews. The idea is good, but we are not Swiss and our bickering will not end so easily. Moreover, our neighbors will make sure that we do not get the time to make such complicated constitutional changes . . .

Friday, April 28

Today, photos taken by a passenger on the *Altalena* were published in *Haaretz*. It seems to be the same group pictured in the four snapshots, probably Jews from DP camps and, on the last photo, kids from Ben Shemen who came to greet them on arrival, before the massacre. There was intense hatred between political groups, even then.

To this day, it remains difficult to apportion blame for the killings that cost the lives of sixteen of the passengers of the ship. I was one of the passengers on the *Altalena*, probably the youngest. Whatever good reasons Ben-Gurion had for destroying the ship, there was no cause for shooting people who had leaped into the sea and were swimming toward the shore, and even less for declaring afterward that the gun which sunk the ship was "a blessed gun."

Saturday, April 29

Tens of thousands are gathering for the demonstration in Tel Aviv. Thousands are protesting all over the country. In Netanya, two opposed groups will demonstrate facing each other. Tomorrow the Knesset reconvenes for three months; while Netanyahu wants to put the judicial overhaul on a backburner, it is not certain that he will succeed.

If the budget is not approved within exactly a month, new elections have to be held.

Sunday, April 30

In opening the summer session of the Knesset, Netanyahu declared that he is convinced the compromise talks at the President's Residence can succeed and that he fully supports them. This was a quasi-direct answer to Levin's declaration at the Jerusalem demonstration that the overhaul has to be voted now and that the PM should stop giving in.

Right-wing activists planned to protest in front of retired Chief Justice Aharon Barak's house in Tel Aviv. This was enough to bring hundreds of people to his house to demonstrate their solidarity. All in all, fifty right-wing activists remained. In the Knesset, the Orthodox parties agreed to postpone the discussion of the law regarding the military service of the Yeshivot students. The discussion of the budget should bring them massive benefits; this is therefore a priority for them, as for the other coalition parties.

An astonishing new poll. If elections took place today:

Gantz's party: 30 mandates.
Likud: 25 mandates.
Present Coalition: 51 members out of 120.
Present Opposition: 63 members out of 120.
Whom would you prefer as PM?
  Gantz: 43 percent.
  Netanyahu: 33 percent.

If the compromise discussions do not succeed, what should be the fate of the judicial overhaul?

Abandon it: 55 percent.
Push ahead: 29 percent.

Quite sensational indeed! If only the discussions about the budget could fail.

Monday, May 1

In Israel, there is no international workers' day celebration anymore, only relentless internal fighting. It will probably reach its most intense moment during this Knesset session: Gantz said today that there was no real progress in the president's talks and that the opposition will not allow the coalition to play for time. But what can he do, except leave the talks? Netanyahu declared that an understanding was possible; he is almost certainly playing for time. The whole situation is quite explosive, since no solution is in sight.

Edelstein, a senior member of the Likud, declared that the party responsible for the failure of the talks will not find him with it. It is encouraging, but one MK is not sufficient to change the majority. Hopefully, some more will follow. In yesterday's poll, only 8 percent considered the judicial overhaul a priority. On the other hand, among the demonstrators against Aharon Barak, one heard a voice shouting: "The people voted Yariv Levin."

Tuesday, May 2

For now, the Orthodox Degel HaTorah party refuses to accept the postponement of the law concerning the military service of *yeshivot* students. They want it now, before discussing the budget. "If you cannot deliver it now," Rabbi Meir Porush, the grand old man of the party, declared to Netanyahu, "then, go home." They argue that it was promised to them in the coalition agreements. Will they be ready to leave the coalition?

As I said before, I have known very liberal and gentle religious people, but they were not typical of the Orthodox community. This is a community closed in upon itself, focused upon its own interests and very little else. As long as it was but a relatively weak group among much stronger parties, it adapted to the will of the majority, but now that it is a strong component of the coalition, it will insist on getting all that has been promised to it.

The self-imposed isolation of Orthodox Jewry is an attitude steeped in age-long tradition. Before the second half of the eighteenth century, the immense majority of Jews followed various strands of Orthodoxy and lived in isolation from surrounding non-Jewish society, out of duress and, partly, out of choice. During the Shoah, Orthodox rabbis tried to save themselves at whatever cost and, after the war, they accused the secular parties of all possible wrongdoing. Even the commemoration of the Shoah in Israel was exclusive for a long time, as far as the Orthodox were concerned. To this day, as I have mentioned several times, the Orthodox parties recognize the state only as long as it can fulfill their own interests.

It would be a mistake to identify the Orthodox with the Mizrahim. A segment, the followers of Shas, are so by definition. But in fact, in the Lithuanian *yeshivot*, as in the Hasidic ones, there is an unspoken *numerus clausus* against Mizrahi candidates, one of the reasons for the foundation of Shas. In a sense, the would-be Purim film of the twelfth-grade girls belonging to the religious school Horev in Jerusalem, which created such a scandal, may not be far from the general atmosphere.

Among the religious friends that we had in Jerusalem and who were profoundly liberal were the professor of Jewish philosophy Stéphane Mosès and his wife, the painter Liliane Klapisch. But this wasn't the common attitude among the Orthodox immigrants from France after the Six-Day War. This "Alsatian" immigration was both Ashkenazi and Orthodox. Over the years, the Mizrahim became the majority among the religious junior officers in the army: not so Orthodox as to shy away from military service, but enough to introduce a distinct and growing tendency in an army which, before that, had been essentially nonreligious.

Wednesday, May 3

Let me return to the present political situation: a crisis that was in the making for some time has erupted between the Likud and Ben-Gvir's Jewish Power. The evil clown complains about not being invited to meetings of the security cabinet, the weak reaction to the shooting of rockets from the Gaza Strip, the disregard of measures he had advocated against terrorists, etc.; in reprisal, his party has abstained from participating in Knesset voting. Jewish Power will open new headquarters in Sderot, one of the towns that suffers most from sporadic attacks from Gaza. A Likud spokesperson told Ben-Gvir that if he further abstains from participating in Knesset votes, he can leave the coalition, to which he answered: "You should dismiss me." That would be the end of the coalition. In short, Netanyahu has to face threats from the Orthodox party and from Ben-Gvir's. Is the end approaching?

Over the last few weeks, several main figures of the Israeli cultural scene have died: the poet Meir Wieseltier, the novelist Meir

Shalev, the popular composer and writer Yonatan Gefen. They were all politically engaged, on the left, or even the extreme left. They follow a number of other writers, among them Amos Oz, who were trailblazers on the cultural left. Only A. B. Yehoshua was often undecided, yet never on the right. Since the crazy days of the Six-Day War, when a series of Israeli writers temporarily became advocates of seizing the whole land of Israel, the Israeli cultural scene has been on the left. The only main figures remaining of that group of writers are David Grossman and Etgar Keret. I am sure that there are many others, but I am too far away to follow the political choices of a much younger generation. It does not seem that there is any significant voice on the right.

It's not that I read much of the poems and novels of the deceased, as I have difficulties in reading Hebrew quickly and get impatient after a while. But years ago, I read Amos Oz's autobiography and some of his political writings, as well as A. B. Yehoshua's novels, Grossman's ones and a few of Etgar Keret's stories, and liked them. It is difficult for people who came with a baggage of very good literature in a language that they consider as their primary one (in my case French) to adopt a totally foreign culture and its literature, sometimes not as good as that of the primary one. I guess that this was an obstacle encountered by many immigrants from Germany in the 1930s and by the Russian immigration in more recent years.

In that sense, the kids born in Israel have a natural way of creating and consuming the new Hebrew culture. For most of them, it is the only one they are aware of until their teens; for many adults who arrived with the early immigration waves, it was partly a culture they already knew and, mainly, a cultural and ideological obligation. Although Hebrew was used throughout the centuries in religious education and in all religious ceremonies and rabbinical scholarship, a Hebrew nonreligious culture existed in the flourishing Jewish community in Spain during the age of Muslim domination, particularly from the tenth through the twelfth centuries, and in Eastern Europe from the "Haskalah" (Jewish Enlightenment), mainly through the nineteenth and early twentieth centuries. Some of the literature written in both periods entered the Israeli cannon.

I was quickly made aware of all that and did my best, once I entered the high school in Netanya. I even got a first in writing an essay on *The Travels of Benjamin the Third* by Mendele Mocher Seforim (a pseudonym meaning "Mendele, the itinerant bookseller"), a Yiddish and Hebrew writer in Russia in the second half of the nineteenth century. But, as I have mentioned elsewhere, during the months that preceded I used to go to the beach and, in a quiet corner, read my only available French book, *Dominique*, a novel by Eugène Fromentin.

Thursday, May 4

Gantz's interview on *Ynet Radio* is worth remembering for its idea of a plea deal for Netanyahu: the indictments would be canceled, but he would leave political life. Hard to believe that Netanyahu would accept this. But the fact is that he faces crisis after crisis and is unable to govern without being confronted by stupendous demands from his coalition partners, both religious and nationalist. Today, Shas also decided to abstain from Knesset voting, because the law that would bring Deri back was put on the backburner: "We do not want to continue without Deri." Does it mean that all three coalition partners of Likud will abstain from voting?

The main demonstrations for and against the judicial overhaul took place today in front of retired Chief Justice Aharon Barak's house. Supporters of the overhaul played Moroccan music and distributed Moroccan sweets to passers-by, under the pretext that Barak was the justice who initiated the activism of the Supreme Court and who supposedly said that he did not know of any Moroccan judge who could sit on the Supreme Court. On the other side of the street stood the demonstrators who came to support Barak. The resentment of the Mizrahim that Netanyahu so cleverly utilized in the elections has spread deep and wide, and it now penetrates every crevice of Israeli life.

Three Palestinians who took part in the killing of the mother and her two daughters some weeks ago were killed today in the casbah of Nablus.

Friday, May 5

A very detailed profile of Justice Minister Yariv Levin in *Haaretz* comes to the conclusion that, notwithstanding all the denials, he now seeks the first place in the Likud and thereafter to replace Netanyahu as prime minister. In the article he is called "the snake with glasses"; he is a poisonous snake with glasses.

Saturday, May 6

This evening, the eighteenth week of demonstrations against the judicial overhaul. We shall see whether Netanyahu's implicit plan to postpone the final push for a few months, to give some time for compromise negotiations and then to evaluate the public's attitude while lowering its desire for demonstrations, will work. It would ultimately be a victory for Yariv Levin and the various architects of the overhaul, both nationalists and Orthodox. It would certainly be the end of democracy in Israel.

The truth is that the decisive step for the end of democracy came with the decision to prolongate sine die the occupation of the West Bank and to begin the settlements. It is not at all clear whether that is reversible. Can a courageous decision for a two-state solution still be feasible to save Israeli democracy? Each day that goes by without a solution is one more day in which the hope for a true democracy fades. In the meantime, the pervasive surveillance of the Arabs gets more technologically intricate by the day: according to news outlets, face recognition cameras are now the name of the game; they are supposedly everywhere that Arabs live.

I don't know of an obvious period of democracy before the fateful Six-Day War and the conquests that followed. Before that, all levers of the administration, the army, and the police—and, of course, all major political decisions—were in the hands of Mapai (Party of the Workers of Eretz Israel), the majority party in the iron hands of Ben-Gurion, with the brief Moshe Sharett interlude (of the same party) and the somewhat more liberal Eshkol years (of the same party again), after Ben-Gurion's decision to retire from politics. In the Ben-Gurion days, the new immigrants from North Africa were more or less ordered to vote Mapai and were promised various advantages if they did. They didn't know any better and usually followed instructions. As for the Arabs, they were of course voting Mapai, or else.

I have told elsewhere how after a few months in my village, I received a visit from a local Shin Bet man who told me that, to make up for my coming on the *Altalena*, I had to report on anything of interest in the conversations of newcomers from

Czechoslovakia. Of course, I did, to make good on my crime. My career as a snitch ended very soon, as I had nothing worthwhile to tell about.

About 150,000 demonstrators in Tel Aviv and thousands more all over the country.

Sunday, May 7

The funeral of the young Arab killed after a road dispute in the Gilboa area by a Jew living nearby brought thousands of local Arabs onto the streets and was punctuated by a series of pro-Palestinian and anti-Israeli outbursts. Does it mean that, in Israel too, the hatred goes on, unabated? Probably.

Two new roads are planned in the West Bank: one for Israelis, one for Palestinians. Moreover, there are plans for the construction of new housing units in the territories. The settlement policy and its apartheid dimension go relentlessly ahead.

Ben-Gvir plans to speak at the yearly reception hosted by the diplomats of the European countries in Israel to celebrate the anniversary of the EU. Why did Netanyahu delegate the evil clown to speak at the event? Probably to make up for reining him in on other matters and to keep the coalition afloat.

Another maneuver is the stupendous amount of money allocated to the Orthodox parties in the projected state budget to be discussed in two weeks. This means severe cuts in ordinary state expenses such as education and health services. What is going on in all domains is hard to believe. It is clear that Smotrich, as finance minister, is behind all of this. There is a common front between all of the Orthodox parties in favor of their own interests, and against the needs of the state.

Monday, May 8

European Union diplomats have canceled the reception to avoid a speech by Ben-Gvir. In the meantime, the tension surrounding the debates on the budget is growing, as Ben-Gvir continues to boycott the various Knesset forums. Even Smotrich has called on him to show good will for the sake of the common cause. I guess that he will wait until he is offered adequate compensation. In the meantime, he managed to restore to the service a policewoman who was found guilty of having attacked a Palestinian woman.

Tuesday, May 9

The army liquidated three of the most senior military commanders of Islamic Jihad in the Gaza Strip. A reaction is expected, and security measures have been taken in the villages and towns within a given perimeter around Gaza.

A second attack in Gaza, against a unit that was about to fire anti-aircraft guns. In the first attack against Islamic Jihad, ten civilians were killed in addition to the three commanders; in the second, two civilians lost their lives. The UN has condemned this, but that is irrelevant; they will automatically condemn Israel. The question is: was the first attack necessary, or was it one more maneuver by Netanyahu to hold his coalition together? Ben-Gvir is ready to join the team, and he has already announced that it was his badgering that compelled Netanyahu to act. I wouldn't be astonished if he were right for once.

In Israel's short history, war has been an integral part of its existence. In most cases, the wars appeared to be vitally necessary; in a few cases they were results of complete misjudgment or, worse, of political maneuvers (the Second Lebanon War is possibly the most striking example). The trouble is that the unavoidably opaque character of Israeli defense policy makes external judgment almost impossible during the events and sometimes for long afterward. In the present case, it is particularly difficult to take a clear view.

The country is possibly getting ready for a significant war, and people have been warned to prepare their air raid shelters. Moreover, there is a massive evacuation of the inhabitants of the Gaza periphery. What is new is that, for the first time, the country will get scant international support. Moreover, a headline in *Haaretz* expressed quite correctly what many feel: "In their missions, our pilots will not know whether they are fighting for their country or for the government of Israel." Netanyahu has poisoned the atmosphere to such a point that suspicion is the name of the game.

Wednesday, May 10

Islamic Jihad has reacted with a hail of rockets on central Israel, but without much effect. The situation may either develop into a wider conflict or lead to a truce.

It seems that, notwithstanding the rockets from Gaza, a truce brokered by Egypt is in the making, although the demands of the Palestinians seem difficult to accept. In the meantime, the head of Jihad's rocket command has also been killed.

As a TV Israeli commentator said quite correctly, all these are tactical successes, but they do not change anything on a strategic level. What is changing is the patience of Netanyahu and the Likud in the face of constant self-congratulation by Ben-Gvir. It has reached the point (which even I have noticed) that the TV transmits images from cabinet meetings in which almost all members are depicted except Ben-Gvir. But how will Netanyahu

get rid of the evil clown without bringing the coalition down?
Will Gantz be ready to save him?

There are previous cases of entrenched disagreement between
a prime minister and an independent-minded member of the government: Ben-Gurion versus Pinhas Lavon and Sharett, Begin
versus Sharon, Rabin versus Peres. Either the confrontation ultimately brought the removal of the head of government or of the
independent-minded minister, or it led to a pseudo-reconciliation,
but it did not affect the ascendency of the major party and the
governing coalition. Now the situation is by far more critical.

Let me repeat: the present internal situation goes far beyond a
purely political crisis. We are facing a major social crisis, whereby
the country is divided between a liberal and liberal-observant, in
majority Ashkenazi, part of society, facing a mostly Orthodox
segment, in part Mizrahi (but not only), and with both sides
having to contend with the aggressive policy of the prosettler
party. In other terms, deep social resentment and fanatic messianic
dreams are mixed with political calculations. All this has existed
for a long time but was papered over until this fragile concealment collapsed thanks to the demands of the various parties of
the present coalition.

In the meantime, the attacks on and from Gaza have certainly
put an end to demonstrations. It won't be easy to renew them,
and if this was engineered by Netanyahu, it was clever in the
immediate term, but not in the long run. The trouble is that we
don't know the real causes of this so-called war.

Thursday, May 11

No truce yet.

The social resentment of the Mizrahim has bothered me for a long time. On the one hand, I do not like the political options of Shas; on the other hand, I know that the—often automatic and unconscious—rejection which the Mizrahim have suffered was real. It is true that in some of the most demanding functions in the army one didn't find many Mizrahim for a long time, because those who became pilots, for example, had to show abilities that most Mizrahi candidates had not yet acquired. I am not sure whether, nowadays, the situation is more balanced. The protest of the air force mechanics, several weeks ago, that they were second-class citizens was unjustified because probably nobody considered them as such, but it was justified in their own eyes, because the most prestigious positions in the air force were not yet equally theirs. And, as I mentioned before, among part of the ultra-Orthodox, the rejection of Mizrahim by their *yeshivot* was conscious and voluntary.

Friday, May 12

For what is this whole thing good, except for consolidating—temporarily—Netanyahu's coalition? Islamic Jihad is not an organization of choirboys, and in the event of real conflict, there would be no reason not to deal with them as severely as necessary. But at this moment, for nothing? Incidentally, it is interesting to see that Hamas abstains from joining the fray. It wants to spare the civilian population for which it is responsible, while Jihad is exclusively fixated on the military struggle against Israel. The whole episode would be ridiculous, were it not for the civilian victims on both sides.

Saturday, May 13

Hard to understand whether the shooting has stopped or not. It seems that the US is sending signals that it is time to put an end to the game.

A few days ago I spoke to somebody who, like me, has not lived in Israel for quite some time, but who visits once or twice a year and shares my ideas about politics in the country. He confirmed what I sensed: the official politics were unpalatable, but on the other hand, the demonstrators are kindred souls, at least some of them, and, mainly, there are the friends, those friends whom one knew sometimes from grade or middle school and, more often, from the army, companions that sometimes accompany you for your entire life. In that sense the role of the army in Israel is quite unique. Notwithstanding its brutal behavior in the Occupied Territories, together with its function as a melting pot which it generally fulfills, it very often creates strong bonds and lifelong friendships. I did not share this experience, as I left immediately after my military service for studies in Paris, and it was there that I made a friend for many years. My case was not typical, but that of the person I talked to recently, is. What is sure is that one cannot stay indifferent to what happens in the country.

A truce with Islamic Jihad has taken effect.

Monday, May 15

According to Simcha Rotman, if the negotiations at the President's Residence—which are resuming tomorrow—fail, part of the judicial reform could be voted during the present Knesset session, that is, before July 30.

Netanyahu, who attributes to himself the success of the latest operation against Islamic Jihad, thanks the chief of staff and the army, but systematically avoids mentioning Gallant, the defense minister. The Likud has slightly benefited in the polls and the coalition today would get fifty-four votes.

Netanyahu declared that the "flags march" will take place in Jerusalem on Thursday, May 18, as usual. Ben-Gvir will participate. Every year, it is an occasion for trouble. There is no doubt that Israeli society is moving to the right—not to the extreme-right, but to the right. Probably not beyond what the US would allow, but, let's say, to a moderate Republican right. If Biden wins next year, Netanyahu will have to accommodate him, but if the Republicans win . . .

I have seen the whole cycle: it's not that the socialist phase was a period to remember, except, as far as I am concerned, in the case of parties like Mapam and particularly Meretz, which were more interested in finding some arrangement with the Palestinians than in any other left-wing goal. Yossi Sarid and Shulamit Aloni were my preferred politicians, but their influence was minimal. The left of the 1960s and the 1970s was infinitely preferable to today's right. Today's right has to be fought by all legal means. I hope that the demonstrations will start again, in strength.

Tuesday, May 16

The budget as it is currently planned, with all its perks for the ultra-Orthodox and additions for the settlers, will seriously slow economic growth and lower the standard of living of a majority of Israelis. That factor may help the protests.

You may not know our ultra-Orthodox method of negotiating: now that they have received enormous perks, they are suddenly asking for 627 million shekels more. Either they will receive it or some substantial equivalent. And they didn't forget anything, either: where is the law exempting the yeshiva students from military service? It should be voted now, even before the budget! How will our Houdini get out of that?

A worrying report about antisemitism in Europe. Apparently, some 38 percent of European Jews are considering emigrating. I do not know whether the statistic is correct. As I said previously, not all criticism of Israel is antisemitism, and you mostly recognize antisemitism by a tone (or an undertone) of sheer hatred.

Wednesday, May 17

Ben-Gvir again boycotts voting (because of insufficient budget allocations for the Negev and the Galilee) and thus allowed a law introduced by the opposition to pass. Netanyahu says he will solve the problem. In a meeting of Jewish Power, Ben-Gvir has also criticized his ally—up to now, Smotrich—as a result of the impossibility of finding additional amounts for the evil clown's demands. As for the ultra-Orthodox, they continue to demand their 627 million shekels. In short, the budget debate has become an unseemly circus.

Tomorrow, the provocative flags march will take place in Jerusalem. The police are on high alert. Hamas is threatening. The evil clown will take part.

Thursday, May 18

The march of thousands in Jerusalem took place without major incidents, but showed once more the ugliest face of Israeli nationalism and racism: you should have heard the anti-Arab insults and the attempts at violence (stopped by a massive police presence) while hundreds of Jewish youngsters marched through Arab quarters of Jerusalem. Ben-Gvir was there and it is his party that was essentially represented among the most vociferous and most violent.

The budget circus goes on without anybody giving in, but Netanyahu seems confident that it will get through on the legally required date of May 29. The governor of the Bank of Israel announced that next week the interest rate will go up again because of the persistent inflation.

Friday, May 19

An interesting report in the evening news: more and more ultrareligious young males—but still a minority—turn to studying what they were forbidden up to now in their milieu: secular topics such as English, mathematics, and other such subjects. Otherwise, they will have no access to the economy and remain living off their wives' meager salaries, from alms, and from governmental allocations.

Incidentally, as I have indicated, if the budget does not get through by the given legal date, the government will fall. The evil clown will not dare to bring the coalition down, but the ultra-Orthodox may.

Saturday, May 20

Today, for the twentieth week, demonstrations all over the country, after they had to stop during the military operations against the Islamic Jihad, for security reasons.

Sunday, May 21

The evil clown Ben-Gvir cannot let a day go by without some provocation: now he has gone to the Temple Mount. Of course, several Muslim countries are up in arms. What a disgusting type! His former political partner Smotrich, who is supposed to attend a meeting of the OECD finance ministers in Paris, is unable to schedule any meeting, either at the French Finance Ministry or with officials of the City of Paris. One may wonder in what language he will speak if he opens his mouth at the general meeting. The two clowns are not talking to each other anymore, because of the budget. Ben-Gvir accuses Smotrich of discriminating against the minister for the Negev and the Galilee, Yitzhak Wasserlauf from Jewish Power, to whom he allocated a mere fragment of what was decided in the coalition negotiations, while he allocated huge sums to Minister Orit Strook, of his own Religious Zionist Party, much beyond what her new ministry can use.

All eyes are riveted on the three days of budget discussions and on the votes starting tomorrow. If no solution is found by the end of the week, one last day will be granted to the coalition: the following Monday, May 28. The comic side of this dramatic situation comes from the fact that the coalition partners do not believe in any promises about future compensation that Netanyahu could give, because they know that his promises are simply not kept.

Monday, May 22

In a speech in Herzliah yesterday, Gantz alluded to a compromise in the making in the negotiations at the President's Residence. The coalition doesn't want to publicize it before the vote on the budget.

In a conversation between Netanyahu and the minister of Torah Judaism, (the ultra-Orthodox) Yitzhak Goldknopf, a deal was reached: the party would get the amount they wanted from the surpluses in the overall budget at the end of the year. Either there were some unpublished additional aspects to the deal, or the ultras have decided to let go of their demands.

Ben-Gvir pretends that he doesn't yet know whether his party will support the budget or not, but it is hard to see him bringing down the only government that gives him a spot and the opportunity to perform his antics.

Netanyahu has promised Ben-Gvir a further 250 million shekels for the Ministry of the Negev and the Galilee, and the evil clown will vote for the budget. The crisis is over.

With the budgetary question resolved and a possible compromise regarding the judicial overhaul, the governmental coalition will sail on for some time and we can say goodbye to the hopes raised by the popular demonstrations. Israel will be poorer over the next few years and its vibrant economy will be a thing of the past; some of its technological experts will leave the country, as will some of its most impressive high-tech companies; the level of its education will go down and elements of its cultural life will have to move to underground (for example, to samizdat).

This is not the worse of it. Religious influence will weigh on life and leisure: public transport on Shabbat will be limited, possibly abolished, and who knows what else will not be allowed. The tech specialists who leave will be followed by part of the scientific and artistic elites, by some of the best medical practitioners, and, more generally, by those able to find a better way of life outside the country.

If this trend is not reversed at the next elections, if this nationalist and aggressive political alliance stays in power, the question of who will defend the country will soon have to be faced. The ultra-Orthodox will do everything to avoid service in the army; the question is whether, in a country under their growing dominance, the secular and liberal part of the population will show much enthusiasm for carrying that heavy burden alone.

Wednesday, May 24

This morning, a few hours after the budget passed, Netanyahu declared that the judicial overhaul could be considered again. Shortly afterwards he declared that he believed a compromise could be achieved. What should we conclude? Are the compromise negotiations gone with the wind? Or is the first declaration just one more maneuver to avoid a split within the Likud? It won't take very long to tell.

Thursday, May 25

The immigrants from Germany were often made fun of in the 1930s and 1940s by the then great majority of Jewish inhabitants of Eretz Israel of Polish or Russian origin. They were so stiff in the eyes of the locals, with such strange (polite) manners and what not. At the outset many of them had to work wherever they could, for example, on building sites. When you approached such a site you thought you heard the strange sound of a steam engine: "Bitte schön, Herr Doktor, danke schön, Herr Doktor" . . . In fact, these *yekes* formed from the outset the intellectual elite of the country; they set up, among other things, the Jewish judicial bureaucracy within the British mandatory system and, later on, after the creation of the State of Israel, an outstanding judiciary and Supreme Court. And, indeed, after 1948, many of the top members of the legal establishment were taught and then chosen from within that restricted pool, to fill the higher positions of the Israeli system. They were usually highly regarded and no professional objections were raised against them over the years. Could the selection have been different in due time as potential "Moroccan" candidates came of age? I am unable to tell. Now the battle over appointments to the Supreme Court may start again, and ethnic arguments will lurk once more behind the political and legal ones.

I touched upon the periphery of the periphery of the legal system by pure chance. When I graduated from my high school in Netanya, in June 1950, I was a few months away from my army service and in the meantime had to find work. There were jobs for youngsters like me at a reduced salary and one of them was that of messenger boy in the office of the legal adviser of the Foreign Ministry, at that time still located in Tel Aviv. The legal advisor was a jurist called Shabtai Rosenne, who was originally an English Jew. His second in command was American, and his young assistant, Canadian. The main secretary was of German origin and her own assistant, Mizrahit, but I do not remember from which country. This gives some idea of the palimpsest of nationalities of origin, in a small government office in Israel at its beginnings. We all worked well together and even went on an outing to Jerusalem—to the Supreme Court—where the main secretary knew one of the justices. He invited us to a court session. These were the limits of my judicial experience, but not the reason for my telling this story.

I met Rosenne again in the early 1970s when he was appointed ambassador to the United Nations in Geneva, and I was teaching there at the Graduate Institute of International and Development Studies. We became quite friendly, and I had discussions with him on international law, not on its theoretical aspects of course, but on the multiple interpretations of this or that event which he had to deal with, particularly in his tiffs with the UN Human Rights Commission. By then, my attitude to the Palestinian issue was probably to the left of his, but, in any case, he had an official position to defend. It taught me that law was not only in the text, but in its interpretation. And, to get back to our present situation, whatever the results of the compromise negotiations may be in our current conundrum, they may depend on the interpretation given to them by a political majority.

Iran displayed a ballistic missile that could reach Israel.

Friday, May 26

Yesterday, President Biden published his program to fight growing antisemitism in the United States. Nothing very new, except that such a program, as well-meaning as it may be, will be of little help against a millenary hatred.

My criterion of "hatred" to identify antisemitism is much too rough. Various degrees of antipathy or animosity against Jews can lead to the spewing of antisemitic rantings; defining where to set the line between objective criticism of Jews or Israel and antisemitism can be tricky. To keep silent because of indecision about the nature of the anti-Jewish criticism is even trickier. See, these very days, the case of the Roger Waters display in Berlin.

Jill Biden, on her visit to the Middle East, will tour Jordan and Egypt, but skip Israel.

Saturday, May 27

Not a day passes without a member of the coalition engineering some provocation. Now MK Ariel Kellner of the Likud has proposed a law concerning Palestinian institutions that would impose heavy taxation on any foreign humanitarian contributions. It has immediately brought sharp protests from the US and all major West European countries. Netanyahu has scheduled an internal meeting for tomorrow.

The law on Palestinian institutions will remain under wraps at this stage, as a result of the international protests.

The twenty-first Saturday of demonstrations in reaction to Netanyahu's declaration, after the budget vote, that the judicial overhaul can now be brought back. Some 80,000 demonstrators in Tel Aviv, and tens of thousands all over the country.

Sunday, May 28

A trove of documents about the Yom Kippur War was published today. The most sensational (although well known) among them was the detailed description, after the events, by Yoel Ben-Porat of how he transmitted, two days before the war, warnings "from the horse's mouth" that "war was imminent," warnings sent to the chief of intelligence and to the head of the Mossad and not transmitted to the political level, Prime Minister Golda Meir and Defense Minister Moshe Dayan, nor to Chief of Staff David Elazar.

I knew Ben-Porat from the time in the early 1950s when we served together in the same intelligence unit, in which he remained and had reached a command position by 1973. After the war, he came to visit me in Jerusalem on several occasions and told me of his warnings, although not about "the horse," the Egyptian Ashraf Marwan, Nasser's son-in-law. Marwan, incidentally, may have been a double spy; whatever his role, many years later, he fell from the seventh-floor balcony of his apartment in London . . . The incomprehensible aspect remains the refusal of the chief of intelligence, Eli Zeira, to take the warnings seriously and transmit them at least to the chief of staff. Ben-Porat died in 2007.

I don't know why this has turned into a sensation, since all of it has been known for many years. Could it be to warn of some similar lack of vigilance?

Avi Maoz, the archenemy of the LGBTQ community, is back in his old position as a kind of inspector-supervisor of educational programs, fighting against his enemies and also supervising the strengthening of Jewishness in education, thanks to Netanyahu, who made sure that he got some budget contribution. In short, the full coalition is back. Only the judicial overhaul is still on hold. For how long?

Monday, May 29

We are getting very close to the outcome of the conversations at the President's Residence. Netanyahu has declared that the judicial reform is not dead, but that he believes in a consensus. Gantz makes clear that all eyes will be open to look for any hidden clause. All eyes are vital when we deal with a master liar of Netanyahu's caliber.

The coalition has turned the Homesh settlement, which it had promised to leave empty, into a religious school. The Americans expressed their opposition; it seems not to help.

Tuesday, May 30

I do not understand exactly what the attorney general rejected in relation to Netanyahu's trial, but it seems to make the trial more threatening for him. It may make him even more intent on getting the judicial overhaul through the Knesset. The only way for him to get a plea deal is to leave the political stage, which he will never agree to do. His situation is not unlike that of Trump, except that Trump has not much chance of getting back to power, while Netanyahu is desperately clinging to power.

June 14 has been chosen as the deadline for the negotiations at the President's Residence. In the meantime, it seems that the representatives of the opposition will reach an agreement about who will be their delegate in the Knesset commission for the election of judges.

Wednesday, May 31

The fateful negotiations gain in intensity with each day; the focus is on the Judicial Selection Committee, which Justice Minister Levin threatens not to convene if he does not get the changes to it that he wants (the date for convening the commission is June 14, which is why this was chosen as a deadline for coming to a compromise at the President's Residence).

Tomorrow, the yearly march of the LGBTQ community will take place in Jerusalem, under heavy police protection. Ben-Gvir plans to be present, but it is not clear why. The great-grandson of Rabbi Ovadia Yosef (the late Sephardi Chief Rabbi of Israel and founder of Shas) will participate in the march; he is a rabbi and an educator. The country needs more people like him.

Thursday, June 1

Thousands are marching in Jerusalem. The American ambassador launched the march, and Lapid spoke; no significant incidents. A counterdemonstration took place some streets away. The police managed to keep both groups separated.

Actually, Israeli society has been divided into quite a number of hostile segments from the beginnings of immigration to the country, as I already mentioned, on ideological, ethnic, religious, and all other possible grounds. Yet a sense of shared fate as Jews and objects of steady hostility, then as targets of successive aggressions, of wars and constant terror attacks, created a feeling of community stronger than any divisions. I wonder whether the present dissensions would disappear in case of another war, probably a costlier one in lives and destruction than the previous ones. Israel's enemies may be counting on an internal fracture deeper than ever before within the national community, one that no attack would heal and that would affect its ability to defend itself as effectively as in the past. Could they be right?

On a similar note, in the news there is increasing talk of the growing danger of Iran getting its atom bomb and of Israel having to launch an attack against the Shiite state's nuclear installations, with or without American help. This would be the most dangerous and complex operation that Israel ever undertook. In the present atmosphere, it is not clear at all that the Jewish state would get any external help.

US Secretary of State Blinken is in the region and was planning to visit Israel until this morning, when he canceled his stopover. Strange, but one more signal of American displeasure with Israeli policies.

Friday, June 2

I never thought much of Hugh Trevor-Roper as a historian. For most people he reached his nadir when he confirmed the authenticity of the Hitler diaries in 1983, an incredible hoax. For me, he had reached it long before then, when he opened his *New York Times* book review of Arthur Hertzberg's 1968 *The Origins of Modern Anti-semitism*—which saw its roots in the ideas of the Enlightenment, mainly Voltaire's antisemitism—with the not-so-rhetorical question: what if the Jews were responsible for the hatred they provoke? Jews may have had their share of responsibility for many things, but to consider them responsible for the hostility they provoked was a little too much, twenty-five years after Hitler. I am delving into this, because it is not uncommon to hear opinions according to which the Jews are responsible for the violence they cause, particularly in Israel. I agree regarding the consequences of the occupation, but that is as far as we liberal Israelis are ready to go. Today Palestinian violence is aiming at the very existence of Israel, and that, of course, none of us can accept. And, beyond that, classical antisemitism is rearing its head: see Elon Musk and what he is spewing against Soros, and so on and so forth.

Actually, I started with this train of thought after speaking of the possibility of Israel launching an attack against Iran, as I remembered an old discussion, also bringing us back to the late 1960s or early 1970s, with a French author arguing that Israel needed war, as an unconscious way of keeping united against the centrifugal forces tending to rent its national fabric. It was a clever idea, but I would not countenance it nowadays.

Levin threatens not to convene the Judicial Selection Committee; the Orthodox demand an immediate vote on the law about the nonconscription of yeshiva students; the Americans have renewed negotiations with Iran for restoring the treaty limiting the ayatollahs' nuclear ambitions. The treaty considerably worries Israel, which does not believe in Iran's peaceful intentions. Moreover, the US is not pleased at all with the installation of a religious school in Homesh, notwithstanding the Israeli promise to keep the place empty. It seems that relations with the US are moving from bad to worse. In short, Netanyahu has a few issues to take care of, more or less simultaneously.

Saturday, June 3

Three soldiers killed near the southern border by an Egyptian infiltrator.

Tens of thousands of demonstrators in Tel Aviv and all over the country for the twenty-second week.

Sunday, June 4

You probably know that old joke about the Jew who was shipwrecked, and who finds refuge on a desert island. When he is discovered, his saviors are astonished to find that he built two synagogues. "Why two?" they ask him. "One is for me," he answers, "the other, I never would set my feet in." From the amusing to the tragic: when getting ready for the revolt, the remaining inhabitants of the Warsaw ghetto and their fighting units remained divided to the end in three political groups: Socialists, Bundists, and Betar. With the third one, the two others never agreed to cooperate and they hardly cooperated among themselves. The survivors made sure to write diverging histories, trying to garner all recognition for their own group. This does not bode well for the hoped-for reunification of the two segments of society fighting in present-day Israel, in case of external danger. But how can one come to terms with enemies of democracy and supporters of religious fanaticism? Lapid declared that his party will not vote for any law agreed upon in the compromise negotiations until the Judicial Selection Committee is convened.

Monday, June 5

Very firm speech by Blinken against the expansion of Israeli settlements and the destruction of Palestinian homes, to a meeting of the American Israel Public Affairs Committee (AIPAC, a pro-Israel lobbying group). But the present Israeli government speeches do not help. A two-state solution is still the American official goal; it is the only rational one, but is less and less within reach.

Today the Likud is supposed to vote on whether it will enable the opposition to nominate one of the candidates to the Judicial Selection Committee. If Netanyahu wants to reach a compromise in the negotiations at the President's Residence, he will have to make sure that the vote of the Likud goes the right way.

Tuesday, June 6

Levin agrees that the coalition will have only one representative in the Judicial Selection Committee. Was it the result of a nudge from Netanyahu?

Yesterday Netanyahu agreed take upon himself the chairmanship of a committee set up to deal with crime in the Arab community in Israel. Since the beginning of the year some ninety cases of murder have been registered. The police, if it intervenes at all, has been totally overwhelmed. It seems to be the "work" of four major gangs. If they are so well known, why has none of their bosses been arrested? Because they are Arabs? Because as the chief of police, Shabtai, once famously said to Ben-Gvir: They are used to murdering each other? As I mentioned previously, Israel's Arab citizens were considered as second-class citizens at the outset. In the meantime, much has changed: they enroll in universities, they work in all walks of life, they have four parties in the Knesset, they are about 2 million now, out of 10 million; there are even intermarriages with Israeli Jews, and yet they harbor not-so-hidden grudges against the Jewish community, although they apparently prefer living in Israel to eventually becoming citizens of a hypothetical Palestinian state. A complicated situation, to say the least.

Wednesday, June 7

Today, in an aggressive speech to the Knesset, Levin gave the expected indication that he won't convene the Judicial Selection Committee. How long, Levin, will you abuse our patience? But it may be his swan song. On June 14, the Knesset has to vote on the composition of the committee: if it sticks with the usual formula of adding one candidate from the coalition and one from the opposition, then Levin's overhaul is dead.

It so happens that, as I am writing this, I am reading Ulrich Boschwitz's novel *The Passenger* about the travails of a Jew in German society on and after Kristallnacht. It is astonishingly gripping, even for somebody whose life's work has been studying and writing about these events and beyond. When, these days, I reflect on even the prewar Nazi years, I cannot help cringing, on the one hand, at the pettiness of our ongoing debates and, on the other, being taken aback by the blindness and ignorance of part of our present generation of Israelis regarding the meaning and consequences of a country's eliminating its independent justice system, in an atmosphere of political aggressiveness and ideological fanaticism.

Actually, pettiness is not the right word. Of course, every political debate is petty when compared to the issues of life and death confronting the Jews during the Nazi years, but fighting for democracy is certainly not petty and fighting for a society that refuses to submit to religious domination is far from being petty. Never mind the right word—the idea should hopefully be clear.

Two days ago, Iran unveiled what it claimed to be its first hypersonic ballistic missile, capable of reaching Israel.

Thursday, June 8

Five killed in the Arab community, near Nazareth, in what appears to be infighting between criminal gangs. Another Arab victim elsewhere. This is a complete loss of control and a scandal. It shows the total incompetence or, worse, the total indifference of the police and of the minister for internal security, the evil clown Ben-Gvir. Netanyahu wants the Shin Bet to get involved, but there is opposition from the organization since that would weaken its campaign against terror attacks and possibly disclose some of its operational strategy.

Netanyahu informed Blinken that a nuclear deal between the US and Iran would not limit Israel's freedom of action in any way.

Friday, June 9

In an interview with Sky News, Netanyahu expressed doubts about the possibility of reaching an agreement in the negotiations at the President's Residence. He dismissed the economic consequences of a stalemate and spoke enthusiastically of the possibility of an agreement with Saudi Arabia.

As a consequence of the wave of killings in the Arab community, the consensus among commentators is that Ben-Gvir should be sacked. He, as is his habit, accuses in response the police and particularly its chief, Shabtai: instead of spending his time on the appointment of friends, he should deal with crime. Ben-Gvir will not be dismissed, but he is generally distrusted and despised.

In poll results broadcasted by Channel 13 on the evening news, Gantz tops Netanyahu as favorite in all essential positions (prime minister, minister of defense, etc.). Lapid is also ahead of Netanyahu at times.

Saturday, June 10

For part of the Israeli electorate, the present coalition is truly a gift from heaven that has to be squeezed dry for all its potential benefits. They will not let go easily. For the other part, apparently a majority, it is the result of dirty tricks engineered by Netanyahu to escape his indictments. If he can be saved, nothing else counts and the world can perish (*pereat mundus*).

Today, demonstrations against the judicial overhaul took place all over the country, for the twenty-third week. The former chief of staff and prime minister, Ehud Barak, called for civil disobedience.

The 102nd victim of the killings in the Arab community in Israel, in the last five months.

Sunday, June 11

The calm before the storm.

Monday, June 12

Two days to the decisive vote in the Knesset on candidates for the Judicial Selection Committee. Gantz declares again the readiness of his party to come to an understanding if the principles agreed upon are respected, while no public pronouncement has yet been heard from Lapid. Wednesday, June 14, is indeed a decisive date that will indicate in which direction Israel will move for the next four years. If the judicial overhaul gets through, it may be difficult to undo it, even under a liberal coalition.

In fact, Lapid, the formal head of the opposition, was quite busy today, as he had to take the stand at Netanyahu's corruption trial.

Tuesday, June 13

Waiting for tomorrow's vote. There is a division within the Likud between the liberal right and the fanatics. Ultimately Netanyahu will decide and the party will have to follow.

At times I feel like "the man from the country" (which in Hebrew means the ignorant) who comes to the gate of the law, as in Kafka's *The Trial*. The number of laws that will follow the choice of candidates to the Judicial Selection Committee is truly mysterious (at least to me), to such a point that I feel barred from understanding what will ultimately remain intact of the overhaul and what could be compromised on in the negotiations at the President's Residence.

Notwithstanding US opposition, Israel goes ahead with the planning of 4,500 housing units in the West Bank. And yet Herzog will probably meet with Biden in Washington sometime next month.

Wednesday, June 14

Drama at the Knesset. The secret elections to the commission took place. Netanyahu tried to delay them, but a Likud candidate refused to stand down. The coalition hopes that no candidate will be elected and demands new elections in one month's time. The opposition is furious, sees it as a trick, and threatens to put an end to negotiations.

Even greater drama! The candidate of the opposition was elected by fifty-eight votes against fifty-six; it means that four members of the coalition have voted against their own side and against Netanyahu. Or, maybe, Netanyahu, the super-trickster, wished secretly for this outcome . . .

The shekel fell steeply after the initial indecision at the Knesset, only to regain its losses after the final vote. It says a lot about what the business community wishes for.

The trouble is that the commission cannot meet without a second candidate and therefore will only meet one month from now. Gantz declares the negotiations for a compromise are suspended for the time being.

Thursday, June 15

Nahum Barnea, a foremost political commentator, tells the old story of the frog and the scorpion who arrive at a river they both want to cross. "I will get on your back," says the scorpion to the frog, "and you will swim across with both of us." "But," answers the frog, "you will sting me." "Why should I do that?" responds the scorpion. "Then we would both die." The frog is convinced and they set on their way. In the middle of the river, the scorpion stings the frog. "Why did you do that?" asks the dying frog. "It's my nature," answers the dying scorpion.

I heard this story in 1961, from a soon-to-be-uncovered Soviet spy, Israel Beer, about Dayan, whom he detested, mainly because Dayan suspected him. Today, it's told about Bibi, who cannot help thinking in tricks, even when these land him in a stinging defeat. Never mind: new tricks are on the way.

It appears that 30 percent of the budget of the religious school at the Homesh settlement (which the US protested against) is paid by the Ministry of Education.

Friday, June 16

For the coalition, the negotiations at the President's Residence will not resume; the plan is instead to vote on those laws that the coalition says have been agreed upon (and which the opposition does not consider as such). Obviously, this hides some other and more devious intention.

In the meantime, the Likud is sinking in the polls. In yesterday's estimate, published by Channel 13, in case of new elections, the coalition would receive fifty seats, the opposition would reach sixty, and nine would be undetermined (Arab votes). Quite a crash for Netanyahu.

Saturday, June 17

The twenty-fourth week of protests: tens of thousands of demonstrators in Tel Aviv and tens of thousands more all over the country.

Sunday, June 18

Today, Netanyahu announced that active steps would be taken to bring back the judicial overhaul, after weeks of waiting for the results of inconclusive negotiations at the President's Residence. If he can be believed for once, it means that the crisis is back, in full force.

Given the present situation, each vote inside the commission for the appointment of judges counts. In two days from now, elections to the national lawyers' committee will take place and, in principle, they have two delegates on the Knesset commission. If the Likud manages to have its candidates appointed . . .

Monday, June 19

President Herzog denied the coalition's assertion that an agreement was reached on several points that could now be debated and voted on in the Knesset, for example, regarding the "plausibility argument." This, among other things, has allowed the Supreme Court to annul a government decision because it was not plausible. Thus, the appointment of Deri as minister was annulled, as it was highly implausible that somebody guilty of a felony could be minister. Now, according to the law in preparation, governmental and ministerial decisions will be immune from such annulments, while bureaucratic decisions would still be subject to them. The change could allow the reappointment of Deri as minister of the interior and of health.

An army operation in Jenin went wrong and several soldiers were wounded. The military chiefs of Hamas and Islamic Jihad are in Tehran for talks.

Tuesday, June 20

Four Israelis were killed in a terror attack in the occupied West Bank, as revenge for the killings in Jenin. Settlers set fire to Palestinian houses and fields to avenge the Jewish dead. The vicious circle goes on, unabated.

The candidate of the opposition won the elections to the national lawyers' committee by an immense majority.

Wednesday, June 21/Thursday, June 22

The three judges in the main Netanyahu court case, who have dealt with the issue for over two years, declared that the indictment for corruption against the prime minister was weak and that it was recommended, also to appease the public, to seek a plea deal. A turn of events that may lead to changes in the general atmosphere.

Sunday, July 2

Very large military operation in the Jenin refugee camp. Special forces and paratroopers with support from the air. Apparently, the largest operation in twenty years. Large quantities of armaments and explosives have been found. The question is: will this help in the long run, or even in the short run? Or will it help Netanyahu?

Monday, July 3

Terror attack in Tel Aviv. Some eight people wounded, several of them severely. The assailant was a Palestinian working illegally in the country, declared that it was to avenge Jenin. He was killed. Hamas declared that the attack was to avenge Jenin.

The operation in Jenin is drawing to a close. One soldier killed at the last moment. Netanyahu declared that such an incursion will be repeated in the future, as often as necessary. Twelve Palestinians were killed. According to CNN, the damage done to the infrastructure is considerable, but, as I wrote and as many others say, will it change anything in the longer run? Most commentators doubt it. Someone dubbed it Acamol (acetaminophen) administered to a terminally ill patient.

Such operations make me wonder each time anew how many Israelis carry this semi-conscious wish to control the whole of Eretz Israel. While the fight for democracy is that of a majority, I am not sure whether the one for a gradual two-state solution would get the support of the same proportion of the population. That, in my opinion, is our basic problem. International pressure will maintain the status quo for some time, but it is most doubtful that it can achieve more.

Regarding the fight against the judicial overhaul, I fear that the opposition won't succeed without major civil disobedience, as has been strongly advocated by the former prime minister and chief of staff Ehud Barak, today head of a small left-wing party. At least it is being publicly aired. Reserve officers' refusal to report for duty is a manifestation of that intention.

This was total anathema in my time. When Begin's government made noises about annexing the West Bank, I stated on Abba Ahimeir's political news program that were this to transpire I would refuse to report for reserve duty. The reaction was immediate: Ahimeir didn't speak to me for the rest of the discussion, nor did the three other participants. My phone remained silent that evening and the following day. And even a friend such as Chief Justice Haim Cohn privately shared his disapproval. In that sense, the atmosphere now is different, but will there be a greater readiness to act?

Tuesday, July 4/Thursday, July 6

Multiple demonstrations, both in reaction to the renewed drive for the judicial overhaul and because of the dismissal of Tel Aviv's police chief, who was deemed too liberal. Large protests at Ben Gurion Airport, in front of ministers' homes, in Tel Aviv, etc. It does not seem to deter either Netanyahu nor the hardliners among the coalition.

Saturday, July 8

Some 150,000 demonstrators in Tel Aviv. A very large protest is planned for this coming Tuesday.

Sunday, July 9

President Biden has openly criticized Netanyahu's policies. In a CNN interview, Biden stated that Netanyahu had problems with the most extreme elements of his government, that the situation in the West Bank was partly Israel's responsibility, that normalization of relations between Israel and Saudi Arabia was a long way off, and that there would be no invitation for Netanyahu for the time being.

In the meantime, coalition ministers unleashed an unprecedented assault against the attorney general, with four of them asking for her dismissal. This, of course, is not yet on the cards. On the other hand, Ben-Gvir and Smotrich managed to scuttle the defense minister's plan, supported by Netanyahu, to strengthen Abbas's Palestinian Authority as a dam against the West Bank militants; the PA will be maintained, but not given special economic assistance.

The public largely disapproves of current policies regarding the judicial overhaul. According to the results of a poll published today, if elections were held now, the Gantz-Lapid opposition would receive sixty-one votes, the coalition only fifty-four votes. It shows that the Jenin operation did not help the PM.

President Herzog criticized the attack against the attorney general and called for a return to discussions under his aegis before any step is taken.

Monday, July 10

The coalition is preparing for a first vote on a measure to repeal most clauses of the plausibility law. Will they postpone the second and third vote and accept Herzog's call for a renewal of talks?

It seems that we received the answer regarding Herzog's urgent proposal: the coalition voted unanimously for a first reading of the plausibility law repeal. Netanyahu informed the president that the coalition would not return to the conciliation talks.

Tuesday, July 11

Huge demonstration at Ben Gurion Airport. Tens of protesters arrested in similar demonstrations around the country, but for the time being the Histadrut isn't ready to call for a general strike.

Wednesday, July 12

On the morrow, the country seems to be returning to normal. How strange. The US is possibly reconsidering its relations with Israel. What could it mean?

The coalition appointed a second delegate, this one from Jewish Power, to the commission for the nomination of judges. This is a very bad omen. One cannot be but aghast at what looks like a wild drive by Israel toward self-mutilation, or possibly self-destruction.

Thursday, July 13

New protests are taking place in front of Netanyahu's residence and in front of the American Embassy to bolster the stand of the US administration.

Hundreds of pilots opt for various forms of resistance, and the country's physicians are threatening to strike. But for the time being, essentially nothing has changed and the present stalemate can last for quite some time.

Saturday, July 15

The PM felt ill and was rushed to the cardiology department at Sheba Medical Center in Ramat Gan. A cardiac monitor was implanted. After a brief observation period, the patient was sent home.

Thursday, July 20

The division of the country has worsened in the last few days: 1,142 pilots and other officers of the air force declared in a letter that they wouldn't report for service if the cancelation of the plausibility law passed a second and third (final) vote next week, as planned by Levin, Rotman, and Netanyahu. The letter said that if the threat is concretized, the air force will not be ready for war. It has rightly been called "an earthquake" by many commentators. I am not sure that it will suffice to stop the passage of the cancelation of the plausibility law, unless a minimum of five coalition members vote against it.

It looks that this is precisely what may happen. Defense Minister Gallant announced that he will not remain indifferent to the air force crisis and that he plans to announce his response this coming Monday. Moreover, Shas's boss Deri stated that he too is worried and will probably take a stand. In the meantime, we know that some other Likud members will possibly not support the cancelation of the plausibility law. Of course, much depends on what Netanyahu says in secret to them all.

Friday, July 21

It has become the mightiest expression of protests: thousands have joined the march from Tel Aviv to Jerusalem (40,000 as a start, say the protest organizers). They will station themselves in front of the Knesset on the days of the vote.

Eight in the evening in Israel: tens of thousands have reached

Jerusalem and plan to camp in front of the Knesset tomorrow. I am proud to say that my son and my daughter-in-law, as well as my daughter (visiting from Berlin) are among them. I wish so much to have been there.

About 100,000 protesters reached Jerusalem and will sleep under tents in Sacher Park. About 150,000 are gathering in Tel Aviv. The chair of the Histadrut declared that he will call a general strike if left no choice, but he is notoriously unreliable.

All over the country, tension in anticipation of the coming days increases.

Further drama in these already dramatic hours. The cardiologist who took care of Netanyahu last week was called urgently during the night: the PM is in immediate need of the pacemaker implant. The meeting of the cabinet that was scheduled to take place tomorrow morning, which included reports from the minister of defense and the chief of staff regarding the widening refusal of reserve officers to report for call-ups and the danger this represents for the armed forces and the security of the country, was canceled.

The PM appointed Yariv Levin as his temporary replacement and vowed to return by the afternoon for the crucial vote in the Knesset. He had declared beforehand that any Likud members who would vote against the cancelation of the plausibility law would be dismissed on the spot. One fanatic appoints the other fanatic to head the government. As the opposition does not seem ready to back down, this could end very badly.

Saturday, July 22/Sunday, July 23

The chair of the Histadrut proposed a compromise that the Likud rejected under the pretense that it was close to the opposition's stance. Lapid announced that he accepted it. President Herzog returned from his visit to the US and went straight to visit Netanyahu in the hospital. He argues that the national emergency demands a compromise regarding the legislation overhaul.

Netanyahu has recovered from the pacemaker implant and says that he "feels amazingly well" but has been asked by his doctors to stay one more night . . . The vote in the Knesset will take place tomorrow.

Over 900 reserve officers of the Intelligence branch announced that they would not report for service.

Former chief justice Aharon Barak spoke to the protesters assembled in front of the Knesset, as did former Israeli president Reuven Rivlin. In different words, both warned of imminent catastrophe. They, along with many other observers including myself, sense ominous consequences if Netanyahu does not agree to a compromise like the one proposed by President Herzog, which was accepted by leaders of the opposition but staunchly opposed by most members of the coalition.

In three days is Tisha B'Av, the yearly commemoration of the destruction of both Temples in Jerusalem. Nothing could be more symbolic of Israel's present situation. In the seventy-five years of the country's existence, there was never a crisis as critical to its very survival as the present one.

Monday, July 24

The Knesset voted for the cancelation of the plausibility law by the 64 votes of the coalition and total abstention of the opposition. Before the vote, Minister of Defense Gallant and the minister of justice had a sharp exchange, but Gallant ultimately voted with the coalition, even though he purports to be in favor of halting the judicial overhaul in view of the situation in the armed forces. Why? The same question can be asked about President Herzog: why do these people not have the courage to resign when so much is at stake and their gesture would carry so much meaning? Will the decision of the government be brought to the Supreme Court before Chief Justice Hayut retires in a month or so? At this moment, the chief justice is in Germany. She is hastening back.

Netanyahu, in a speech full of lies about the past and a mellifluous description of the future unity of both sides, added his bits and pieces of disinformation. He is a prisoner of the extremists in the coalition and speaks for them. Their voice is his voice. Both Lapid and Gantz answered with firmness and dignity.

Protests continue throughout the country with renewed intensity, and the police is increasing its violent response. A long war of attrition has begun on the streets.

My wife, Orna, and I have different views about the effectiveness of the demonstrations. I said that one of their main and striking aspects was that they were protests without real anger, while the other side was filled with resentment and anger; the best example being the growing brutality of the police. I was astonished that the tens of thousands of demonstrators didn't yet react with anger of their own. Orna argues that this is precisely the beautiful side of our demonstrations: protests *bon enfant*, in a way. For me, without anger you will never ultimately get to the only result that can make a difference: civil disobedience.

Tuesday, July 25

The attorney general opposes the cancelation of the plausibility law: "It is meant to facilitate Netanyahu's personal situation." As a result of the above—and following several appeals to the

Supreme Court against the vote—a forum of eleven judges will debate its legality sometime toward the end of August.

On the other hand, there is some background noise about new attempts between the two opposing sides to reach a compromise.

In the meantime, religious parties are demanding the vote of a new law that would establish equal status between military service and Torah study. Otherwise, they will not support the judicial overhaul. Their usual extortion tactics.

Severe economic consequences are expected following yesterday's vote. Several rating agencies downgraded their estimates of Israeli credit worthiness for investors. The shekel and Israeli stocks are down, etc.

Netanyahu's coalition has slipped to a prospective fifty-two seats according to the latest polls. The Shas party journal warns against proceeding with the judicial overhaul.

Wednesday, July 26

President Herzog has openly pointed to Netanyahu as the person most responsible for the current crisis and the one who has to resolve it, "as he is the one who has the power." The chairman of the coalition, MK Ofir Katz, hastened to call the declaration by the president "unfortunate."

The Supreme Court will start to debate the cancelation of the plausibility law in September. Then it will address Levin's refusal to convene the Judicial Selection Committee. Why so late?

The thousands who spent the last few nights in Sacher Park in Jerusalem express the great spirit felt by all, of the spontaneous friendships, of the devotion and care shown by the people who supplied the protesters with tents, food, and water, and after a few days cleaned the grounds to perfection. Orna says that it is so heartening to see this wonderful side of our people. I agree, it is heartening and it is wonderful, but I am afraid, as I have noted before, that great spirits and exemplary citizenship will not make any impression on the fanatics of the coalition. Maybe the growing refusal to volunteer for call-ups among officers of elite units and pilots will be a decisive factor.

Today, the Knesset voted on a law according to which every community of more than 700 inhabitants could decide who was allowed to live there and who was not: undisguised apartheid.

Before the passage of the first measure of the overhaul, there were some thirty physicians or medical students who had applied via WhatsApp for relocation out of the country. Now there are 2,000. Hard to believe!

The coalition is set to significantly weaken the position of the attorney general by passing a law that would split his or her authority in several parts. However, they will have to wait until October, when the Knesset reconvenes from its summer recess.

It may be the right time to conclude this diary.

I never imagined, when I started, that I would have to conclude at such a terrible time. Yet this is the reality we are facing. Will Netanyahu be able to negotiate some acceptable compromise during the coming two months before the fanatics threaten him with the ruin of his coalition?

I am not competent enough to predict how badly the Israeli economy will be shaken in the next few months, how grievously the country's security will be imperiled, how catastrophically the health system will suffer, whether the two segments of society that are aligned against each other will ever find a path to some unity, and how the rational part of the population will, if needed, maintain its will to protest. These are ultimately the main issues. But let me, nonetheless, turn to the political scene.

Against all my dire prognostics and rational judgment, I wish to end on a whiff of optimism, very mild optimism, because the ongoing protests, if they continue, may ultimately lead to some positive results. Let me suggest, therefore, very tentatively, that in the not-too-distant future, the present governmental coalition will be torn apart from the inside. The Likud will turn into a party of the hard right and will not remain the most powerful party in the Knesset. Sooner or later Netanyahu will be out of politics and likely still busy with his remaining court cases and with his health.

A major question is whether Gantz and Lapid, if they are still around, might be able to establish a viable coalition of essentially liberal, centrist, and secular parties. On past form, it is not certain; their mutual animosity may be too strong for that. Given the usual division of the left, we could be in for a period of political chaos. The usual social resentments and religious and nationalist fanaticism will not, of course, disappear.

It was, I think, the great scholar of Kabbalah, Gershom Scholem, who wondered whether Jews would be able to shift from a messianic level of aspirations to that of practical politics. An active minority in Israel managed to operate at both levels: it adopted the most dangerous realpolitik and infused it with messianic ideology. Together with the hard right and the Orthodox parties, it seeks to dictate its will. This can happen if the covert messianic drive for the whole of Eretz Israel is not abandoned by a majority. It must be opposed by all legal means. This, for a long time, will be the main task of the rational part of our society, the liberal and democratic segment of it, however small it may be at the outset. But will this segment be able, over time, to maintain the necessary strength and steadfastness to defend its convictions and ideals? Will it go on fighting against constant attempts of an adverse coalition to subvert the freedom of our citizens and endanger the possibility of as humane and just a solution as possible to the conflict with the Palestinians?

II
War

Saturday, October 7

Unbelievable! The country is under attack! Hamas has deeply penetrated southern Israel along the border with Gaza. Total surprise and complete pandemonium. Apparently no one saw it coming.

Initial reports mention tens of Israelis dead—maybe hundreds—and dozens of inhabitants from border communities taken hostage and likely taken to Gaza. The replay of October 1973 in October 2023 has taken Israel by complete surprise: the government was asleep, the army was asleep, the specialists who bombard us every day with interpretations of what the Arabs are going to do were all taken by surprise not only with their pants down, but asleep and without their pants . . .

What a disgrace, mainly for Israel's military intelligence, the Shin Bet and the Mossad. And, of course, for Netanyahu and Gallant. Retaliation will be complicated because of the hostages who are now in the hands of Hamas. On top of everything, Israel is in deep internal turmoil, rent between various hostile factions and an internally weakened army.

Hezbollah in the North is probably waiting for the bulk of our forces to move south before opening a second front. Hundreds of thousands of Israelis are being mobilized. The civilian population is in for a very tough time.

Gantz is ready to join Netanyahu's coalition without conditions. Lapid will join if Smotrich and Ben-Gvir are shown the door. I think he is right. It is taking an interminably long time to clear the Sderot police station that five—yes, five—Hamas militants are holding. Incredible! There are endless questions and everyone in the army keeps mum. Where was our sophisticated intelligence, where was the Mossad, what happened to the technologically advanced "smart fence" built around the Gaza enclave? Of course, heads will roll in due time, and Netanyahu and his wife Sara'le will be shown the door at the next election. He would never show the courage that Golda showed in 1974 and resign. The whole government is a bunch of freaks, but at this moment the country has no choice but to keep them.

The number of Israelis killed has climbed to 700 and is expected to rise, as is the figure of more than 2,200 wounded. And at least 130 Israelis have been taken hostage, among them, let me stress, small children, elderly people, and men and women of all ages. The parents and relatives of the hostages are on the radio and on television at all hours and have yet to receive any answer, any news, any support from an official source. Not a syllable. They cry, they implore the government for answers, but no word comes. Nothing.

In all likelihood, Iran helped Hamas to prepare the onslaught, as China may have helped the Vietcong to launch the Tet Offensive that changed the course of the Vietnam War in 1968. It is unlikely that the military balance between Israel and Hamas will be changed, but the course of events in the Middle East seems to be on the brink of modification. This explains the strong US support of Israel. An entire carrier strike group has been ordered close to Israel's shores, and various types of military aid are being dispatched. Of course, Biden's sympathy for Israel plays a role.

But what is more decisive than sympathy is the stand against a probable front in the region, as elsewhere, of Iran, Russia, and possibly China.

Netanyahu spoke and said nothing: "We will break their bones . . ."

Sunday, October 8

Even on Yom Kippur in 1973, the assault against Israel was less brutal and horrific than now. In the midst of this total chaos, official sources have remained silent, either as "policy" or, more plausibly, as a manifestation of their embarrassment about their complete lack of any preparation—or, perhaps even more damning, the absolute failure of these so-called preparations. Online news sources fill the silence, but the general feeling is one of utter official disarray.

One assumes that the army is getting ready to enter Gaza. That move could be terribly costly in human lives on all sides. We will probably know more very soon.

In his first declaration since the beginning of the events, the chief of staff admitted that there were many unanswered questions and much bitterness, "but now was the time to take the necessary measures" (and not to search for answers, if I may complete his declaration). General Herzi Halevi has indeed proven an ill-fated chief of staff, attacked constantly by the country's Ben-Gvirs and their ilk, not defended by Netanyahu during times of relative peace, and now certainly held responsible for the army's unpreparedness. There will be many commissions of inquiry when the time comes. Incidentally, Ben-Gvir and Smotrich are completely silent. They had better be.

A story shared on the radio: a woman, whose young son was

spending time in the South, called him to see how he was faring. A voice answered her call: "My name is Muhammad. Your son is dead." One of the 700. The number of Israelis taken as hostages or prisoners to Gaza has now risen to between 150 and 200. This will horribly complicate the retaliation.

There is something somewhat mysterious about the present situation: Israeli Air Force raids on Gaza, which have the potential to be extremely destructive, have so far been very mild, apparently on purpose. Hamas still has fighters on Israeli territory who haven't been rooted out; all this seems to unfold on an intentionally minor scale. I know that some people think of treason. Instead, I attribute this to US pressure and, thanks to US or Egyptian brokerage, a promise from Hamas not to harm the hostages and prisoners held in Gaza if Israel abstains from drastic retaliatory measures. In short, an attempt to bring these events back to the level of the usual incursions and ordinary responses, if all sides keep to an imposed moderation. That would also explain the overall silence of official Israeli sources. But how long can this go on?

There is another possible explanation: Netanyahu managed to prove that Iran masterminded the Hamas attack and has convinced Biden that this is the moment to strike Tehran, and thereby put an end to various annoyances in the Middle East (Hamas, Hezbollah) and reestablish the predominance of Western influence in the Arab world. It would be a step fraught with dangers, as the ayatollahs of the region will assuredly not go down without a fight. This in itself could explain the American reinforcements, at all levels. Orna holds this bold but logical interpretation. It is quite convincing, except for the risks involved, which do not fit with Netanyahu's usual modus operandi.

Monday, October 9

An estimated 800 Israelis killed. Otherwise, no sign of any major operation. Chaos on the roads: it takes hours for reservists to join their units.

It seems that Abbas Kamel, the Egyptian minister of intelligence, warned Netanyahu a few days before the assault that a major attack from Gaza was imminent; Netanyahu reportedly responded that the army was busy in the Occupied Territories. Indeed, the army was busy "protecting" Rachel's Tomb, as requested by Ben-Gvir and Smotrich. Kamel was supposedly stunned by the prime minister's indifference. If these reports of Egypt's warning turn out to be true, Netanyahu's responsibility is even heavier than previously thought. Netanyahu's office is calling it "fake news." Obviously.

Today I received a copy of my book, a German edition of this very diary, covering January to July 2023: *Blick in den Abgrund. Ein israelisches Tagebuch.* In English: "Gaze into the abyss: An Israeli diary." If, as I hope, I continue this diary to the conclusion of the war, I will strongly recommend its publication in a single volume. The early months do not explain what happened on October 7, but they describe the political blindness in Israel and the horror show that was Netanyahu's coalition. But all that is irrelevant for the time being. Let me turn back to events.

A correspondent in Sderot on this third day of the war reports that Hamas militants are still hiding in a variety of locations on Israeli territory around Gaza. They continue to fight sporadically and appear to be well camouflaged. Tens have been killed, but some apparently remain. The only grocery open in the town is operated by Mofida, an Arab woman who has resided in Sderot for more than twenty-five years. She sells food, clothing, and a wide variety of other basic necessities; her son delivers goods to those who are unable to visit themselves. Mofida says that she is not afraid. After all these years, the inhabitants of Sderot are her family.

It has become increasingly difficult to get a clear picture of what is going on. Individual eyewitness testimonies shared from the region are hard to believe and even harder to stomach. The estimate of the number of Israelis killed is probably close to 1,000. The first two days in the South, where the Hamas terrorists penetrated, was the scene of an unprecedented massacre.

One of the most brutal and appalling attacks occurred on the border, near Re'im, where hundreds of young music lovers had assembled for a festival in the desert, without any protection, any forewarning, in the deepest peace. In addition, there was a change of venue, which Hamas knew all about. After dancing the whole night, many of the young festivalgoers slept for a few hours and were then awakened to the sound of bullets. Some 300 corpses have been uncovered to date. The road leading to the festival is lined with hundreds of their abandoned cars.

In comments by the foreign press, often informed by Israeli sources, one of the recurring themes is the incomprehensible failure of Israeli intelligence, which over the years has been praised to heaven. There are many other examples from other countries over the previous decades, but Israel is too small and fundamentally too weak to be comforted by the precedents of the attack on the Soviet Union, Pearl Harbor, or 9/11. What happened to us?

It appears that Hamas and Iranian military planners developed new ways to coordinate their operations, ones that didn't rely on communication methods that Israel expected and could easily intercept. Moreover, the country was increasingly distracted by recent incidents in the West Bank and the attention lavished on settlers and settlements by Netanyahu's messianic coalition, whose judicial overhaul undoubtedly also bears some responsibility, because of the internal divisions it created.

The European Union put a hold on the annual financial assistance it provides the Palestinians. Up to now, Hamas did not seem to be lacking funds. Netanyahu calls on all parties to join a national coalition government. The official number of Israelis massacred now stands at 900, with 2,200 seriously wounded.

According to the latest news, Hamas militants have again breached the "unbreachable" security fence and penetrated somewhere in the South.

Tuesday, October 10

It has been reported that Hamas used pickup trucks for its first penetration in the South. Apart from transporting the terrorists, these trucks were used to obstruct key crossroads and passageways in a successful attempt to hamper rescue efforts in the area. What does that mean? That in the whole Gaza periphery, there wasn't a single Israeli tank, a single armored car, a single bulldozer! And if there was, apparently no one up or down the chain of command had the presence of mind to order their use.

Emerging details of the attacks are horrifying: they raped some of the female hostages and then killed them, and it is almost impossible to keep a modicum of common sense and remember that Hamas is not the equivalent of Palestinians but a fanatical Islamist faction of the Palestinian people.

This will make a reasonable political solution very difficult, because most Israelis consider Hamas and Palestinians to be one and the same. In my mind, the stage-by-stage creation of a

Palestinian state that will coexist peacefully alongside Israel is the only reasonable long-term solution. It is an opinion that I have held for many years. After this latest Hamas onslaught, many Israelis may point not only to the fact that Hamas are Palestinians, but also that many Palestinians have expressed some form of contentment at Hamas's "achievement," proving that they all want our death and the eradication of Israel, and making any type of peaceful coexistence impossible. That is why I allude to a stage-by-stage process. No doubt the Palestinians will have to get used to the advantages of coexistence and not pay attention to the daily attempts to add more Jewish settlements on the land allocated to them, as was the case under our disastrous coalition government. But back to the immediate events.

In an unusually warm and supportive speech today, President Biden expressed his horror at Hamas's atrocities and reaffirmed America's full support of Israel. The *USS Gerald R. Ford*, the most modern aircraft carrier in the US Navy, is now sailing near Israel's shores with 5,000 marines on board, ready to intervene if needed. Additionally, the first US plane with sophisticated ammunition landed in Israel.

It seems that on the northern border we are also at war. The overall number of Israelis killed is now estimated at 1,200.

Wednesday, October 11

War cabinet established. Gantz is a member, and a slot has been kept for Lapid. Otherwise, the situation remains chaotic, with ongoing uncertainty about the North: will Hezbollah join Hamas or prudently decide to stay on the sidelines? Apparently, some gliders have penetrated Galilee from Lebanon; planes are searching for them. After two hours, however, it was announced that it had been a false alarm. The chaos in Israel reminds me of the poet Christian Morgenstern's wall, built only from holes.

Netanyahu's failure becomes increasingly blatant: American sources confirm that three days before the Hamas attack, the Egyptian minister of intelligence warned our PM about something big coming from Gaza. There was no reaction—or rather, there was total indifference.

Let me return to the problem of attempting to further a two-state solution. One of the early conditions will have to be the exclusion of Islamists and Jihadists, as well as the neutralization of Iran's influence. That will be one of the difficult tasks to achieve. The other will be overcoming opposition to any compromise with the Palestinians from the annexationist part of Israeli society, which supports the present coalition, including the half million settlers who may comprise the wildest group of all. The resistance encountered during the evacuation of Gaza in 2004 was nothing in comparison. And today, of course, there is no Ariel Sharon around.

Tonight we had a tiny preview of what could happen: about 100 members of La Familia, a right-wing extremist group, attempted to break into Sheba Medical Center in Ramat Gan, where a wounded Hamas terrorist was being taken care of. They were contained by police and hospital security. The wounded Hamas member had previously been transferred to a police hospital. Yet this indicates what can be expected on a large scale if steps are taken toward a neutralization of our settlers.

Tomorrow there will be a Knesset vote to confirm the unity government established today: there is no doubt of a positive outcome. Lapid and Avigdor Lieberman have not joined yet. The main advantage, hopefully, should be the sidelining of Smotrich and Ben-Gvir.

Gaza is now under complete siege and Israeli troops have amassed on the periphery, apparently ready for an invasion. In their joint announcement, Netanyahu and Gantz announced the formation of the unity government that they promised would liquidate Hamas. It means entering the enclave, which will result in many more victims on both sides, particularly civilians. Apart from the moral and legal implications, entering the Gaza Strip may be a mistake. But getting rid of Hamas without entering the area may be impossible. And of course there are the Israeli hostages in the hands of Hamas. What a terrible mess!

Official sources are still unable to provide much information to many families about their missing relatives, another scandal, to put it mildly. Unofficial sources report about 400 Israelis unaccounted for.

At present, it remains unclear whether Iran was behind Hamas's attack, or if it had any prior knowledge of operational details of the strike. But apart from such precise involvement, it remains clear that for years Tehran has financed Hamas, supported its general aims, offered it all the weapons it needed, and supported its ideological and strategic aims, particularly the destruction of Israel and the liberation of Palestine by force. Thus, regardless of how one wishes to interpret such facts, its direct complicity is a moot question.

News stories detailing what happened in this or that spot in the South are very hard to bear because the few survivors all tell a similar story of resistance by the inhabitants, who fought the Hamas militants until their homes were reduced to rubble—but not before the children, the women, and the elderly were either slaughtered or transported back to Gaza as hostages. And all this time, the army was nowhere to be seen.

Thursday, October 12

Nothing new on the ground for the time being. A waiting period that may last. *Time* magazine published an article on Netanyahu's responsibility for part of the country's present tragedy. If one stresses the word "part," I agree. Of course the main responsibility for what is going on falls on Hamas. That is clear, but Netanyahu and his coalition's absolute dismissal of the Palestinians meant pouring more fuel on a well-known fire. The Hamas leaders may have calculated that the policies that divided Israeli society and strengthened pro-Palestinian opinion worldwide were the right moment for their attack; they didn't foresee that the atrocities of their "fighters" would shift part of world opinion back in favor of Israel and, most importantly, would unite Israeli society in defense of the country.

According to both Israeli and American estimates, 162 Israelis have been taken hostage. Half of them are believed to be dead.

Smotrich will have to change course or go. It is clear—and an excellent article published today on *Ynet* was merely a warning—that the minister of finance will have to drastically revise his priorities and shift billions to postwar reconstruction of the communities in the South that were destroyed by the October 7 aggression and to psychological, medical, and professional help for the survivors of that trauma. From where will these huge sums be drawn at first, if not from the enormous budgets allocated over the last few months to the religious parties and to the settlements in the Occupied Territories? The end of the coalition bonanza.

Settlers attacked a funeral procession in the West Bank and killed a father and his son, according to Palestinian reports. This is the second incident of this type since the beginning of the war.

Otherwise, there is only waiting regarding Gaza, regarding the northern border, and regarding the West Bank and Jerusalem. Tense waiting. No sign yet of any move regarding the hostages and the prisoners.

Friday, October 13

Israel ordered more than 1 million Palestinians living in the northern part of the Gaza enclave to evacuate their homes within twenty-four hours, probably in preparation for the army's occupation. One can only hope that the present atmosphere in the country will not lead to wanton acts of revenge. Like everything else, discipline in the army seems rather loose.

A former student of mine just posted a heart-wrenching message: members of his family were killed and others taken hostage in the Nir Oz kibbutz. He rightly places part of the responsibility where it should be placed: on the shoulders of the prosettler coalition that has been in charge these past few months. As for Hamas, nobody doubts that they are killers who, on top of their own murderous ideology, made the most of the poisonous atmosphere created by the settlers and their supporters. I am afraid that many people in Israel, even those who participated in the demonstrations against the government, will forget the noxious role played by the coalition and will call for revenge against Palestinians in general. The Americans, Biden, Lloyd Austin, and Blinken, are aware of the explosive atmosphere and call for firmness but warn against revenge. May they be heard.

In the last two days, several articles published in Israeli newspapers have expressed a deep pessimism about the future of our relations with the Palestinians (David Grossman in *Haaretz*, two days ago) and about the future of Israel as we have known it, of the ethos that we dreamed of (Nahum Barnea, today). Both attach the responsibility that should be attached to our horrendous government. I hope that we will have a chance to say to those freaks' faces what must be said. Grossman used the right expression: treason by the government, letting down the people they were in charge of. The key word is "treason."

According to research by CNN, Hamas prepared the attack for months, a few hundred meters from the Gaza border, in constructions that replicated the Israeli border fence and the southern communities in great detail. How these preparations escaped the attention of our wonderful military intelligence is even more incomprehensible than ever. According to the *New York Times*, it appears that Iran was involved in some measure in these preparations.

Reserve units of paratroopers describe a lack of necessary weapons as they mobilize. Elite units apparently lack breastplates. Again and again, one cannot believe the level of unpreparedness, but then it is reinforced by similar examples from alternative sources. The various intelligence agencies were deeply asleep, the army supply system was on a prolonged vacation, the army operational division went home, and all the upper ranks of the IDF were probably in Bali or at least in the Alps. As for the chief of staff . . .

And leading the charge we encounter "King Bibi," as some called him until a few days ago, polishing his crown and smiling to the mirror—with Sara'le at his side, of course. He spoke again today, repeating exactly the same things he has said every day since October 7, that "we will break Hamas's bones." Well, you are no Churchill, sir.

On the news tonight, an inhabitant of Nir Oz shared that

his mother and his son disappeared when Hamas evacuated the kibbutz. To this day, he has not received information from an official source, not a visit or even a word of support. From the tragic to the tragicomic: the army released surveillance balloons in three locations around Gaza. A few days before the attack, the balloons fell. Because the technician who could repair them was busy, they were left on the ground. Now it has become clear that Hamas had shot them down in preparation for the onslaught . . .

The Israeli population includes many admirable people, but its political leadership and many of its institutions have been in a state of decomposition for many months, certainly since the most recent elections, in December 2022, which hoisted the present coalition to power. Many of us hope that the postwar reckoning will be pitiless.

According to a new poll, 86 percent of Israelis, including 79 percent who supported the coalition, think that Netanyahu should resign.

Saturday, October 14

Yesterday's poll has evidently disappeared from the news. But Netanyahu is finished. Nonetheless, according to official news reports, spokespeople from the Likud and representatives of Netanyahu's family are active in the information center in Tel Aviv. One more scandal.

It seems that the army's entry into northern Gaza is now just a matter of hours away. It demanded that inhabitants of the northern part of the enclave evacuate by 4:00 p.m. local time. Two local hospitals refused—they have nowhere to go. In the meantime, Hezbollah and Iran remain on the sidelines; the numerous incidents along the northern border and rockets fired from Lebanon are almost exclusively coming from the Hamas and Islamic Jihad units located there, with Hezbollah's authorization, of course.

US support of Israel, made abundantly clear by the carrier group off the country's shores, is probably the main deterrent that keeps Hezbollah at bay, since Israel has lost much of its own power of deterrence as a result of the catastrophically successful Hamas attack. This enormous psychological loss will remain a major issue for Israel for a long time to come. After 1967, the country emanated an aura of invincibility that contributed to its defense—and also to its delusions. It started to get shaky with the Yom Kippur War, and even more so after the Second Lebanon War. It all came crashing down on October 7.

Based on documents found on the bodies of slain Hamas terrorists, it is becoming evident that the kidnapping of civilians, including children, was always part of their plan: the terrorists entered with detailed maps of the kibbutzim closest to the border. As for the slaughter that took place, the responsibility lies with Hamas and with the rabble that entered Israel in the wake of the first incursion to engage in looting and killing. The motivations may have been different, but the slogan was the same: "Slaughter the Jews." The official number of Israelis killed on October 7 is now set at 1,400; the number of hostages at 220.

Since the beginning of the conflict, the BBC has played its typical pro-Palestinian role. For the British radio and television center, the Hamas people who entered Israel and killed or abducted civilians wherever they could are not "terrorists" but "militants." This seems not unrelated to an antisemitism often attributed to the BBC. Stronger anti-Jewish sentiment will undoubtedly rise again in many countries, and support for

Israel will weaken, as the prolongation of the war increases the
number of Palestinian civilian casualties and suffering in Gaza
and possibly elsewhere.

The humanitarian situation in the Gaza Strip is horrendous.
The number of dead is estimated at over 2,200, and hospitals
cannot cope with the constant influx of wounded. As I already
mentioned, two of the main hospitals in the North of the enclave
have refused to evacuate because they have nowhere to go. This
creates major difficulties for the planned Israeli entry into the
enclave and will demand precautions that may hamper military
operations.

Sunday, October 15

The army still hasn't entered Gaza, eight days after the beginning of the war. There must be a strategic reason, somehow
linked to Iran. Are Israel and the US waiting for some Iranian
intervention in order to strike Tehran? Is the entry into Gaza
just a sideshow that will come later, after Iran is knocked out?
All of this is plausible and could explain why the US is moving
a second carrier, the *USS Eisenhower*, and its strike group to the
eastern Mediterranean.

The chaotic situation on the Israeli side, on the eve of Hamas's
onslaught, is further demonstrated by new information: after
receiving news on October 6 of an imminent attack, the head of
Shin Bet arrived in the South, as did an elite unit of the service.
The commander of the army division in the region was apparently informed (although he denies it), but the commander of the
air force was left in the dark. In other words, the right hand did
not know what the left hand was doing. And don't let us forget:
Netanyahu's personal theory was that Hamas was not interested

in conflict but sought merely an improvement of material conditions in the enclave. If this was the well-informed opinion at the top, why should the civilian and military services be worried? The initial Yom Kippur disaster, on October 6, 1973, stemmed from a massive failure of the various intelligence services; the disaster on October 7, 2023, seems to be due to a similar failure. And these are Israel's most highly praised agencies!

Possibly worse: after their parents were killed, two small children from the kibbutz Be'eri, ages six and eight, hid in a closet and phoned relatives in the central part of the country to ask for help. It took these relatives twelve hours to organize a rescue. Friends and civilians with small arms and maps volunteered to drive to the kibbutz and liberate the children. Civilians! Not a single soldier in sight! The army was nowhere to be seen!

General David Petraeus, the retired commander of US troops in Iraq and Afghanistan, says that Israel's challenge in Gaza is much worse than what the US had to face after 9/11. He warns that troops entering the densely populated enclave would have to face a highly hostile and unpredictable environment, where each room could be packed with explosives, where endless tunnels had been dug and could be full of Hamas terrorists, and so on.

When I get depressed by events and the growing hatred all around, I cannot help thinking that I started in life, in the 1930s and 1940s, under the cloud of antisemitism and that I am coming to the end under a cloud of hatred against the Jews. I know perfectly well that the two situations cannot be compared, but what does rational thinking help in moments like these?

On the other hand, what one hears regarding Netanyahu and his people can only serve to enrage. Apparently an order has come from his office not to give any assistance to the agency that aids survivors in the southern kibbutzim because they were among those active in the protests.

And in a recent public declaration Smotrich took responsibility for "what was" and admitted that "the country's leadership failed to protect the country's people." As well as being the finance minister, he is also minister in the defense ministry and therefore in charge of settlers and settlements. He didn't apologize for hastening the building of settlements by all possible means. There is more: while the minister of education wants to use the money allocated to religious schools to help schoolchildren from the South, Smotrich is opposing it. Words of apology are easily provided, but changes of policy are nowhere to be seen among the most fanatical members of the coalition. As for Ben-Gvir, he has remained mostly silent since the attack.

In the meantime, Iran's foreign minister is touring some of the region's Muslim countries, and in each capital he threatens Israel with more dire consequences if it does not stop its "genocide of Palestinians" in Gaza. As for Iran's supreme leader, Ali Khamenei, he kissed the hands of Hamas's leaders for the defeat they inflicted on Israel. For the time being, apart from its uncertain involvement in the preparations of the attack, Iran seems to be generous mainly with words, probably due to America's unequivocal support of Israel. It could be that the intensification of Israel's fighting with Hezbollah on the Lebanese border will compel it to intervene.

Monday, October 16

Today the Knesset reconvened for its winter session. None of the main speakers (Herzog, Netanyahu, Lapid) said anything beyond the typical generalities. The session was interrupted by an alert but resumed shortly thereafter. It is to be noted that neither Netanyahu nor Defense Minister Gallant said a word about their responsibility in this catastrophe. Do they really hope to escape an immediate verdict as well as the verdict of history? US Secretary of State Blinken will meet the PM for a second time today, and President Biden will probably arrive in Israel during the coming week.

The evacuation from the North of the enclave continues under horrible conditions; Israel promises to open a humanitarian corridor. In the North of the country, Hezbollah and Israel appear to be engaging in a war of attrition. This reveals the limits of open Iranian involvement at this stage.

Biden will arrive in Israel on October 18. Some 2,000 American troops will be deployed to the country in an advisory capacity. What this means, nobody knows. As in most wars, much remains under wraps and will likely only become clear when the war is over.

General Petraeus warned Israel about the dangers linked to staying in the enclave after an initial victory. He used Iraq as an example. Staying would quickly become unbearable in casualties and costs; leaving would allow Hamas to reconstitute. Not entering at all would be difficult to justify to the Israeli population, which is eager for a small victory and some weakening of Hamas. An extraordinary conundrum.

Tuesday, October 17

Exchange of fire in the North. The impression is that Hezbollah is preparing to enter the war, if Tehran decides so, and only if Tehran decides so. For the Iranians, the risks may be too high.

Biden's visit in Israel tomorrow is designed not only as a show of solidarity, which it certainly is, but also as an opportunity to achieve several military, humanitarian, and political goals: avoiding an occupation of Gaza, since it might create a challenging military situation for both Israel and the US; extricating as many Israeli hostages as possible from Hamas's clutches; deterring Iran from intervening; advocating for a two-state solution to the Israel-Palestine conflict; exhibiting Biden's humanitarian side to the progressive members of the Democratic Party, with an eye on next year's elections; and, by avoiding the occupation of the enclave, maintaining public support for Israel and the US. Quite a full plate. We will know more tomorrow.

The chief of Military Intelligence today took full personal responsibility for the lack of vital information ahead of Hamas's attack. Netanyahu and Gallant, the two main culprits, still refuse to accept any culpability. When shall we get rid of these two?

The normalization of relations between Israel and Saudi Arabia may have incited Iran's conflict escalation in the hopes of destroying what Tehran views as a threat to its role in the Muslim world. It certainly succeeded in putting all efforts of normalization on hold. No one seems to know how things may ultimately play out. It reminds me of a sentence in *The Complete War Memoirs of Charles de Gaulle*: "Vers l'Orient compliqué, je m'envolais avec des idées simples." (Toward the complicated East, I flew with simple ideas.) Today, the East is by far more complex than it was in 1941.

Prime Minister Olaf Scholz of Germany arrived in Israel to display his country's solidarity. So did the Romanian prime minister, and the president of the EU, Ursula von der Leyen. British PM Rishi Sunak is expected in the coming days. Each visit is welcome, but the atmosphere in the country is out of control: no one dares tone down the thirst for revenge that has spread;

it may compel the leadership to take political and military missteps. No moderate opinion dares express itself locally regarding the conflict. Today, prominent right-wing television presenter Ayala Hasson threatened *Haaretz*, Israel's only liberal daily, with retribution for its typical anti-Netanyahu stance. *O tempora, o mores* . . . The Israel that will emerge from this war will not be the country that we have known and which found its most recent expression in the vast demonstrations against the policies of Netanyahu's coalition. The war, despite the widespread anger generated by the country's dismal unpreparedness, may be a boon for ultranationalists.

According to the latest estimates, Hamas is currently holding 199 Israeli hostages. That in itself makes an invasion of the Gaza Strip virtually impossible. The hostages are Hamas's shield. For most Israelis, this is a horrible dilemma.

Hamas says that 500 patients were killed in the Israeli bombing of a hospital in Gaza City. Israel claims that the destruction resulted from a misfired rocket by Islamic Jihad. All Arab leaders who were supposed to meet with President Biden have since canceled their participation due to the hospital bombing.

Wednesday, October 18

Biden spent half a day in Israel in a show of solidarity. He relied on information from the Pentagon to say that the responsibility for the hospital explosion lay not on Israel, but "on the other team." He met with the families of hostages and promised to help negotiate their release. All in all, he showed extraordinary warmth in his speeches: "Contrarily to what happened in the Holocaust, this time you are not alone." He promised "unprecedented help" for Israel and $100 million for Gaza. He probably convinced Israel's war cabinet to allow humanitarian aid to enter Gaza and may have helped prevent an occupation of the enclave. "Think about what happens after victory," he said. His last speech ended with the words *Am Yisrael hai* ("The people of Israel live," a traditional Jewish slogan and song).

In the West, the major news outlets cautiously mention a "blast" in regard to the Al-Ahli Hospital, but the pictures of wounded and dead Palestinians tell a story of their own.

Skirmishes on the northern border and rockets on Kiryat Shmona, but nothing more for the time being. It seems that both Hezbollah and Israel are treading cautiously, as for both the price of a misstep could be high. Israel learned in the Second Lebanon War in 2006 that Hezbollah fighters are fierce combatants, and the organization has since accumulated a huge arsenal of long-range, precision-guided missiles provided by its patron, Iran. The fighters themselves have garnered considerable battle experience in civil wars in Syria and Yemen. Hezbollah, on the other hand, realizes that the Israeli Air Force alone can rain destruction on southern Lebanon, and knows quite well the force the IDF can unleash on the ground. In short, both sides have good reason to remain cautious for as long as possible. This said, if a two-front war were to take place, Israel could win it even without American military support, though it would undoubtedly take a long time, entail enormous devastation, and exact an unthinkably high human toll.

It is difficult to know whether, in the wake of October 7, Israelis have lost some of the confidence they had in the army, even in difficult times. After the Yom Kippur War, there was a need to pin responsibility on some of the senior commanders. An investigative body, the Agranat Commission, dismissed chief of staff David Elazar, head of military intelligence Eli Zeira, and the initial commander of the southern front, Shmuel "Gorodish" Gonen, among others, yet shielded the political figures who supposedly made bad decisions on the basis of bad information, mainly Golda Meir and Moshe Dayan. One has the feeling, and this will undoubtedly become clearer in due time, that the present crisis of confidence is worse. This must be taken into account in any planning for prolonged fighting. But of course, Hamas and Hezbollah know this.

In the South, Egypt has not yet allowed the opening of the Rafah border crossing into Gaza through which humanitarian aid will eventually pass, because it wants only Palestinians with dual citizenship to use the crossing. In other words, the Egyptians are worried about a massive Palestinian exodus through the Rafah crossing into their country. "They should settle in the Negev," president of Egypt Abdel Fattah el-Sisi is alleged to have said.

In the meantime, a letter by some thirty Harvard student organizations that declared Israel "entirely responsible," when the news came out about the Hamas atrocities, created a chain of backlashes. Some are comparing the reactions of Jewish donors canceling their financial support for Harvard, as well as the publication of personal identifying details of the students involved, to Senator Joe McCarthy's anticommunist campaign in the 1950s; others point to the implicit or explicit antisemitism in the position of pro-Hamas supporters and allude to the fearfulness of some heads of major universities to take a stand against pro-Hamas, mainly leftist organizations.

I always considered myself as being on the center-left in politics, mainly due to my support for the two-state solution. In Israel, I voted for a small party, Meretz, which advocated this. Nowadays, however, one has to be careful: part of the left has become so radicalized that one has to tread very carefully when defining one's political leanings. The process started in the 1960s, but in many cases traditional social democracy has steadily been emptied of its content, so when you say that you are on the left today, that places you somewhere else.

Thursday, October 19

As of this morning, which is already midafternoon in Israel and the twelfth day after the Hamas attack, there is nothing to report in terms of military operations. This may indicate a cleverly camouflaged next step or basic indecision. This situation cannot go on for long because it has a negative impact on the morale of the hundreds of thousands of reservists who have been called up for an operation in Gaza. And if the bombings of northern Gaza continue without any end in sight, international public opinion will undoubtedly become ever more critical of Israel. If Israel does nothing, Hamas and its allies will claim victory. And what happens to the hostages and to the prisoners? Will they be bartered for several thousand Palestinians held in Israeli prisons?

Israel has agreed to let humanitarian aid enter Gaza tomorrow. By an over 90 percent majority, the European Parliament expressed its support for the country's right to defend itself against Hamas. British prime minister Rishi Sunak has arrived. He may not have practical aid to contribute, but he may share with Netanyahu his concerns about the potential massive influx of Gaza refugees the UK may have to face, and also about a further rise in the price of oil, if Iran decides to abandon its relative restraint. But, as I said before, these visits, as well as the European Parliament's vote, are welcome for whatever psychological boost they may provide Israelis.

Tonight, in an address to the nation from the Oval Office, President Biden will reportedly share concrete details of the US financial and military aid for Israel and Ukraine. The aid package will apparently be as large as $100 billion. In the meantime, a US plane with armor-plated jeeps landed at Ben Gurion Airport "to replace those destroyed," according to an official statement. In online comments, somebody asked the right question: how could it be that after just ten days of fighting, the army's armor-plated jeeps have all been destroyed? The answer is simple: as other equipment was found missing, no jeeps were ready . . .

The evil clown Ben-Gvir declared, in a speech encouraging civilians to acquire arms, that wherever in the Gaza periphery there were armed groups of civilians, these areas incurred smaller losses on October 7. This is pure propaganda, argue survivors: small arms couldn't do much, even a tank in the courtyard couldn't do a thing against hundreds of Hamas assailants. Ben-Gvir, the most despicable member of a despicable coalition, cannot miss an opportunity to say something, as stupid and false as it may be, to remain in the news. He is not alone. Thus the communications minister announced today that Israel would "decrease" Gaza's territory after the war. Did he possibly express the settlers' intention of reinstalling Jewish communities on part of Gaza's territory? Nothing coming from members of our coalition astonishes anymore.

Today, Gallant issued some sort of half-baked apology for what happened. Totally insufficient. As defense minister, he will have to pay the full price. In the meantime, he told soldiers "to get ready to see Gaza from the inside."

In his speech to the nation, President Biden grouped Hamas with Putin, in terms of their attempts to destroy two democracies. He made clear that international law and humanitarian rules had to be respected, clearly addressing future Israeli operations in Gaza. Tomorrow, he plans to ask Congress for a package of $14 billion in military aid for Israel. All in all, the president will be asking Congress for $105 billion. An American destroyer located in the northern Red Sea, the *USS Carney*, downed nineteen long-range Houthi missiles directed at Israel.

Friday, October 20

The missiles fired at Israel from Yemen came very shortly after Iran threatened that new fronts would be activated against "the Zionist entity"; their interception by an American destroyer showed that the United States was ready to intervene. Iran probably wanted to check whether the Americans would stand by their word. The Americans sent a clear signal that they would. Now comes the hard part—to get really involved or not. For the time being, the answer seems to be to stay on the sidelines, but the real test will come with Israeli ground forces' imminent entry into Gaza. This will be the turning point of the war.

For Israel to be ready to take the next step, it needs strong leadership. It does not have any at all. The government is a chaotic heap and its head is a dead man walking. Thus, Israel's entry into Gaza could become a tragedy, for both the soldiers and Palestinians. A new poll has confirmed what a previous one had already made clear: more than 80 percent of Israelis consider Netanyahu and his coalition as partly responsible for the Hamas attack and want him out. Unfortunately, that cannot happen now. In short, Israel is facing the worst crisis of its history, under the worst possible internal conditions.

Gal Hirsch is the Israeli official appointed to supervise the hostage issue. Today Hirsch invited foreign diplomats to his office and shouted at them that the "Oslo Agreements" were responsible for the present situation. None of these diplomats had anything to do with agreements signed in the 1990s; some of them had not even been born by then. They left the meeting aghast. Hirsch's performance is an allegory for what goes on.

It is extremely difficult to get a clear picture of Israeli public opinion right now. The polls give some indications and so do multiple other sources, but any attempt at an overall assessment reveals a set of contradictory trends. The October 7 attack certainly revived a sense of a community of fate that had not existed in the country for a long time. The polls point to the persistence of widespread anger against the government and, more widely, against all individuals in positions of leadership, including military leaders, who demonstrated such horrendous incompetence, lack of preparation, and misplaced confidence. If the aforesaid is correct, one cannot avoid asking the obvious question: can the sense of a community of fate sustain a readiness to fight and bear unavoidable heavy sacrifices, despite simmering anger against the country's leadership? In October 1973, the same question could have been asked, but the war was short, and defeat turned into victory rapidly enough not to put the country to the test. This time one speaks of prolonged fighting for weeks and possibly months. On top of it, many commentators report that Netanyahu has not "been himself" since October 7, and some have pointed to the photo of his embrace with Biden, in which he seems to lean into the arms of the American president. Of course, the mere pounding of Gaza does not put the country to the test, but the expected ground operations will necessarily change the parameters, and anything beyond that is shrouded in uncertainty.

The same uncertainty shrouds Israeli attitudes toward Palestinians in general and those of Gaza in particular. The attitude of

Israeli Arabs is not considered relevant. (According to a poll from the Truman Institute at Hebrew University, nearly 80 percent of Israeli Arabs denounce Hamas's actions.) The fanatical prosettlement ideologists, and many Israelis, enraged by the atrocities of October 7, will demand some sort of retribution and may possibly vent their rage upon the Palestinian population. On the other hand, by now there are many Israelis who understand that the prewar policy of the settlers and their supporters (shown by Huwara) fueled Palestinian extremism, but that most Palestinians want to live in peace with Israel and merely go on with their daily life and regain their dignity, as the Truman Institute poll seems to demonstrate. These contradictory trends will find their contrary expression during the ground war. What is allowed and what is forbidden will depend on the decisions of a leadership that, in the eyes of many, has to be done away with.

In the meantime, there seems to be a serious rift between Netanyahu and Defense Minister Gallant. According to Israeli commentators, Netanyahu opposes an Israeli operation against Hezbollah, whereas Gallant is in favor of opening a second front in the North. If Hezbollah remains passive during the ground offensive against Gaza, Netanyahu will reap the praise; if not, this will be one more of his many mistaken assumptions and just another of the many questions he will have to answer.

Two female hostages, Judith (Yehudit) and Natalie Raanan, mother and daughter, were liberated thanks to the mediation of Qatar. They are American citizens who plan to settle in Israel. It may bolster the expectation that if nothing happens on the ground, more hostages will be freed. According to an IDF estimate there are still 210 hostages and prisoners in Gaza. "Our aim is to bring all of them home." Will that postpone the imminent ground offensive?

Saturday, October 21

Humanitarian aid was allowed to enter Gaza today through the Rafah crossing. Strangely, UN and other humanitarian sources confirm that the shipments did not undergo any screenings for weapons or other contraband before entering the enclave. In Israel, the twenty-fifth American cargo plane landed with military and medical equipment.

American and Israeli officials are considering various political futures for Gaza after the elimination of Hamas. Among such possibilities, they envisage a temporary government with some form of UN participation and the support of Arab countries. How this support might be achieved, nobody knows for the time being. The Americans seem to be worried by Israel's focus on short-term military objectives, without sufficient thought being given to what could happen after these objectives are achieved. President Biden, during his trip to Israel, warned of repeating the mistakes the US made after 9/11.

Even the best postwar preparations cannot ensure that the ground offensive in Gaza will lead to a good outcome. Without such a ground offensive Hamas cannot be destroyed, and if it is not destroyed it will claim victory and repeat an October 7–style operation in due course. But the ground offensive may, under the existing conditions in the Muslim world, draw in Hamas's allies and its patron Iran, which in turn will necessitate American involvement. And what the sequels of an American involvement may be, no one can predict.

Israel has evacuated about 300,000 civilians from communities near the Gaza border in the South and the Lebanon border in the North. It has suffered approximately 1,400 deaths since Hamas unleashed its attack. The Gaza population has, according to the

Health Ministry, suffered some 3,800 deaths from Israeli Air Force attacks. Unfortunately, the ground offensive cannot take place without exacting many more human lives, on both sides.

Sunday, October 22

The summit meeting in Cairo of European and Arab countries, convened by Egyptian president el-Sisi to find a solution to the crisis, ended without any resolution because the two main actors, the United States and Israel, had not been invited.

Nothing new on the Gaza front, except ongoing pounding of the enclave from the air with the catastrophic humanitarian consequences it entails. Skirmishes in the North. Netanyahu threatens Hezbollah with dire consequences if it dares join the war. Further American forces are deploying to the war zone.

Israel's warning that northern Gaza should be evacuated led to a massive exodus, with no place for residents to go (Egypt is keeping its borders closed) except for a growing tent city in the southern part of the Gaza Strip near the Khan Yunis refugee camp. For the desperate evacuees this is a reminder, as the present exodus brings them near a camp of refugees from the first Arab-Israeli war. It is remarkable that the neighboring Arab countries refuse to open their borders to the desperate Palestinians.

The most recent estimates set the number of hostages at 212. In Jenin, in the West Bank, a group of alleged Hamas terrorists reportedly made plans to capture hostages, as on October 7. They were arrested in time.

While the first humanitarian convoy of trucks entered Gaza yesterday, it remains unclear what the present situation is. It seems that the seventeen trucks that comprised today's humanitarian convoy have not yet crossed into Gaza. It is probably related to the reported "accidental" shelling of an Egyptian position at the crossing by Israeli tank. Hamas is getting its arsenal of Iranian weapons via Egypt through a well-oiled system of bribes. By shooting at the Egyptian position, Israel is signaling that it is well aware of the traffic. Whether there were weapons hidden in today's humanitarian convoys remains an open question. Later, President Biden and Prime Minister Netanyahu agreed that humanitarian aid to Gaza would continue.

From day one of the conflict, the arena of Western public opinion, particularly the European one, has been engulfed in a free-for-all—in fact, in a mud-slinging match—the likes of which haven't been seen for many years. On each side, raw emotions have taken over and feelings of belonging to a community, in some cases dormant for a long time, have suddenly resurfaced. And from day one, people who do not belong to either community have also joined the fight, either because of vague affinities with one side or the other, or because it allows them, indirectly or explicitly, to push an agenda that couldn't as easily be peddled in quieter times, or even that, in normal circumstances, would be considered a hate crime: anti-immigrant rhetoric and Islamophobia on one side, antisemitism on the other. Of course, there are also hardcore ideologists on both extremes. That's where we are, in the UK, France, and Germany in particular. For the time being, there haven't been major explosions of violence. But in such volatile circumstances, it can be enough to strike a match to create a firestorm.

Netanyahu is holding off on a ground invasion of Gaza for the time being, probably at the request of the American president.

Monday, October 23

According to Israeli officials, instruction booklets were found on dead bodies of Hamas terrorists killed in the South detailing how to use cyanide to prepare explosives for chemical warfare. The information was repeated by President Herzog in an interview with Sky News two days ago. The booklets are actually al Qaeda booklets from the early 2000s.

Another humanitarian aid shipment was allowed to enter Gaza today. Apparently, such shipments will be allowed daily from now on, after Israeli inspection.

Despite repeated denials, it seems that there are differences of opinion between Defense Minister Gallant and the IDF on the one hand, and Netanyahu and people close to him on the other. Gallant and the army are convinced that Hamas cannot be destroyed without a ground offensive but warn that military operations in Gaza may take months. Netanyahu seems hesitant to launch a ground offensive that may be drawn out and deadly. The fact is, as Shas leader Deri admitted today, that no military plans were ready and everything has to be prepared as events are unfolding. This total lack of foresight is the direct result of Netanyahu's view that Hamas was only interested in economic advantages, and that as long as you feed the beast it remains quiet. Interestingly enough, Bennett, who was the temporary head of a pre-Netanyahu centrist coalition, offered his mea culpa today. Netanyahu, who engineered most of prewar Israel's policies during his repeated premierships, remains silent on the matter.

According to an article by Nahum Barnea, one of Israel's most reliable political commentators, previous suggestions of a crisis of confidence between Netanyahu and Gallant, as well as between the PM and his senior military commanders, are correct.

Netanyahu detests Gallant. Several months before the war, he wanted to dismiss him for speaking against the judicial overhaul and its disastrous impact on the army but had to let him remain due to the vast support for the defense minister among the opposition, which was so vocal on the streets at that time. Moreover, the PM holds the army command responsible for all the blunders that led to October 7. That will certainly be his defense when the hard questions are asked after the war. In the meantime, this lack of confidence hampers any effective civilian-military collaboration and formulation of policy. It explains in part the increasing US influence on Israeli decisions, particularly on the priority given to hostage release over the launch of a ground operation against Hamas.

Incidentally, Netanyahu's future line of defense was confirmed in an interview given to Channel 14, the mouthpiece of the Likud, by cabinet member Miri Regev, the prime minister's most faithful follower. When asked about the PM's responsibility for October 7, she replied that the prime minister cannot dismiss the head of Shin Bet, the head of Mossad, or the chief of Military Intelligence; they are the specialists, they offer the assessments. Netanyahu may try, but he will be forced to resign.

Two female hostages were released today: one aged eighty-five, the other eighty. They were brought in ambulances, on stretchers.

Notwithstanding my dislike for Netanyahu and my desire to see him out of the door, at the moment I prefer his prudence to Gallant's insistence on a ground operation in Gaza and, earlier, on an immediate offensive against Hezbollah. A ground operation in Gaza could be disastrous, since Hamas has dug miles of tunnels that would take months to clear and result in a considerable number of casualties on all sides. During that time, growing international pressure would be exerted on Israel, demanding an end to the Gaza warfare. After a while, the US would probably have to join these demands. In a declaration he made today, ex-president Obama seemed to adopt such an attitude. And, as horrendous as this would sound to most Israeli ears, Hamas could then strut and fret and claim victory.

Tuesday, October 24

The Israeli chief of staff repeated that the army was ready for a ground operation, but the decision is not his, as we know; it depends on Netanyahu and the Americans. Iran-supported groups have fired rockets targeting American bases in Iraq and Syria. The possibility of a wider war seems closer than ever.

In the past two days, additional negotiations have taken place with Hamas regarding the release of hostages. Their demand: fuel for the enclave in exchange for hostages. A few moments ago, the Israeli military spokesperson announced that no fuel would be allowed into Gaza, which most probably means that something went wrong in the negotiations. Does it mean that the ground operation is on its way? We should know very soon.

The incandescent atmosphere that is spreading through Western countries is overwhelmingly pro-Palestinian. This leads to a series of questions. First, what is the role of overt, but mostly covert, antisemitism in this blatant difference of reactions toward the documented atrocities perpetrated by Hamas on the one hand, and the bombing of the Gaza Strip and the civilian casualties it entails on the other? Will we see the spreading of a new series of satanic images of the "enemy of mankind?" Will we hear and see that Jewish lives don't matter? It almost happened in Duisburg, Germany, where a would-be *shahid* reportedly planned to drive a truck into a pro-Israel meeting to kill as many participants as possible. He was arrested in time.

It is for this general reason that it never occurred to me to be a pacifist like my uncle Hans. He became a follower of Rudolf Steiner, and in 1939 reached Sweden, where he became director of an anthroposophical institution for youngsters with mental disabilities. He was a convinced pacifist and attempted, gently, to convert me when I spent a year, in 1956–57, at his institution. To no avail. I was totally at peace with my three years in the army and never thought that Israel could exist without a strong national defense. It has become more obvious now than ever. Unfortunately, we have always had a lunatic fringe for whom violence against the Palestinians was acceptable as long as they occupied the land "promised to the Jewish people." I am afraid that a situation like the present one encourages them, but they remain a small minority.

Second, an essentially political question is of the essence: will the tilting of public opinion in the Palestinians' favor influence decision-makers? This is mostly a problem for European leaders, although the US president cannot but take into consideration the looming 2024 elections, particularly if the progressive segment of the Democrats comes to play an increasing role. There is also a very different aspect to the surge of pro-Palestinian sentiment: its overestimation in Tehran. The launch of attacks against Israel and the US could cost the ayatollahs the survival of their atrocious regime.

In their effort to retrieve whatever was left behind by the victims of October 7 and by their murderers, Shin Bet and Military Intelligence say they found the cell phone of one of the victims near Re'im, which her killer used to call his parents in Gaza (the conversation was recorded on the phone): "Dad,

I call to tell you that I killed the Jew whose phone I am using, and with my own hands I killed ten other Jews—yes, ten—with my own hands. Open WhatsApp and you will see all the dead." The father: "May God protect you." The killer then shared his feat with his mother and got her blessing. Foreign Minister Eli Cohen read a transcript of the phone call to the UN Security Council, on the occasion of a special debate regarding the Israel-Hamas war.

Wednesday, October 25

According to various reports, mainly American ones, it seems that to this day, Israel has no clear military plan for its ground operation in Gaza. Will it use special forces and limit its operations to surgical strikes, or will it instead stage a massive show of force? How does one avoid large numbers of military and civilian casualties? Where is the exit plan? How does one get out of Hamas's tunnels—the "Gaza Metro," as they call them? It appears that President Biden is trying to help Netanyahu "use his head and not only his heart." The arrival of US advisors in the country brings experience with urban fighting in Iraq, particularly in Fallujah and Mosul. But what use is technical expertise in the face of a complete lack of preparation in the army and ongoing chaos at all levels of government? Netanyahu, in today's allocution, still spoke with certainty of the coming operation, the date of which will be decided by the war cabinet. As for his responsibility, he merely declared "that after the war, all will have to give answers," he too. That can be called "drowning the fish" (noyer le poisson). How will this affect the country's mood?

On October 7, the sudden Hamas attack was apparently accompanied by a near-total paralysis of Israel's cyber network. This operation was so sophisticated that it was well beyond Hamas's or even Iran's capacity; only Russia may have such expertise. So much for Netanyahu's "my friend Putin" ... In short, wherever you look, you find traces of our PM's lack of foresight: a failure far worse than what was imagined.

According to the *Wall Street Journal*, some 500 Hamas fighters were trained in Iran by the Quds Force in preparation to the October 7 attack. In any case, the Hamas operation seems to have been thoroughly planned for quite a long time. That it totally escaped our celebrated intelligence agencies is an incredible failure.

Qatar and Egypt have announced a breakthrough in hostage negotiations with Hamas. In Israel, this information is confirmed. Specific details should be revealed very soon.

The US has apparently requested a postponement of a ground operation in Gaza until sufficient antimissile defense systems have been installed at all American air force bases in the Middle East. In the past few days, about forty Americans have been wounded in bases in Iraq and Syria.

A friend of mine, an Israeli who teaches at an American university, was informed that his uncle had been killed in one of the kibbutzim overrun by Hamas, the wife badly wounded, and their teenage daughter taken as a hostage to Gaza. During the two weeks he spent in Israel, no official got in touch with him, nobody came with information, nobody tried to reach him, nothing. It was only when he was back in the States that he learned, from one of four female hostages who were released, that his cousin was alive in Gaza.

Thursday, October 26

Israeli armed forces made an overnight incursion into northern Gaza in readiness for the wider ground operation. There were no casualties among the soldiers. Simultaneously, suspected military and civilian leaders of Hamas are being identified, found, and executed.

Still no news about the hostage deal. Could it be a release of all hostages in return for an end to the Gaza operation? Such a proposal would confront Israel with a terrible dilemma: sacrificing the lives of about 200 of its citizens and waging an uncertain campaign against Hamas, or letting Hamas survive and saving the lives of the hostages. Undoubtedly, the hostages are the national priority.

A poll published on October 13 shows a dramatic downslide of Netanyahu to only nineteen mandates, while Gantz has climbed to a stunning forty-one mandates. Lapid would garner fifteen mandates. Shas would lose half its mandates, and Religious Zionism (which merged the Jewish Home and Religious Zionist Parties) together with Jewish Power would garner a mere nine mandates. The poll also gives six mandates to Meretz and another six to Yisrael Beiteinu. In short, a tremendous surge of the center and center-right and an amazing downfall of the hard-right and religious right. This explains of course why Netanyahu declared, after the publication of these results, that he would finally answer questions about what happened on October 7. Too little and too late.

In a press conference with the Australian prime minister today, President Biden sharply admonished the Israeli extremists who killed several Palestinians in the West Bank in acts of so-called retaliation. He also called for a humanitarian pause to allow more aid to be shipped to Gaza. Whether Israel will agree remains unclear.

Israelis have been arming themselves in record numbers: some 150,000 applications for gun licenses since October 7, compared with 42 applications in the same period last year. This signals a loss of confidence in the armed forces' ability to respond quickly enough in the face of an emergency. It looks like a frantic response to a situation that is unlikely to repeat itself but which can lead to ominous consequences, such as an intensification of settler violence against the Palestinians in the West Bank.

Russia is taking a clear stand on the side of Iran and Hamas, both at the UN and in talks being held in Moscow. In Israel, Putin is accused of "organizing an axis of terror."

Friday, October 27

While US planes were pounding targets in eastern Syria in retaliation for attacks on American targets, Israel launched a second ground incursion into northern Gaza. No casualties were reported among the raiding troops. A rocket launched from Gaza hit a building in Tel Aviv: four people wounded. The number of Israelis taken hostage on October 7 is now estimated at 229.

These limited incursions seem to be the only ground operations against Gaza for the time being. The lack of confidence between the army and Netanyahu's entourage seems to run as deep as ever. Clearly the PM doesn't want to take responsibility for a ground war that could fail. The hostage issue—which Hamas may be postponing on purpose—is a powerful argument against a hasty incursion, but so are the military uncertainties of tunnel warfare. Notwithstanding the early bluster, it appears that the IDF is lacking vital equipment for prolonged warfare. One shortcoming after another. Netanyahu is aware of the political battle he will have to fight against enormous odds after the war, and this prospect appears to paralyze him, even beyond his usual procrastination and caution.

Regarding the IDF, its lack of readiness on October 7 is obvious. On the other hand, it may have been preparing for a war in Gaza for quite some time, as a recent article published by the *Telegraph* appears to confirm. According to the *Telegraph*, the Israeli army some time ago set up a replica Gazan city in the Negev Desert near Tze'Elim; it's even known as "Little Gaza" and mimics the enclave's terrain and infrastructure, including its tunnels. The article also mentions that the army has "sponge bombs": bombs or explosives projecting foam that immediately solidifies and which can seal passageways in or between tunnels. The article doesn't offer any precise indication for its assertions but gives the impression that the IDF is not entirely unprepared for a ground assault.

According to several commentators, Hamas has already achieved what was possibly its major aim: a renewed international awareness of the Palestinian issue. Over the last two years or so, there has been a distinct possibility that the Abraham Accords between Israel and a number of Arab countries, coupled with a potential normalization of relations between the Jewish state and Saudi Arabia, would marginalize the Palestine issue, and perhaps even make it irrelevant. October 7 drastically changed the situation: now, the Palestinian issue and particularly the setting up of a Palestinian state is on the minds of everyone, including President Biden. For the present Israeli government this may be the most unwelcome perspective.

In a special briefing for foreign correspondents, an IDF spokesperson disclosed considerable intelligence materials intended to prove that Hamas's operational headquarters is located beneath Gaza's largest medical complex, Al-Shifa Hospital.

Apart from its overall political goals, Hamas seems to have three specific demands for the release of hostages: an end to the bombing of the enclave, the delivery of fuel, and the liberation of Hamas and Islamic Jihad prisoners in Israeli jails. In response, Hamas could liberate children, women, and old people. Facing this possibility, the Israeli war cabinet is divided between two positions: postponing a ground invasion to prioritize the partial liberation of hostages, or beginning a ground assault and negotiating release of the hostages after achieving some strategic military advantages.

Israeli ground forces are fighting in the enclave. A spokesperson for Netanyahu announced to foreign correspondents that "the turning point has arrived and Hamas will feel the intensity of our anger." It is impossible at this stage to know exactly what is going on and whether the ground operation is "surgical," as the Americans have demanded, or whether it is massive. Iran has declared that fighters in Lebanon "have their finger on the trigger," to use its terms, but one does not know whether Hezbollah will join the war or only fight with Iran's empty words.

Saturday, October 28

Little information about the IDF operation. This is understandable. The *New York Times* writes that Hamas has stockpiled enormous quantities of fuel and provisions in anticipation of a protracted war, even as the population in Gaza lacks the essentials. The organization's constant demand for fuel was just camouflage: it seems to have all it needs for a long war stored along hundreds of miles of tunnels. It has become clear that

Egypt was the pipeline for all this hidden traffic. Despite el-Sisi's goodwill facade, hatred of Israel seems to run very deep on the shores of the Nile.

The families of the Israeli hostages are worried about the fate of their loved ones during a ground operation. It appears that after he was informed of a planned meeting between Gallant and the families of the kidnapped, Netanyahu decided to meet with them immediately. The meeting took place this evening, without anything new coming of it.

The dilemma between ensuring the safety of the hostages and expanding the ground operation remains, even if it is not explicitly acknowledged. It seems that the army is seeking a limited ground operation in northern Gaza as a basis for negotiations. But how limited is limited in a ground operation that has a dynamism of its own? More or less simultaneous with the beginning of the operation, Yehia Sinwar, the head of Hamas in the enclave and planner of the October 7 attack, offered a deal: all for all. In other words, exchange of all the hostages for all Hamas members held by Israel. An Israeli military spokesman rejected Sinwar's proposal, calling it "psychological terrorism." Israel prefers a step-by-step negotiation via Qatar and possibly other mediators.

In a press conference held this evening with Defense Minister Gallant and war cabinet member Gantz, Netanyahu refused once more to take responsibility for the events that led to October 7. He denied again that there was a lack of trust between him and the defense establishment. He repeatedly reaffirmed his certainty of future victory, after which "all the hard questions would be asked." It seems that he has no intention of being held accountable for anything and will fight tooth and nail to keep his position.

Sunday, October 29

In the North, exchanges of fire, but it doesn't seem likely that Hezbollah will join the war beyond that. Iran remains silent for the time being. In Gaza, very little information about the ongoing ground operation. Among the population, there seems to be growing frustration and panic: widespread looting of UN warehouses has been reported, and no electricity, apart from private generators.

No news about the hostage negotiations. Qatar's role is apparently crucial but very ambiguous, to say the least. For years now, the tiny Gulf state has played host to Hamas's political leadership on the one hand, as well as to US Central Command headquarters for the Middle East and Central Asia on the other. For the oil-rich monarchy, this means a permanent and precarious balancing act. It means talking out of both sides of their mouths.

As was to be expected, Netanyahu criticized the head of Military Intelligence and the head of the Shin Bet for not warning him of the dangers brewing on the eve of October 7. Soon afterward, he apologized. Despite the apology, this may be his defense tactic from now on. The Israeli public will not be swayed so easily. Anger against the PM is accumulating, including indignation at the luxurious lifestyle he's flaunting while many Israelis suffer. One of the most unbelievable aspects of Netanyahu's behavior, one that has been documented countless times, is that his criticism of his two senior commanders was apparently expressed against the opinion of a senior advisor.

As I am writing all of this, a question, in fact *the* question, is constantly on my mind: will this war convince the Israeli population that it won't be possible to reach an authentic peace settlement with the surrounding Arab states without moving toward a two-state solution? It is true that we have had peace with Egypt and Jordan and the Abraham Accords without any settlement of the Palestinian problem. But as the attitude of their populations and the declarations of their leaders make clear, in the present situation this is a brittle peace, one that may crumble at any moment. Will steps toward a settlement of the Palestinian issue ensure a more stable acceptance of Israel by the Arab world? Nobody knows. The Oslo agreements looked like a first step, but nonetheless we faced a "refusal front." All that must be taken in consideration, but Israel has to show a readiness to move beyond mere words and more settlements.

What is new in the equation, and perhaps should not be taken into account but is of major importance for me, is the enormous outpouring of hatred against Jews, in other terms the identification of Israelis as Jews in an outburst of antisemitism not seen in the West since the heyday of Nazism. Actually, it should be very much taken into account, given, for example, what happened today at the airport in Dagestan, where a crowd mobilized by an antisemitic channel rushed to find Israeli passengers on a plane arriving from Israel. We know that the crowd got out of hand and that armed police had to intervene.

In the US, after Harvard, Cornell is making a splash: a student there is accused of openly calling to kill Jews. Nice, isn't it? The Anti-Defamation League reported a 388 percent rise in antisemitic incidents nationwide since October 7, in comparison to the same period last year.

Monday, October 30

The number of hostages in Hamas's hands is estimated at 239. One of them, a young Israeli-German woman named Shani

Louk, whom Hamas paraded and filmed in her underwear in the streets of Gaza, is now confirmed dead. Today, Hamas published a short video of three kidnapped Israeli women and their statements (most probably obtained under duress) against Netanyahu.

Yesterday, the largest aid convoy yet entered Gaza: 33 trucks. It is manifestly insufficient. Therefore, Israel agreed with the US that, from today on, 100 trucks would be permitted to enter the enclave daily. The ground operation is systematically widening, according to the military spokesperson, but obviously one gets very few details.

This morning it came out: in 2016, Avigdor Lieberman, then defense minister, informed Netanyahu that Hamas was preparing an operation inside Israel that included the taking of hostages. The document was apparently extremely detailed, and Lieberman and the army command also prepared a detailed plan for preventive action. The cabinet shrugged it off. The general complacency was based on Netanyahu's belief that Hamas was interested only in improving the material conditions in the Gaza Strip, nothing else.

Great news! A female Israeli soldier, Ori Megidish, a hostage apparently held alone, was found and liberated by the advancing troops. She is back in Israel.

Turkey's president, Recep Tayiip Erdoğan, attacks Israel in daily salvos. During one of his pro-Palestinian rallies, he promised to denounce Israel as a "war criminal." Coming from the Turkish president, this is quite a threat. Israel recalled its ambassador and will reconsider its relations with Turkey.

Harvard's president, Claudine Gay, announced the establishment of an advisory group to help eradicate antisemitism on campus. It took President Gay some time; let us hope that these aren't mere words.

A friend wrote to me from Paris: "Numerous swastikas drawn on the streets. French public opinion is desperately fractured." In France, the supporters of Israel nowadays are the extreme right (Marine Le Pen), as at the time of the Algerian War. Yesterday's antisemites are temporarily pro-Israel out of hatred against immigrants, as they were then, out of hatred against Algerians.

Tuesday, October 31

The Israeli ground offensive is progressing, deep in the enclave. No concrete information about military developments, except that from the moves reported by foreign correspondents, one may gather that the army aims to isolate Gaza City by cutting the north-south highway.

There has been a significant increase in the number of anti-Palestinian incidents in the West Bank. Blinken is coming to Israel once again to discuss this worrying development. The responsibility is first and foremost on the settlers, the direct culprits, but also on a government that is unwilling or unable to stop this rabble.

This war against Hamas may be different from those that preceded it in scope and scale, but essentially Israel is waging one and the same war against enemies that want one and the same thing. It is necessary to recall the sequence of conflicts in order to grasp the true depth of the issue and the difficulty one may encounter in finding a permanent solution.

As for the wars' sequence, it is quickly summed up:

The 1948–49 independence war was but the first of the struggles waged against the new State of Israel, but also the last of the repeated assaults against the "Zionist entity," since it was now here to stay. The Balfour Declaration of 1917, which promised the establishment of a Jewish national home in Palestine, was in fact the true founding charter of Zionism, even if the dream of a Jewish state, born of the growth of antisemitism in Eastern and Western Europe, predated it by three decades.

Under the British Mandate beginning in 1920, a spate of Palestinian attacks against Jewish communities, resulting in several hundreds of deaths, did not stop the growth of the Yishuv, which led to the proclamation of the State of Israel on May 15, 1948.

The War of Independence, which Israel won against five Arab states, was followed by a period of constant Palestinian incursions and Israeli reprisals and the short-lived Suez Crisis in 1956, that strange alliance of Israel, France, and Great Britain against Egypt, after Gamal Abdel Nasser's posturing led to his closure of the Suez Canal to Israeli shipping. A few years of relative calm followed until Egypt, this time allied with Syria and Jordan, moved troops into the Sinai Desert and directly challenged Israel, triggering the fateful Six-Day War of June 1967.

Israel's victory was swift, crushing, and fateful. The Jewish state was now master of conquered territories from Suez to the Golan Heights and from Gaza to the Jordan Valley, and master of a Palestinian population that would soon number over 2 million.

Six years later, Egypt and Syria attempted to restore the military balance in the Yom Kippur War in October 1973. The sudden attacks were announced, on television to an Israeli public in total shock, by Defense Minister Moshe Dayan and Prime Minister Golda Meir. The turning point came with Israel's counterattack, the crossing of the Suez Canal by Sharon's forces and the encircling of the Egyptian Third Army.

Peace with Egypt and Jordan did not mean peace with the Palestinians and did not change the overall situation. Wars with the Arab neighboring states were replaced by escalating conflicts with Palestinian resistance organizations.

The First Lebanon War, in 1982, was launched by Israel against Yasser Arafat's Palestine Liberation Organization, which had mounted attacks on Israel from southern Lebanon. The war aims, planned by the wily defense minister Sharon under the formal leadership of PM Menachem Begin, led to the uprooting of the PLO from Beirut and its relocation to Tunis, but little more than that. It also produced a fragile and short-lived alliance between Lebanese Christians and Israel. The siege of Beirut bears some resemblance to the present Gaza War: it was short and led nowhere.

The Second Lebanon War, in the summer of 2006, was even closer to the present situation. It started with Hezbollah kidnapping and killing Israeli soldiers on the northern border with Lebanon. The ensuing Israeli-Hezbollah conflict was difficult for the IDF: it faced a tough Shia opponent, fully armed and trained by Iran. It also led to growing Israeli disillusion with an aimless war. An end to the fighting was brokered by the UN in August 2006, but without any real resolution.

Today, the Arab states of Egypt and Jordan have partnered with Israel in fragile peace agreements. But the increasingly militant Palestinian "refusal front," under changing monikers, is the present justification for a decades-long struggle against an enemy that may change names but is pursuing the same aim: pushing the "Zionist entity" out of the Arab Middle East.

These are military confrontations, but in this instance, war is not only the belligerents' politics by other means, but much more: it is religious passion and world politics by other means.

Among Jews, the religious motivation has been present in the yearning for a return to Zion since the High Middle Ages. It found its expression in prayers, of course, but also in an abundant literature from that time on. Theodor Herzl, the author of *The Jewish State* and founder of political Zionism, was not attuned to it, but a significant segment of East European Jewry, who joined the Zionist movement, were aware of these religious roots and in part motivated by them. The religious dimension of Zionism did not play a crucial role until the Six-Day War and the Israeli conquest of the biblical territories and the whole of Jerusalem. Afterward, it surged as a messianic movement, with Zionists convinced that these conquests were the beginning of redemption.

On the Arab side, the religious presence is more directly linked to political and military action against Israel. Hamas was established in Gaza in 1987 by the imam Ahmed Yassin, its full name being the Islamic Resistance Movement. In many ways, Hamas descended from the Muslim Brotherhood, and in Gaza it became the herald of refusal politics, of the rejection of any political arrangement with Israel. Its stance led to a direct confrontation with Yasser Arafat's Fatah, which agreed, after the Oslo Accords of 1993 and 1995, to recognize Israel and work toward a two-state solution of the conflict. In 2006, Hamas won the elections to the Palestinian Legislative Council. In 2007, Hamas evicted Fatah and took control of the Gaza Strip.

Hamas, although autonomous, depends for its struggle against Israel on the aid of the religious Shiite regime of Iran and its fanatical stance against the "Zionist entity." Thus, the religious dimension is playing an important role in the politics of Netanyahu's extremist coalition, and even more so in the uncompromising militancy of Hamas, Hezbollah, and their patron, Iran. This doesn't exclude political calculations on both sides.

Wednesday, November 1

The Yemeni Houthis have declared war on Israel. Yesterday, Israel bombed the Jabalia refugee camp in an attempt to kill a senior Hamas leader hiding there, killing dozens of civilians in the process. Foreign nationals are leaving the enclave. Jordan has recalled its ambassador from Israel.

The enormous upsurge of anti-Israeli sentiment in Western countries is astonishing. The horror of the attack by Hamas did not create any significant change of opinion; the war that it triggered merely accelerated the anti-Israeli and antisemitic surge.

How long can this go on is anybody's guess. Israel will be able to withstand the tsunami of international hostility as long as the United States is backing its progress in Gaza—notwithstanding the growing number of civilian casualties it entails. But how long can we rely on America's stand? And do not mistake the situation on the home front: the Israeli population has no confidence in its leadership, to say the least. This also reminds us of the two Lebanon wars, but it is worse. For the time being, anger motivates Israel, an understandable anger. President Biden understands it, as do other Americans.

Yesterday, Secretary of State Blinken spoke at a Senate hearing to remind us all of the starting point of this war: the October 7 Hamas aggression, which led to the killing—and often the torture—of 1,400 Israelis and the taking of 240 hostages at the last estimate.

Thursday, November 2

On the ground, the slugging goes on without any solution in sight. It is worrisome as such and because of the mounting number of hapless civilian victims. The knowledge that so many innocent Palestinians are caught in the rubble and getting killed cannot be sustained for much longer. And we know nothing about the fate of the Israeli hostages (242, as of today). The United States will propose a pause in some of the fighting to allow delivery of humanitarian aid. The *New York Times* writes that Netanyahu is open to the suggestion. In Israel, this is denied. Secretary of State Blinken will meet tomorrow with the Israeli war cabinet. We shall hopefully know more by then.

American Jews are divided. The majority supports Israel unconditionally, but a growing number on the left have become increasingly critical, even extremely so. One hopes that Netanyahu knows what he is doing if he rejects even a limited pause. The total eradication of Hamas is an aim dictated by the desire for revenge, but one cannot eradicate an ideology, and a religious one at that. Netanyahu probably hopes to appear as the victorious leader in battle, something he has not achieved before. How much do personal calculations enter his "detached" assessment of the situation? Does the "war cabinet" have any influence on his decisions?

The ground operation goes on without any concrete details released, except that Gaza City is now completely surrounded. This of course means that the leaders of Hamas are in danger of getting caught. It probably explains the sudden trip by the political leader of Hamas, Ismail Haniyeh, to Tehran, obviously in order to ask Iran to induce its client, the Hezbollah leader, to intensify his military intervention. Indeed, Nasrallah is supposed to speak about the conflict tomorrow. He will most likely hint at what his organization plans to do and, indirectly, give some idea about Iran's intentions. The tension in the North is palpable, with the Israeli chief of staff warning Hezbollah of dire consequences in case of increased involvement.

In the meantime, as the fog of war is as dense as ever, let me return to my prior remarks about the basic factors that seem to determine the conflict between Israel and this or that actor, either an Arab state or the Palestinians. I pointed to the influence of religious motivations on both sides, but, of course, political considerations have played the major role in shaping the conflict.

On both sides we see a similar pattern: actors intent on finding a peaceful solution on one hand, and actors who do not believe in such a solution and consider striving for security (or taking aggressive initiatives) as the only viable policy.

On the Israeli side, there have been leaders who believed in the possibility of a peaceful solution and have endeavored to achieve it. First and foremost among them was Moshe Sharett, a longtime foreign minister and prime minister for a very short period in 1954–55. Such was also, to a lesser degree, Levi Eshkol, prime minister from 1963 to 1969, although he was more or less compelled to launch the opening gambit of the Six-Day War. Yitzhak Rabin will enter history as the leader who brokered the Oslo Accords and offered Israel a peaceful perspective regarding the Palestinian issue, and he was assassinated because of it. So too will Shimon Peres be remembered, to a lesser degree.

Most other political leaders in the country were determined security-first advocates, like the preeminent national leader David Ben-Gurion, or involuntary peacemakers like Menachem Begin, who was basically a hawk. Ariel Sharon, the most extreme hawk of all, also has this dual image, for taking Israel out of Gaza and planning to retreat from parts of the West Bank. There remains the weird figure of Golda Meir, the American-raised prime minister who, as I described in an earlier entry, denied the very existence of a Palestinian people. And also the captivating figure of a man who, although never prime minister, had immense influence as chief of staff, minister of defense, and, in his later days, foreign minister: Moshe Dayan.

In 1966, on a visit to Israel before my appointment at Hebrew University, I met Moshe Dayan and we talked. It was my friend the journalist and later biographer of Ben-Gurion, Shabtai Teveth, who took me on a visit to Moshe in his house in Zahala. He was a private citizen at that time, before becoming a key figure as defense minister in the cabinet that was to launch the chain of victories in the Six-Day War. In the 1950s, he had given a memorable speech at the tomb of a friend killed by a Palestinian infiltrator from Gaza (at the time belonging to Egypt). I have already mentioned how he prognosticated that there would be no peace with the Palestinians and that Israel would have to survive by the sword. I asked him about that.

The Palestinians are peasants whose land we took, he explained, and peasants never forget their land until they have taken it back. It was basic and cogent. For Dayan, living by the sword was nothing to be afraid of. Many years later, after bearing the brunt of popular anger as defense minister during the Yom Kippur War, he became foreign minister in Begin's cabinet and partly engineered the peace with Egypt. Dayan was a loner who didn't mind changing political camps. I guess that he didn't change his views about the Palestinians.

In this gallery, where does Netanyahu stand? I have amply shown in the early diary entries what I, along with 60 or 70 percent of the Israeli population, think of Netanyahu as prime minister, mainly as far as internal politics are concerned: he is a despicable self-serving type who, in order to save his skin, has been ready to set up a religious ultranationalist coalition with catastrophic results for the country. Insofar as he has backed the settlers' program, Netanyahu has been ready to endanger the precarious balance of relations with the Palestine Authority to keep his coalition afloat. On the other hand, he strove to bolster the Abraham Accords and reach an agreement with Saudi Arabia. All of this is now in ruins, or nearly so. And yet, one cannot deny that throughout his several premierships, Netanyahu was anything but a firebrand. In fact, he was extremely cautious during previous outbreaks of hostility with Hamas, postponing moves that could have led to a wider conflict. His present refusal to opt for a limited ceasefire stems, in my opinion, from the pressure of the minister of defense and the army, who expect tangible results within a short time. To make his procrastination palatable to the Americans, he uses the liberation of the hostages as the prerequisite for a ceasefire, but how long will he be able to use this argument against US demands?

Smotrich, our despicable finance minister, tried to withhold the payment of tax money Israel owes to the Palestine Authority. Today, the cabinet decided on transferring the money after a strong intervention by Defense Minister Gallant.

Friday, November 3

Nasrallah's speech did not disclose much: on the one hand, he described the Hamas aggression as 100 percent Palestinian, even mentioning that he had not been warned of it. On the other, he did not exclude the possibility of widening the conflict. In this guessing game, I would venture to predict that Hezbollah will keep to its present limits and not start a full-scale war.

The troops engaged in Gaza seem to be progressing inside Gaza City itself. One of the units is getting close to Al-Shifa Hospital.

Despite the general progress of ground forces, there are repeated warnings from Israeli military spokespeople that the operations will take a long time. Is that intentional disinformation? It had better be, as Israel does not have much time. The United States will soon ask for not only a humanitarian ceasefire but a cessation of the military campaign as such. Nobody has said this up to now, yet that is the impression one gets. In this context, it seems to me that Secretary of State Antony Blinken's warnings are of much greater significance for Israeli military goals than Nasrallah's bluster. The US is flying MQ-9 drones over Gaza to help Israel locate the hostages.

Israel can nonetheless count on the United States in the face of the international anti-Israel coalition that is taking shape. For the time being, this coalition is essentially active in the propaganda domain and the transfer of some weapons systems to Hamas. Apart from Iran, which is fully engaged against the "Zionist entity," the participants are Iran's ally, Russia (since the Ukraine war) and, increasingly, China. These three powers are united in a global confrontation with the US. This is the fundamental reason for American support of Israel in the present conflict.

As if all this weren't enough, Israel has leaked a position paper formulated by Military Intelligence proposing the transfer of the Palestinian population from Gaza to northern Sinai—an idiotic idea that has caused an outcry in Egypt and from all possible international aid agencies. It shows that nobody knows what a safe postwar solution could be.

Israel's proclamations about the long fight to come may have been disinformation, as later news indicates some panic in Hamas's ranks. The organization attempted to smuggle its people among the American citizens who were allowed to depart through the Rafah crossing to Egypt. The Al-Shifa Hospital is apparently encircled.

Saturday, November 4

Demonstrations against Netanyahu resumed in Jerusalem, Caesarea, and other small cities. People who lost family members on October 7, or whose family members were taken hostage on that day, consider him responsible. The release of the hostages is an obvious goal for Israel. It is not clear what price will have to be paid for their release.

For the time being, no Arab country seems to be ready to side with Hamas, not even in words. To understand Abdel Fattah el-Sisi's abstention, one must remember that since Nasser's ill-fated belligerence and Anwar Sadat's initially successful war of October 1973, Egypt's policy toward the Jewish state has been decidedly peaceful. Sadat's role in this decisive departure from the policies of his predecessor cannot be stressed enough. It led to a peace agreement. Like Rabin a few years later, Sadat, in 1981, paid the price of his peace policy with his life. His successor, Hosni Mubarak, followed Sadat's policy from 1981 to 2011, when he was ousted during the Arab Spring upheavals.

It seems unlikely that the belligerent stance of the Muslim Brotherhood, briefly in power in Cairo from 2013 to 2014, echoed deeply among a growing Egyptian middle class that can only benefit from a policy geared to economic development rather than to Islamist militancy. In any case, as I pointed out, el-Sisi, who was appointed president in 2014, follows an extremely cautious policy in this respect.

Sunday, November 5

I was somewhat astonished by the highly positive response to the publication of my prewar diary in Germany some ten days ago. Now the real opinion of the country seems to be taking a different turn: there is probably no patience for talk of a two-state solution to the conflict between Israel and the Palestinians. And yet, whatever way you look at it, no other solution is realistic.

It so happens that today an interesting proposal was posted online. It was apparently written by a retired senior member of the Mossad. In a nutshell, his idea is that after the conclusion of the Gaza War, Jordan should become an active partner in negotiations regarding the future of the Occupied Territories. In place of the direct negotiations with the Palestine Authority that have been proven hopeless, the talks would be with a Jordanian-Palestinian confederation that would be responsible for the West Bank and Gaza. The degree of autonomy of the Palestinian entity within such a confederation would be determined in arrangements between Jordan and the Palestinians.

This sounds like a very reasonable step on the way to a solution of the Palestinian question, but to be feasible it needs both Jordan and the Palestinians to be on board. First and foremost it needs a different Israeli government (a precondition mentioned by the author) and some kind of acceptable solution of the settlements issue. All this is fraught with immense difficulties, but preferable to an endless stalemate with recurring eruptions of violence.

Netanyahu is manifestly playing for time. He rejects the humanitarian pause, does everything to appear the tough leader of his embattled country, calls Sinwar "a little Hitler in his bunker," and in short is ready to sacrifice the interests of Israel by jeopardizing its close alliance with the United States, just to save his political skin.

Just how despicable Netanyahu is he proved again today. He apparently declared that Sinwar attacked us because pilots and other elite units refused to serve due to their opposition to the judicial overhaul. Gantz stated in response that launching such accusations in a time of war was weakening the country. Netanyahu denied the reports.

Strangely enough, lack of confidence in the country's leadership did not exist to such an extent in 1973. I was in Jerusalem on that Yom Kippur day when the shock came, but then our Pugwash group at the Hebrew University organized to help the Ministry of Foreign Affairs in its effort to mobilize support for Israel overseas. On October 10 I was sent to France to get our narrative across. It was generally accepted, even on the left. And, during all those days, there was no desire to hold Golda Meir responsible, although she was, knew it, and resigned. What a difference!

The *New York Times* published the Israeli proposal that I mentioned a few days ago to transfer several hundred thousand Gaza Palestinians to Sinai. The US, Great Britain, and Egypt have rejected the proposal, which comes from the hardcore Likud party (and not from Military Intelligence, as was first announced). It is an insane proposal that can only lead to a growing rift with Egypt. That is exactly what Israel needs at the moment!

It seems that the US administration has its own plan for postwar Gaza, which Secretary of State Blinken discussed with Mahmoud

Abbas on his current visit. According to this plan, after the war the Palestinian Authority should be extended to Gaza. Abbas will accept the proposal, if it comes with the establishment of an independent Palestinian state. How will Israel react? The present coalition will reject the proposal, of course. Does it mean that the plan is dead from the outset, or that the US will try, with the support of a majority of Israelis, to get rid of the present coalition? It is not out of the question.

The Pentagon announced that a nuclear submarine has been sent to the Mediterranean. This show of strength is in line with President Biden's policy. But a poll taken a few days ago indicates that a majority of Americans are not in favor of the president running again in the forthcoming elections, mainly due to his age.

Monday, November 6

Yesterday, pro-Palestinian demonstrations all over the US, particularly in Washington. Were it not for the chant of "from the river to the sea," and the widespread anti-Israeli calls, one could agree with the demand for a humanitarian pause of the bombing in Gaza. But what about the hostages? What are the conditions for their release? Is Israel's argument that only growing military pressure will lead to their release tenable, if the military operations have to go on for months, which means no end to civilian casualties in the enclave? I admit to feeling hapless in the present conundrum.

What is sure is that the settler attacks against Palestinians in the West Bank have to stop, but nobody seems to lift a finger. And do we have to hear another idea from Knesset member Amihai Eliahu, who suggested dropping an atomic bomb on Gaza and had to be suspended for a month? Unfortunately, there is more than one madman in today's Israeli politics.

IDF ground forces in Gaza report seizing an important Hamas underground compound, killing a senior Hamas leader in the process.

South Africa recalled its ambassador from Israel. The growing diplomatic isolation of Israel among non-Western countries can be sustained as long as the United States has Israel's back. In Washington, the "progressive" segment of Democrats is as vocal as ever and threatens the president with dire results for his pro-Israel policy on election day. Such an outcome is tangible in a swing state like Michigan, with its population of 200,000 Arab Americans. Very few of them, according to researchers, would support Joe Biden today. In western Europe, Ireland and Norway are for the time being the only outspoken anti-Israel countries, Ireland more extremely, Norway with greater hesitation.

The US can demand that Israel be more pliant insofar as a humanitarian pause is concerned, but it cannot abandon its pro-Israel policy, because Israel's main enemies are also enemies of the United States. Thus, whether one likes it or not, the global context for relations between Israel and the US is a given.

IDF ground forces are in action close to Al-Shifa Hospital.

Tuesday, November 7

The fog of war is denser than ever. We only know that IDF ground forces are fighting in the heart of Gaza City, near Al-Shifa Hospital. Ironically, the hospital was built by Israeli architects in the 1970s, when Israel was occupying Gaza. But the tunnels below the hospital were not built by Israel. We do not know whether the fighting has reached the tunnels.

That Israel's war against Hamas has to take place in a densely populated urban setting, with countless innocent victims, is highly distressing. That Hamas is using the civilian setting and constantly broadcasting Israel's inhuman behavior is in line with its strategy from the very outset. That Israel has decided to pursue a campaign, the aim of which is to destroy Hamas's ability to repeat its attack of October 7, is evident. That the majority of public opinion in the West willfully ignores this justification and turns against Israel is hard to take. That the Israeli ambassador to the United Nations found it necessary to wear the yellow star of Nazi times on his coat is plain stupid, as it ignores the difference between then and now.

There seems to be some divergence of opinion within the Israeli war cabinet. While Defense Minister Gallant announced that there was no way of interrupting the fighting, Minister Gantz declared that every effort would be made to hasten the release of the hostages, either by military or political means. It was later confirmed that Gantz had suggested holding a joint press conference, but Netanyahu refused. Thus Gantz and Gallant each held separate press conferences while the PM spoke without journalists being present and, as usual, offered only a general declaration about the necessity for Israel to control the security situation in Gaza for an indeterminate period after the war. That is the national unity of our war cabinet.

Wednesday, November 8

Whereas the two fanatics, Smotrich and Ben-Gvir, demand more extreme measures against the Palestinians of the West Bank, the members of the war cabinet, including Gadi Eisenkot, Gantz, Gallant, and the top commanders, want to ease the situation of the Palestinian population. It is reported that Netanyahu will use a high-level conference this evening to criticize the chief of staff and the head of Shin Bet.

It remains unclear whether the ground operation in Gaza has reached the tunnels or whether the fighting remains on the streets. From well-informed sources, it seems that Hamas has managed to retain most of its military strength and that the IDF will need much more time if it aims at the thorough destruction of the terror organization. Getting the time needed may become difficult in view of international pressure and particularly American internal constraints. The solution could lie in tactical pauses in military operations that would allow more humanitarian aid to get to the population, without necessitating a general ceasefire that would seriously hamper pursuit of Israel's objectives. Hamas was apparently ready to liberate ten to fifteen hostages in exchange for a three-day pause in the fighting. Israel is asking for the release of many more hostages and a shorter pause.

I feel deeply depressed about the situation. From the information one can gather, Hamas is far from broken, and if we take an overall view, Israel is faced with a series of extremely difficult challenges that may already be influencing the general course of the war.

First, the families of hostages want the return of their loved ones to be a priority, but this probably doesn't fit the strategic goals of the IDF. It is often repeated that only military pressure will compel Hamas to liberate all the hostages, but things don't look that way. A general exchange of all the Palestinians kept in prisons by Israel for all of Hamas's hostages seems achievable, but it would mean a psychological and military success for Hamas. This option was rejected by Israel.

The lack of trust between Netanyahu and part of his coalition on the one hand, and the military and security heads on the other, is a second rift, felt in policy toward the Occupied Territories. With demonstrations in front of Netanyahu's house, one notices a resurgence of the deep distrust of most Israelis toward the present coalition and its head, notwithstanding the war.

The external challenge has already been mentioned. It is the growing pressure for humanitarian pauses, which may turn into a ceasefire that allows Hamas to regroup and replenish its arsenal.

Brazilian authorities foiled an alleged terror attack by Hezbollah against synagogues, on a tip from Mossad.

Thursday, November 9

After a ten-hour fight, a unit of the Nahal Brigade took control of a Hamas underground tunnel in the Northeast of Gaza. It found considerable intelligence material and the organization's battle plans, and killed Hamas's commander of antitank operations. Yesterday, some 50,000 additional inhabitants of the northern part of Gaza evacuated to the South, many more than in the previous days.

Germany has banned all Palestinian organizations supporting Hamas, particularly the Palestinian Samidoun group, which organized celebrations for the Hamas terror attack of October 7.

In an article in the *New York Times*, Tom Friedman, on a visit in Israel, calls Netanyahu "the worst leader Israel has ever had," on the basis that for the sake of maintaining his extremist right-wing coalition, he rejects any possibility of a two-state solution that would not only garner support from moderate Palestinians but give Israel the public backing of moderate Arab states that it lacks now. It would also give President Biden the political justification for all-out support of Israel. Friedman is absolutely right, and hopefully the country will get rid of Bibi at the first opportunity. There is enough anger going around to dump the PM many times over. My worry is that even a moderate center-left or center-right coalition will balk at the two-state solution from the get-go. The proposal for such a solution has to come with very clear security guarantees and a stepwise implementation, particularly in light of the trauma of October 7.

It is difficult to know how far Hamas or Islamic Jihad have penetrated the Palestinian population of the West Bank. Repeated Israeli operations in Jenin suggest a strong implantation of terrorist cells in the city and the refugee camp. Today Israeli forces killed fourteen Palestinians in the city and four more in clashes in other parts of the West Bank. A strong Hamas presence in the Occupied Territories would make the two-state solution almost impossible. That is what Hamas wants and also what people like Smotrich and Ben-Gvir wish for.

Israel has agreed to daily four-hour pauses in the fighting to allow inhabitants of the northern part of the enclave to evacuate to the South. The US and Qatar have apparently reached a deal for the liberation of tens of hostages; Hamas wants the liberation of a number (we don't know how many) of its prisoners from Israeli jails. The deal depends on an agreement about the numbers.

Friday, November 10

Secretary of State Antony Blinken said it in New Delhi and the *New York Times* quoted its own sources: the US is getting impatient. This is going on for too long, too many civilians are being killed, the risk of a wider conflict is growing—in short, American all-out support is reaching its limit. What will Israel do? It cannot stand alone against the whole world, but it also cannot cease its military operations and let Hamas claim victory. Accept a ceasefire? Change the nature of its operations and reduce the scope and scale of its fighting? Is that possible? In the meantime, Israeli military correspondents on the front lines in Gaza report that the discipline in Hamas's ranks is weakening and that some of their people are running away. Could it be the beginning of the end? Thirty-eight Israeli soldiers have been killed since the beginning of the ground offensive in Gaza. The scenes from Al-Shifa Hospital and its surroundings are heartrending. The Palestinian civilians' plight is awful. Israel is convinced that Hamas tactically established its headquarters in tunnels under the hospital compound, and that Yahya Sinwar, the Hamas chief, is holed up there. Time will tell, but in the meantime civilians are getting killed.

The negotiations in Qatar about the exchange of hostages for Hamas prisoners in Israel go on, but the information about agreements is contradictory.

In a poll of the Israel Democracy Institute, 70 percent of Israeli Arabs feel close to the country in the present time of war; in June, the identification was only 40 percent. Strange but encouraging. On the other hand, a poll taken in mid-October by the Peace Index of Tel Aviv University showed a sharp increase of hawkish opinion among Israeli Jews. Whereas in September more than 40 percent of respondents were in favor of negotiations with the Palestine Authority for some peace agreement, the proportion fell to 24 percent in October. This was to be expected.

Each time I see or hear reference made to the Holocaust in regard to the ongoing war, I cringe. When pro-Palestinian demonstrators use the term, I mostly get upset by their stupidity and total ignorance of what they are talking about; when our people use the Holocaust as a comparison to what this or that person said or did, I feel shame and disgust at such wanton use of Nazi criminality to vilify our present detractors. The immediate example that comes to mind is the use by our ambassador to the UN of the yellow star of Nazi times to denounce the supposed antisemitism of the secretary-general of the organization. How silly and shameful!

Saturday, November 11

Half a million anti-Israeli demonstrators in London. Jeremy Corbyn, the former Labour leader, harangued the crowd.

Did the British example influence the French president, who, after an early show of friendship for Israel, unexpectedly took a decisive anti-Israeli position in an interview with the BBC, demanding a ceasefire in Gaza and accusing Israel of murdering women and children in its ruthless bombing campaign? Or is Macron worried about potential trouble among France's large North African immigrant population?

In Riyadh, a two-day meeting of the Arab League and the Organization of Islamic Cooperation commenced. The aggressive rhetoric in Riyadh is not new, but the handshake of Mohammed bin Salman, the Saudi leader, and of the Iranian leader Ebrahim Raisi could signal the emergence of an Islamic bloc that may become dangerous for Israel.

In Gaza, the battle will have to go on for a long time—contrary to my bouts of optimism, here and there—since Hamas still controls the essential part of approximately 500 kilometers of tunnels, built at the cost of approximately $1 billion, with reserves of fuel and food that can last for a very long time.

A spate of polls proves once more that the Israeli people's confidence in its present government and leaders is at an all-time low. The respondents recognize the harm caused by the attempted judicial overhaul. They have full confidence in the army and want an aggressive center-right government under Gantz. There is very little support for negotiations with the Palestinians.

Yesterday, about 80,000 Palestinians left northern Gaza for the South, the largest number of daily evacuees yet. On videos shot on the scene one sees Hamas people trying to hamper the flight, manifestly without success.

Nothing new was said in the press conference held today by Netanyahu, Gallant, and Gantz. This unusual conference of the three together was probably convened in order to show that Netanyahu is part of a political common front that can bring victory. In fact, the only interesting aspect of the meeting was a photograph of Gallant and Gantz holding each other's shoulders in a friendly greeting, while neither one made such a gesture to Netanyahu. This spoke louder than any rhetoric about unity that the PM has tried desperately to put across. Netanyahu repeated on this occasion that the IDF would be in charge of security in the Gaza enclave after the war, a position contrary to the American wish to give the Palestinian Authority full responsibility, in the framework of a solution to the Palestinian question.

Sunday, November 12

A march against antisemitism will take place today in Paris. President Macron supports it, although he won't participate. The far-right leader Marine Le Pen will attend, which incited the far left to boycott the event.

Representatives of French Jewish organizations expressed their displeasure at Le Pen's participation, recalling that her father, the founder of the Front National, was an extreme antisemite and Nazi collaborator. France's prime minister, Élisabeth Borne, will speak. Macron called President Herzog and more or less apologized for yesterday's declarations.

The situation in the Gaza hospitals is hard to bear. There's no concrete news from the ground operation near Al-Shifa Hospital.

Today the *New York Times* ran a long article about the slaughter near the Re'im music festival on October 7. It described in detail the flight of one group who tried to hide in a bunker built along the road leading out of Re'im. Hamas found it and slaughtered most of them, also taking several as hostages. An escapee told the story. Some of the charred corpses were found a few days ago but were so disfigured that identification was almost impossible.

In a series of interviews with American networks, Netanyahu refused once more to answer the question of his responsibility for the October 7 events. Did anybody ask this of Roosevelt after Pearl Harbor? Did anybody ask this of Bush after 9/11? These were his standard answers. He promised that after the war all questions would be dealt with, including that of his responsibility. We know what his defense will be: no one in the army or his entire defense and security establishment gave him a warning. How could he know?

By declaring for the nth time that Israel will keep control of security in the Gaza Strip after the war, Netanyahu wants to appear as the strong, no-nonsense leader that he failed to be before October 7. But he is running into a trap that the Americans know well, after Iraq and Afghanistan. By refusing to share power with the Palestinian Authority or promise it the possibility of a two-state solution, Israel will face a growing radicalization of the Gaza Palestinians and those of the West Bank, and the rebirth of Hamas, be it under another name. Nobody can be assured that this will not occur in any case, but there is a much better chance of avoiding such radicalization by showing a readiness to support what most Palestinians demand: a state of their own.

According to the *Washington Post*, maps and instructions that were found in possession of one of the Hamas units that attacked Israel on October 7 show that the aim of the attackers was to reach the West Bank, which would have represented an immense victory for Hamas, not only against Israel but also against the Palestinian Authority. In their eyes, it would have demonstrated their ability to liberate the whole of Palestine.

As a complement to this rosy picture, it became apparent over the last days that, although there is a war cabinet for social and economic matters, there is complete chaos and indifference all around, as if there were no war and no urgent matters to deal with. In short, those responsible are deeply asleep and Finance Minister Smotrich has more important matters on his agenda.

Monday, November 13

One hundred US officials from the State Department signed a document dissenting with the president's policy in the Israel-Hamas war and accusing Joe Biden of spreading misinformation when, three days after Hamas's attack, he characterized it as "pure evil." It is interesting to note that the State Department has traditionally been anti-Israeli and, during World War II, antisemitic (Breckinridge Long), when it tried to impede immigration to the United Stares of Jews fleeing for their lives.

It is perplexing, somewhat unsettling, and sad to witness these substantial instances of antisemitism suddenly popping up in so many places, including from within the State Department. This is not frightening anymore, as it was for centuries, but certainly perplexing. Why this hatred? I won't start answering here: it demands more than a few sentences, and a lot of thought. Apart from the State Department example, there is the notorious one of the Harvard student organizations. That, however, has triggered the response of some 1,600 Jewish alumni who now threaten to end their donations. That will probably rattle the university's leadership.

During the last two weeks, as all attention has concentrated on the fighting in Gaza, a low-level war has ensued on the Israeli-Lebanese border, with Hezbollah and Israel exchanging fire and inflicting casualties on both sides.

A strange symmetry: more than 70 percent of Gazans were critical of Hamas and wanted a peaceful agreement with Israel, according to a poll by Foreign Affairs taken just before October 7. And about 70 percent of Israelis wish to be rid of Netanyahu and his coalition, and want a center-right government, probably under Gantz. Although there is no desire for negotiations with the Palestinians, the very fact that we shall get rid of Netanyahu and his coalition will open many possibilities.

According to Defense Minister Gallant, Hamas has lost control in the northern part of Gaza; the inhabitants are looting the organization's reserves and its militants are fleeing to the South. If that is so, the fighting should soon be over. But where are Yahya Sinwar and company? I hope that Gallant doesn't mistake his wishes for reality.

According to the Israeli foreign minister, the IDF still has two or three weeks before support from allies wanes due to the loss of civilian lives. If Hamas is not defeated, what then?

An Israeli force entered Al-Rantisi Hospital. President Biden spoke about the liberation of hostages and the conflict with the emir of Qatar but did not mention a ceasefire at this point.

Tuesday, November 14

The armed wing of Hamas offered to liberate seventy hostages in exchange for a five-day ceasefire. It means that Hamas is in dire straits and needs a respite. It doesn't seem that Israel will agree to such a lengthy pause.

The idea outlined by two Knesset members of a voluntary population transfer of Gaza inhabitants to neighboring Arab countries, supported by Smotrich and angrily rejected by Egypt's foreign minister, is of course a nonstarter, coming from the Israeli extremists of Netanyahu's coalition. Another aspect of the coalition's intentions can be seen in the particularly aggressive policy enacted in the West Bank. The evil clown Ben-Gvir is encouraging this policy with the distribution of weapons and creation of self-defense groups all over Israel, particularly in the West Bank settlements. Some of the settlers wear army uniforms and act as if they were soldiers; more often than not, they are backed by the army in their acts of violence against the population. Seven Palestinians were killed yesterday in one of the antiterrorist operations that go on day after day, with Hamas members killed each time. In short, the coalition's policy is to use the war situation in order to get a total grip on the Occupied Territories, one way or the other. But the more pressure used, the greater the danger of radicalization among the population.

A march supportive of Israel and against antisemitism will take place this afternoon on the National Mall in Washington, DC. Tens of thousands of participants are expected. Pro-Israel marches in several European countries have garnered the support of hard-right political figures such as Marine Le Pen in France and Suella Braverman in England (dismissed yesterday as home secretary by Rishi Sunak). As already mentioned, the pro-Israel stance of these supporters is merely another way of expressing their hatred of immigrants, mainly from the Middle East and North Africa. In the US, there is no sign of this specific kind of alliance, but Israel is strongly supported by another sort of extreme right wing: the evangelical Christians, because of their messianic expectations. Incidentally, the messianism of the evangelicals does not fit exactly that of Ben-Gvir and his ilk. According to the latest reports, some 300,000 people participated in the march in Washington.

There is little doubt by now that the IDF ground operation in Gaza is successful. But does this mean that Hamas as an ideology and even as an organization will disappear? If it survives, the main task must be to impede it from reforming as a terrorist force, close to Israel and capable of attacking it again. That is why Netanyahu wants Israel to keep control of security in the Gaza Strip after the war. How does one achieve that without reoccupying the enclave?

Wednesday, November 15

Israeli ground forces entered Al-Shifa Hospital. Moreover, they captured the Hamas parliament building and other sites that symbolized the organization's control of the enclave. A new proposal from Hamas for the liberation of some of the hostages: fifty women and children for three days of ceasefire and the same number of Palestinian women and children from Israeli prisons. No answer yet. Israel authorized the delivery of 25,000 liters of fuel to Gaza. Strong critique from some coalition members: "Fuel equals weapons."

The military operations within the Al-Shifa health complex must protect the patients and the refugees as much as possible. It is a moral imperative and would also give Israel the legitimacy it needs.

The BBC, generally rather hostile to Israel, interviewed an Arab physician and a journalist as well as some international health personnel after an Israeli commando backed by tanks occupied Al-Shifa. Until now, all of them, including the director of the hospital, confirmed that there was no fighting on the premises. The IDF was systematically checking the identity of all males between sixteen and forty to make sure they were not members of Hamas or Islamic Jihad. According to a military spokesperson, the troops found weapons and uniforms left on the floor, indicating that the militants planned to flee as civilians. No trace of the hostages was found.

According to Reuters, in their meeting a few days ago the supreme leader of Iran Ali Khamenei informed the political head of Hamas, Ismail Haniyeh, who had come to Tehran from Doha to ask for help, that Iran would not intervene in the war because Hamas had not informed it of its attack of October 7. The same argument was used by the head of Hezbollah, Hassan Nasrallah, in his response to Hamas's pleas.

After being presented to Congress, a video recording of the Hamas attack on October 7 was screened to 70 members of both Houses of the British Parliament. In both cases, the incredible brutality of these images made a deep impression. However, there are 650 members in the House of Commons alone and more than 750 in the House of Lords. It is probable that no member of the Labour Party attended the screening . . . The negative (or shall we say, somewhat negative) attitude toward Israel and, often toward Jews, in the UK nowadays remains puzzling.

Thursday, November 16

Israeli Defense Minister Gallant says that evidence was discovered inside Al-Shifa that linked the facility and the fate of Israeli hostages. It would be helpful if Gallant could be more precise in his frequent announcements. For the time being, there is no evidence proving that Al-Shifa was a Hamas command center and that its senior leadership was holed up there. Repeated announcements without proof do not help the Israeli information campaign, a campaign increasingly important and not very successful up to now. One point in Gallant's announcements was sadly proven correct: the corpse of Yehudit Weiss from Kibbutz Be'eri, who was taken hostage on October 7 and whose husband was murdered on that day, was found near Al-Shifa. Yehudit was diagnosed with breast cancer a few months ago. She was murdered by her kidnappers and weapons were found nearby.

Israel allowed some fuel to be delivered to Gaza. The chief of staff, in a conversation with the troops in Gaza, said that Israel was ready to widen its operations to other parts of the enclave. Gallant had said as much previously. The extension of ground operations to the south of the enclave will depend in some measure on the attitude of the US. The dire situation of the population needs to be taken into account. And what about the hostages in all of this? Forty-eight soldiers have been killed so far in the campaign.

The rise of antisemitism in western Europe and the US shows that hatred of Jews was merely dormant since World War II and the Holocaust, and that any pretext can revive it. This hatred is being amalgamated with social conflicts that have nothing to do with it. Jews are portrayed as oppressors, either directly oppressing the Palestinians or using the money they have supposedly accumulated to oppress any possibly disadvantaged social group. Antisemitism certainly is the oldest hatred, and it does not end. In the US, at least, the Jews react forcefully, although there is no way to stop the constant tirades of well-known personalities such as Elon Musk.

Friday, November 17

Under American pressure, Israel's war cabinet has permitted a daily supply of fuel for Gaza, which has unleashed anger among the most extreme members of the coalition. I have the feeling that the government does not have any clear idea how to pursue the operations, how to rescue the hostages, how to keep some American and some west European goodwill despite the increasing chaos and misery in Gaza, how to fend off growing international hostility . . . Mainly, Israel does not seem to have any plan regarding the fate of Gaza after the war. To declare that it wants to keep control of the security in the enclave is no plan. What governing authority is foreseen for Gaza? None? In the meantime, the settlers are let loose in the West Bank. Apart from giving interviews to American networks, Netanyahu doesn't give a lead anywhere. As the head of the opposition Lapid demanded a few days ago, Netanyahu should go.

The US has warned Israel that without an exit plan from Gaza after the war, the IDF will face the long guerrilla warfare that Americans faced in Iraq and Afghanistan. Both the US and moderate Arab states certainly do not want Hamas to remain in charge, but the only solution they have is a Palestinian Authority government within the context of a two-state solution that Israel—at least under the present government—rejects.

The *New York Times* and the *Guardian* both express doubts today about the evidence provided by the IDF regarding Hamas's military activity at Al-Shifa Hospital. Apart from the corpse of Yehudit Weiss, which was found near the hospital, and the weapons and uniforms that supposedly belonged to Hamas fighters, the IDF uncovered a shaft with steps leading down to tunnels that could not yet be explored because of the danger of booby traps. Only such hard evidence would justify the Israeli incursion into the hospital with its thousands of patients and refugees.

Saturday, November 18

Netanyahu, Gallant, and Gantz explained in a press conference that, in response to demands by the US and other friendly nations, and on the recommendation of the army and Shin Bet, they have approved the daily delivery of 130,000 liters of fuel to the enclave, the minimum necessary for avoiding the spread of diseases and other catastrophic developments. The decision has been met with protests in the ranks of the coalition. In order to discuss the matter, Netanyahu will convene the wider cabinet in the evening. The decision was approved.

The *New York Times* has confirmed that the IDF has lowered a camera down the opening of the tunnel uncovered under Al-Shifa. At the bottom of a short flight of stairs, there was a short passage of approximately fifteen meters leading to an armored door with a slit through which to fire weapons, but only from the inside out.

Sunday, November 19

The Yemenite Houthis hijacked a cargo ship in the Red Sea. The ship, the *Galaxy Leader*, is somehow linked to an Israeli company. The crew was taken hostage, but there are no Israelis among them. This is an escalation of the conflict, although the Iran-backed Houthis have already launched missiles at Israel that were intercepted by an American destroyer and, later, by Israeli missile interceptors. Beyond missile interception, Israel will not be dragged into a war with the Houthis.

Yesterday *Haaretz* published an article reporting that several female military personnel who were stationed on the border between Israel and Gaza before the war had warned of unusual activity on the Gaza side for several days—warnings that were not heeded, in their opinion, because they were young and also because they were women. Some of them, incapacitated after the attack, could not immediately rejoin their units and received warnings that they would be considered deserters and could get ten years in prison. They now have to be treated for post-traumatic stress. A very sad and revolting episode in many ways.

According to Hamas, a ceasefire of several days will start tomorrow at 11:00 a.m. and fifty hostages will be freed. Israel denied that an agreement had been reached, but a confirmation from Qatar was submitted to the war cabinet.

Danny Cohen, formerly BBC's director of television, has demanded an independent inquiry into the BBC's blatantly anti-Israel reporting since the October 7 attack by Hamas. The anti-Israel attitude of the corporation has been noticed on several occasions in the past and it seems that its journalists covering Middle Eastern affairs are a priori hostile to Israel.

Ben-Gvir cannot miss an opportunity to be seen and heard and to promote something, anything, as long as it is repulsive. Now he has found it necessary to speak to the families of hostages and to use the occasion to promote a new law imposing the death sentence on terrorists. The families protested and pointed to the danger for their loved ones, who are still held by Hamas. The evil clown did not relent. No such law will be discussed in the Knesset anyway, but Ben-Gvir has had his publicity stunt.

Tuesday, November 21

A hostage deal is now seriously in the making: 53 hostages, mainly children, their mothers, and elderly women will be exchanged for 150 Palestinian women and youngsters and a four-day ceasefire. The war cabinet and the government will discuss the proposal this evening. The key to future exchanges is a one-day ceasefire for ten hostages and three Palestinians liberated for each Israeli hostage. All Israeli military and security entities are in favor of the deal.

One speaks more and more of a war that will last for a full year. Quite a somber view of the future. For now, the hostage deal is very encouraging. Otherwise, the daily announcements on television of the names and pictures of soldiers and officers killed are very depressing. I remember that the same daily postings in newspapers took place during the "war of attrition" of 1969–70 until they were stopped because of their impact on the population.

Watching the endless march of tens of thousands of Palestinians evacuated from the northern to the southern part of the Gaza Strip is heart-wrenching. They proceed slowly, carrying whatever they can, in a dense procession of the dispossessed. Soldiers are watching the march to find any Israeli hostages. To no avail.

According to the army, almost all inhabitants of northern Gaza have moved to the South.

Of course, Ben-Gvir and Smotrich are against the hostage deal. It won't change anything, but how long shall we have to suffer the revolting presence of these two freaks?

Wednesday, November 22

The Israeli Cabinet has agreed to the ceasefire and hostages exchange with Hamas. According to Hamas, the ceasefire is supposed to start tomorrow (Thursday, November 23) at 10:00 a.m. Let us keep our fingers crossed. Many of us hope that it will happen and that it can be followed by further days without fighting in exchange for further releases, but naturally we worry lest some incident impedes the process. The head of Mossad is in Qatar and tonight he will get the list of hostages to be liberated. Yet the names will not be released before their formal identification tomorrow, to avoid any disappointments. Netanyahu declared that the liberation of a further group of hostages is not certain at the moment.

In the government session that approved the exchange, Smotrich and Religious Zionist ministers decided to vote in favor. The finance minister aimed at separating his party from Ben-Gvir's Jewish Power and showing that he and his party were acting responsibly. Ben-Gvir railed against the agreement; he and his ministers left notices "against" and did not wait for the end of the meeting. He knows that even in this government he is done once the war is over.

An illegal settlement that had been erected near Ofra was forcibly evacuated today by the army; the temporary constructions were dismantled. The settlers sent a virulent protest letter to the military commander of the West Bank. Thank God for this courageous initiative. The settlers' daily rampages against Palestinians are unbearable.

What can take the place of Hamas in postwar Gaza is the unresolved and essential issue. The most obvious answer is that some form of Palestinian authority should be in charge, but not one governed by the old and corrupt Mahmoud Abbas. Two potential candidates are regularly mentioned. Mohammed Dahlan was once the Fatah security chief in Gaza, until Hamas overthrew the Fatah leadership. He fled the Palestinian Authority territory in 2011 and lives in exile in Abu Dhabi. He is generally considered the rival of Mahmoud Abbas for leadership of a future Palestinian state and, needless to say, there is not much sympathy between Abbas and Dahlan. The other candidate, Marwan Barghouti, is in prison in Israel. Israel hasn't said that it agrees to either one of them, and in any case, Hamas is far from uprooted.

At about midnight in Israel, it was announced that the liberation of the hostages was being postponed until Friday, since the list of those to be freed has not yet been handed over and a formal agreement hasn't yet been signed. What the true reason for the postponement may be is not clear.

Thursday, November 23

The ceasefire starts tomorrow, Friday, at 7:00 a.m. local time, with a first group of thirteen hostages to be released at 4:00 p.m. Fifty hostages will be released during the four-day truce, and 150 Palestinians imprisoned in Israel will be liberated. During the ceasefire substantial humanitarian aid will be delivered to the enclave. One assumes that further groups will be liberated if the ceasefire is prolonged. The families are on edge, understandably so. Netanyahu declared that the war will continue until Hamas is destroyed. It does not look that way. The one to promise death and destruction all around is Gallant. Yesterday he prophesied that the leaders of Hamas are living on borrowed time. It is nonsense and does not absolve Gallant for the abysmal lack of preparation in the defense forces to deal with the catastrophe of October 7.

The director of Al-Shifa Hospital has been arrested by the Shin Bet for interrogation about Hamas's alleged activities in the hospital.

Omer Bartov, a former student of mine in the 1970s, who over the years became a professor and a well-known specialist in the Holocaust, has caused a firestorm by accusing Israel of genocidal intent in its attacks in Gaza. The trouble is that Israel cannot let Hamas survive with its 1988 charter (revised in 2017) advocating the destruction of the Jewish state, as it will, in one way or the other, repeat its murderous attacks.

I understand Bartov's motivation in the face of so much death and destruction, but I do not agree with his accusation. What is the alternative for Israel? I actually am for a cessation of hostilities, but it is because I see the human catastrophe involved and not because I think that Israel has to stop its operations forthwith because it is committing genocide.

It is impossible to know, in the midst of the fighting, which Israeli operations are militarily necessary, and which are dictated by sheer indifference to civilian casualties. It seems that some operations, like the bombing of the Jabalia refugee camp, are more likely the latter. "It is worse than a crime," as Talleyrand said about the killing of the Duke of Enghien, "it is a mistake."

Ultimately, the decisions implemented by the military are taken at the political level and, there, as I have already wondered, how much does Netanyahu have to say? I have described him as a cautious politician. He was that in the past. But did the catastrophe of October 7, and the responsibility he carries for it, change him to the point of rejecting US appeals for greater caution in unleashing whatever violence is feasible? It could be. If so, Israel risks paying the price for Netanyahu's need to justify himself with yet another series of miscalculations. Or can one rely on the levelheaded members of the war cabinet to tell him when enough is enough?

Israel is caught in a horrible dilemma for which there is only one solution, a most improbable one: Hamas has to abandon its goal of destroying Israel and recognize its right, like that of every other state, to live in peace with its Palestinian neighbors, who also have the right to a state of their own. In other words, the two-state solution has to come with the cessation of hostilities and the acceptance of it by Hamas and Israel. But in Israel there are too many right-wingers to accept a two-state solution, and Hamas would have to stop being Hamas to accept a peaceful solution. What then is in store for the next decade at least and probably for a whole generation? There will be truces which can last for a few years, with the certainty of further explosions.

Today, another kind of explosion: the letter sent in March by the chief of intelligence to Netanyahu, outlining in detail the strategic conjuncture for an attack on Israel, has been published. The analysis uses general terms but is correct in its conclusion: the enemies of Israel can use the internal turmoil in the country to attack it. Netanyahu disregarded any kind of such warning and, instead, opted for the dismissal of Defense Minister Gallant. He was compelled to rescind the dismissal because of the huge protests it provoked, but he didn't pay any attention to the warning from the intelligence services.

The chief of intelligence himself was or was not aware of the extremely precise details that a female intelligence officer had forwarded about Hamas's preparations for an attack. She observed and analyzed all the methods they used to avoid any Israeli suspicion of some unusual behavior. We shall know soon enough whether her repeated warnings reached the top or remained stuck in the intelligence bureaucracy.

Friday, November 24

The first group of thirteen Israeli hostages was freed today. The event was broadcast from its very beginning on both radio and television. The emotion in Israel is immense. All ten hostages from Thailand and one from the Philippines were also freed.

Much has changed in the country since October 7. From what I hear from any number of friends who are there or have visited over the last few days, the major change is in the loss of a sense of security. The previous feeling of total normality was probably foolhardy, but what else could be expected? The majority of Israelis lived in relative economic well-being, owned a house or at least an apartment, took vacations in Eilat or Greece, and often further afield, etc. This sense of total normality was reinforced by a leadership that was, like the Netanyahu family, living the good life to the full. The normalization of the relations with the Gulf states and Morocco, and the possibility of a normalization of relations with Saudi Arabia strengthened the sense that the traditional security problems had been solved. Most Israelis were involved, over the last few months, in the internal conflicts that I've discussed here. October 7 has radically changed all of that. The insecurity felt by many is deeper than the bouts of anxiety that occurred after the previous wars. There is war in the South and in the North. There is growing restlessness among the Palestinians of the West Bank. There is the deadly hatred of the ayatollahs not far away. There isn't much support for Israel in the world. In short, the country is in many ways fighting for its existence or, more precisely, for its acceptance as a state like any other state.

What now mobilizes all news outlets—and rightly so—is the liberation of hostages. Hamas will almost certainly use the possibility of liberating further groups to extend the ceasefire from its original four days to a much longer period that will make a resumption of war very difficult. The organization can then claim victory, as it will emerge unbroken from a war that Israel proclaimed it would pursue until Hamas's complete destruction. For Israel the dilemma will be difficult. Yet even if it opts not to resume the fighting, Israel will have learned a very precious lesson: not to be caught sleeping anymore. And, in the meantime, to start working on a solution to the Palestinian problem, even if its implementation takes many years, possibly a whole generation.

Saturday, November 25

Another swap of fourteen hostages for forty-two Palestinian prisoners is supposed to take place today, although there seem to be some difficulties. Over the last two days, 400 trucks with humanitarian aid entered the enclave. Today a Qatar delegation arrived in Israel to discuss the possibility of prolonging the truce. There seems to be willingness on both sides.

Yesterday the Egyptian president spoke of the possibility of establishing a demilitarized Palestinian state including Gaza. It is possible in theory, but el-Sisi did not say where Hamas would be in the meantime. Does he imagine that Hamas will simply evacuate Gaza and allow for some other authority to govern the enclave? Or did he just say anything, for the occasion, which was a press conference with the prime ministers of Spain and Belgium?

Will the progressive wing of the Democrats lead to the defeat of President Biden in the forthcoming elections, because of his staunch pro-Israeli policy? It's quite possible. The progressives ask that the aid for Israel be linked to various conditions; the president avoids being pinned down and stays the course. Biden's stand is decisive in many ways.

After some gut-wrenching delays the second group of thirteen hostages was freed and a group of forty-two Palestinians liberated. In addition to the Israelis, four foreign hostages were also freed. Two more identical swaps are expected before the ceasefire expires. Let us hope for additional days of ceasefire, with the liberation of ten hostages for each peaceful day. It is difficult to imagine a resumption of hostilities with such massive civilian presence all around. The result could be a humanitarian disaster. Israel should find other ways to deal with Hamas, like liquidating its top leadership.

Sunday, November 26

Fourteen Israeli and three foreign hostages are being liberated today. Among the Israeli children liberated, there is four-year-old Abigail Eden from Kfar Aza, whose parents were murdered on October 7. Her father protected her with his body. He was killed and she was kidnapped and taken to Gaza. Her two little brothers hid in a closet for ten hours before they dared to phone for help. The grandparents will be their family.

President Biden spoke of Abigail in very moving terms: "Thank God that Abigail is home. I wish I were there to embrace her," he declared. He also talked to the grandparents. His support of Israel is genuine and, of course, of utmost importance.

Biden spoke with Netanyahu. Both seem to accept Hamas's demand to prolong the truce, which will allow them to liberate all the hostages and bring essential humanitarian aid to the enclave. Does it mean the end of the war? It looks that way, although in the long run Hamas may try again.

Tomorrow there will be a cabinet session about a partial allocation of the budget for 2023. Netanyahu and Smotrich want to keep intact the "coalition moneys" that were decided upon before the war, with billions for Orthodox education and the settlements, while Benny Gantz wants the whole budget to be devoted to war-related expenditures and help for the communities that had to be evacuated. In a letter to Netanyahu, Gantz made clear that if his demand was rejected, his party would have to consider its next steps.

Some 100,000 people marched in London against antisemitism. It was high time.

Monday, November 27

Eleven more Israeli hostages should be liberated today, but again there seem to be some difficulties. The Egyptians are optimistic, the Israelis less so. It seems, however, after hours of uncertainty, that the hostages will be released as initially foreseen. Six citizens of Thailand will also be released. There are negotiations for a prolongation of the ceasefire. Yet the mutual hatred between both sides is such that a resumption of hostilities is only a matter of time. Where is the kind of leader that Yitzhak Rabin was? What we have now is a self-centered trickster.

According to American and Qatari sources, after today's exchange, the ceasefire will be prolonged by two days, which means the release of twenty more hostages. Today's exchange almost didn't take place, as Israel refused to accept the initial Hamas proposal that included nine children and two older women but not the children's mothers. Finally an agreement was reached, thanks to President Biden's energetic intervention: the two elderly women were replaced by two of the children's mothers.

It is hard to believe that after prolonging the ceasefire for two more days, the war will resume and some 160 hostages will still be in the hands of Hamas. This will cause serious turmoil in Israel, and Netanyahu certainly doesn't want that. President Biden will put a lot of pressure on Israel and Arab states to get a further prolongation. That could also help his reelection in due course.

Benny Gantz and all members of his National Unity Party voted against the budget for 2023, supported by Netanyahu and Smotrich. Netanyahu also went from one Likud member of Knesset to the another to promise that he will make sure no Palestinian state sees the light of day.

Today, I feel shame. Yes, shame. The unit of the army I was a proud member of, the famous Unit 8200, which should have been the first to warn that something was happening on the other side on October 7, was probably asleep: instead of warning hours ahead of the attack, they mumbled something at 8:30 in the morning, some two hours after the attack. The whole intelligence force was a disgrace on that crucial day.

Tuesday, November 28

Further information about the complete unpreparedness of the army on October 7: the head of intelligence was on vacation in Eilat, and the head of the air force not asked to participate in a perfunctory phone conference with the chief of staff as vague indications came in about something happening in the South. This shows that the failure was not one of intelligence only, but one of the commanders of many branches of the IDF, from the very top.

The chief of staff said as much: "The army and the intelligence failed on October 7, but it isn't right for officers to deal with their responsibility today," he declared during a visit to the Northern Command.

The *New York Times* today published an article detailing the horrendous conditions in which the inhabitants of the northern part of the enclave moved to the South. I do think at times that Israel engages in such massive destruction because it is the most obvious way of getting at Hamas's tunnels and their concealment behind civilian structures. The pity of it all!

The transfer of ten adult female hostages has started. The head of the CIA, the head of Mossad, and the head of Egyptian intelligence are all in Doha to discuss turning the partial truce into a permanent ceasefire that would allow the return of all hostages.

The cabinet is meeting. I guess that they will decide to agree to prolong the truce and a return of as many hostages as possible. This is probably the American wish.

Wednesday, November 29

It seems that the truce will be prolonged by several more days. In the meantime, hostages are being liberated and so are Palestinian prisoners. Humanitarian aid is rushed into Gaza. In other terms, the US is setting the tone.

Horrible news: the Bibes family hostages, a baby of ten months, a boy of four, and their mother, cannot be released: they are dead, says Hamas. It may be psychological terror, as there is no proof. The IDF tries to find out.

Nine-year-old Emily Hand, who was also taken hostage on October 7, was released after fifty days. According to her father, Emily now speaks only in whispers. The little girl can no longer speak otherwise.

Secretary of State Blinken is in Israel once more. It is probable that the truce will be prolongated for a few days. Netanyahu declares that the fighting will resume after the release of the hostages and that that is also the cabinet's position. Sure, but it is probably not President Biden's idea. Actually, American officials are warning Israel about the scope of further fighting in the South of the enclave.

Thursday, November 30

Two Hamas terrorists killed four people at a bus station in Jerusalem and were shot dead. Negotiations about another exchange of Israeli hostages for Palestinian prisoners are beginning, but it doesn't seem that the ceasefire will hold much longer.

The coalition government does not enforce any sanctions regarding settler violence against Palestinians in the occupied West Bank. The perpetrators should be put on trial like any other criminals and punished according to the law. Ben-Gvir and his party would oppose this, of course, and probably so would Smotrich. Isn't it high time to get rid of these two? As Netanyahu would probably oppose any disruption of his coalition, he should also be ousted as soon as possible. The trouble is that a change of government in wartime is hardly feasible. Secretary of State Blinken discussed the settler violence with Mahmoud Abbas, and agreed that punishment was necessary.

The ceasefire will be extended through today and will bring the release of ten more women hostages and the liberation of thirty Palestinian prisoners. This is the penultimate release of female hostages under the existing conditions. After tomorrow, the group of hostages should include older Israeli males; Hamas may ask for the liberation of more prisoners for the release of each male hostage and that may put an end to the negotiations and the ceasefire. The Americans seem to understand the Israeli rationale for a resumption of the fighting but insist on the need to spare civilian lives as much as possible and allow for the continuation of humanitarian aid for Gaza.

There is a growing possibility that under pressure from within the administration, President Biden will have to put tougher conditions on its military assistance to Israel. From the outset, and more so as time goes by, Israel has been losing the fight for world opinion. In part, the massive bombing used by the IDF led to this and, in part, the upsurge of antisemitism, linked to hatred of Israel, has had an immense amplifying effect. It is angering and very sad to see this despicable fanaticism spread far and wide.

The liberation of hostages is taking place. Tomorrow the negotiations and decisions will be much more difficult.

The situation is unclear: on the one hand, fighting has resumed on both sides, but is relatively low key; on the other hand, there is still talk of continuing negotiations.

The horrendous failure in IDF readiness before October 7 comes to light more and more starkly. According to the *New York Times*, the IDF had obtained a forty-page document with the title "Jericho Wall" describing in exact detail the Hamas attack plan—a year before it happened. It was dismissed as being beyond Hamas's capabilities. A few months later, a noncommissioned officer of Intelligence Unit 8200 repeated the warnings in full detail and again the warning was dismissed. When she didn't back down and repeated her warning once more, the commander of the Gaza area put an end to it. All of this is being discussed in Israel these days and is not considered fake news. It is not clear whether Netanyahu was informed of "Jericho Wall" or not. In any case, the dismissal of these warnings did perfectly fit with his theory about Hamas being merely interested in economic advantages and nothing more.

Apparently, Unit 8200 has brought in psychologists to investigate what went wrong with the group. It is clearly suffering from excessive homogeneity, collective narcissism, and fear of rocking the boat. My recollections are from the early 1950s, when the unit still went under the name Intelligence 2, but I can at least confirm the extreme homogeneity of that part of the unit I served in. But as far as I remember, it wasn't so in the case of other sections. In any event, much will have to change in the IDF in general.

One hundred and three hostages have been released; 145, mostly men, remain in captivity. A US spokesman declared that the president was intent on continuing the ceasefire and on the release of further hostages. According to the spokesman, Hamas was responsible for the resumption of the fighting because it wasn't able to deliver a list of further hostages for release.

But it's only on Israel that the US can put pressure. When being told by the war cabinet that eradicating Hamas could take months, Secretary of State Blinken supposedly answered: "I don't think you have the credit for that."

Israel is apparently circulating a map of the enclave among Arab countries, with the indication of a demilitarized zone that should separate Gaza from Israel as the basis for a postwar agreement. Some Arab countries have rejected it, but others are ready to take it into consideration.

It is very hard for me to read the individual testimonies of ordinary Palestinians in the areas that are presently attacked. People have nowhere to go, and where they are, they live in horrible conditions. Is there no other way of getting at Hamas?

Saturday, December 2

Nowadays, Israeli kids are unavoidably exposed to short films about the atrocities committed by Hamas on October 7, which are all over the internet. Naturally, they are deeply affected, often traumatized, by this and by the pervasive sense of danger. How do parents deal with the traumas of their children, how do they answer their anxious questions? But I am also told that there has never been such readiness to enlist, even among people who needn't do so. On the one hand, a heightened sense of insecurity, on the other hand, an uncommon readiness to confront it.

In an interesting, perhaps last, interview, Kissinger expressed his skepticism regarding the two-state solution. Gaza could have been a model for the two-state solution, after it had been vacated by Israel in 2005, but instead became what it became. Kissinger saw no feasible solution other than having Jordan rule the West Bank. In my opinion, the former secretary of state's skepticism has good ground, but his solution is questionable. It is anybody's guess whether Jordan would accept the poisoned gift of a West Bank, with its extremists. As for Gaza, what would happen to it? I repeat that the only reasonable solution, after a lengthy de-escalation process under a Palestinian authority, with control of security by an international body in which the US would have a major role, is the setting up of an independent Palestinian state.

Why do I believe that a Palestinian state can eventually see the light of day? Because there manifestly is a national feeling among Palestinians, a feeling strong enough to preclude the acceptance of foreign rule, either Jordanian or Egyptian, not to mention Israeli.

The major obstacles will be Palestinian extremism (Hamas) and Israeli extremism (the settlers). I am told that Ben-Gvir makes sure that weapons are being distributed to the settlers "for their defense." Five hundred thousand settlers armed to the teeth will make any de-escalation process lengthy and difficult, with, from the outset, an exterritorial status for the settlements. A further obstacle may be the overall shift in Israeli politics from the center-left to the center-right, which means that there is very little support for the creation of a Palestinian state.

One of the Houthis' enemies organized an explosion in a shed where they keep armaments. Nonetheless, Israel's main shipping company redirected all its traffic around the Cape of Good Hope. That will lead to a serious increase in prices for a whole range of commodities.

Sunday, December 3

Let's try to get a picture of the overall situation as seen from Israel. Internally, we have a population that has experienced shocking events, that is in part traumatized, but which nonetheless overcame previous deep divisions and is ready to volunteer for service beyond expectations. Yet it is not clear how far this same population is confident in its political and military leadership. Probably, the population bears with the leadership because the country is at war. The leadership itself is deeply divided: Netanyahu hates Defense Minister Gallant; Gallant keeps close to Gantz and as far away from Netanyahu as possible. The extremists Ben-Gvir and Smotrich know that their time is limited and try to accumulate as many advantages as possible. Mainly, the PM holds the army command responsible for October 7 and deftly alludes to its responsibility for the catastrophe whenever he has the chance. Yet most of the population knows that he is the main culprit and that, at the first real opportunity, he has to go.

Externally, Israel is on the eve of a new offensive in Gaza-South, which according to the IDF may take months. However, the US is not ready to give it months—possibly weeks, at most. World opinion will become increasingly hostile as time goes by and the situation becomes more dire for the civilian population of Gaza. Israel may have to stop its offensive without achieving its aims: defeating Hamas, putting an end to its presence in Gaza, and retrieving the Israeli hostages. At the same time, the Jewish state is fighting Hezbollah in the North and is threatened by the Houthis along the Red Sea. As for the West Bank, it is a volcano waiting to erupt. Over all of these threats hovers the shadow of Iran, held back only by the presence in the region of the United

States. For Israel, internally and externally, this is a war for its very existence.

Incidentally, there is something strangely similar between October 6, 1973, and October 7, 2023: our hubris, the sense, in the IDF and Israeli society at large, that the Arabs are incapable . . . in the first case, incapable of overcoming the fortifications that we built on our side of the Canal; in the second case, incapable of such an attack as the one described in the warning documents. We have probably been healed of this disastrous sense of superiority in regard to our neighbors.

Notwithstanding this overall bleak forecast, there are segments within Israeli society that inspire confidence and hope. I became more aware of these bright spots as I heard details from visitors, mainly over the last few weeks. This was indeed a chapter over which I had no clear information previously and which could be summed up as follows. What did actually function on October 7, and during the days and weeks that followed, when many state agencies and mainly the government itself were paralyzed? Who brought help where it was most needed, and saved people in many cases? Those segments of civil society and the networks of volunteers they set up during the demonstrations of the preceding months against the government's attempts to overthrow the country's legal system. These same networks went into action on "Black Saturday," sending help to those people trapped in the villages and kibbutzim on the Gaza border, literally fighting in places that saw no other armed forces, taking care of inhabitants who needed it most and helping them in the most diverse ways. These are the unsung heroes of Israel in its darkest days, and they will possibly set the country on its feet again.

Monday, December 4

The IDF is near Khan Yunis. The war goes on and the population of southern Gaza is its most immediate victim. As today's *Haaretz* reminded those readers who needed reminding, Secretary of State Blinken warned us that military operations in the South of the enclave should not lead to the scale of civilian deaths caused by operations in the North. The US is the only power still supporting Israel. If we disregard Blinken's warning, we shall soon have to bear the consequences. Moreover, has the IDF forgotten the slogan it was proud of: "the purity of arms"? It may belong to a world without Hamas, but Israel has to fight Hamas, without in any way being infected by its brutality and its total lack of humaneness.

According to US sources, a rocket fired by Hamas at the outset of the war hit a military base where Israel keeps some of its nuclear missiles. A fire started at the base but did not reach the missiles. In any case, the warheads are kept somewhere else. Also according to US sources, Israel has installed five pumps capable of filling the Hamas tunnels with thousands of gallons of seawater, which would compel its fighters to abandon their underground hideouts but would also threaten the water supply of the Gaza population. According to the same sources, Israel has not yet decided to activate the pumps.

Hamas keeps ten women hostages, who according to Israel are alive. If Hamas agrees to liberate these women, Israel will be ready for another pause in the fighting to discuss all other categories of hostages (older men, wounded ones, men of military service age, etc.) to be released in exchange for Palestinians kept in Israeli prisons.

Tuesday, December 5

Today, the US decided not to grant visas to settlers convicted of violence against Palestinians. Although quite a few are Americans, this certainly won't deter them.

This morning in Israel, a very painful meeting took place between women who are released hostages and the war cabinet. The women are afraid that measures taken by the IDF to neutralize the tunnels will result in the killing of their loved ones, who are held in those tunnels. Netanyahu, instead of talking to them in a compassionate way, as their situation demanded, read them a declaration prepared ahead of time.

Wednesday, December 6

The IDF is considering the disbanding of the settler unit "Sfar Hamidbar" (Desert Frontier), which was set up some years ago, due to its being the source of repeated violence against Palestinians and left-wing activists.

The battle for Khan Yunis, the main city in the South of Gaza, is continuing. The war may drag on for weeks, if not more. Israel is trying to get at Yahya Sinwar and Mohammed Deif, the two top figures of Hamas in Gaza, so far without results. In the meantime, the civilian population is in dire straits, notwithstanding the aid daily reaching the enclave. For the time being, the US doesn't lean too heavily on Israel, but how long will American support continue before the president pressures Netanyahu for operational limitations and especially on postwar arrangements?

Today Mahmoud Abbas, the old and corrupt head of the Palestinian Authority, announced that he was ready to take over the government of Gaza after the war. Netanyahu responded that this wouldn't happen as long as he is prime minister.

We are not so far along yet. Netanyahu announced that Sinwar's house had been taken, but Sinwar himself is in one of the tunnels. I wonder whether Hamas can be entirely eliminated; as long as it cannot fight or govern, we should be satisfied. Israel's main task is not only to win this war in military terms, but to get a long-lasting peace. This will not necessarily imply Abbas's governing of the enclave; there are other possible formulas, but it will mean a Palestinian state on the horizon. That necessarily means a change of government, without the extremists and without the man who called on them to save his own skin: Netanyahu.

Let me get back for a moment to antisemitism, the real stuff. A few weeks ago, I wrote that I had started my life under the cloud of antisemitism and that I would end it under the same cloud. Actually, this is absolutely not the same cloud, thank God. Let me get back to April 1939, when my parents and I arrived, as hounded Jews, in Paris from Prague, where I was born, and which had just been occupied by the Germans. From my parents' letters I can follow the hours, days, and weeks they went and queued at the Préfecture de Police to get an authorization to stay in Paris, then the months they each spent learning a trade to earn a living (while I was in a children's home). My mother became a beautician, which was useful for two more years, while we lived in central France, having escaped, once more, from a Paris occupied by the Germans. My father, who was an insurance company lawyer in Prague, learned to make cheese in the hope of obtaining a visa for Canada, which he never got; he ultimately gave German lessons. What did they both hope for and never receive? A visa (immigration certificate) for Palestine, where, as my father wrote in one of his letters, one feels like a free person, notwithstanding all the difficulties. They never reached Palestine. They were murdered in Auschwitz. This was the antisemitism that was. Palestine as a hope, and Israel as a reality, are the justification for the existence of a Jewish state on the land of Israel. For me, it is the only valid and fully convincing one, on condition that we show justice to the people we dispossessed and share the land with them. Otherwise, in one form or another, there will always be some kind of opposition, some kind of resistance to our presence. Let's not fool ourselves.

Under US pressure, the Israeli cabinet agreed to allow more fuel to be delivered to the enclave. It seems that the president and an important part of the administration are getting impatient with what they consider as insufficient Israeli efforts to alleviate the sufferings of the population.

Thursday, December 7

Yair Golan, a former general, who was at some point deputy chief of staff, is entering politics and wants to revive the Israeli left, which certainly needs a new life. To my mind, he has the right ideas, but Israeli politics have seen many bright and courageous beginners. Let us wish him good luck!

The son of the former chief of staff and present member of the war cabinet, Gadi Eisenkot, has fallen in Gaza today.

For the first time, the Israeli television has shown images of tens, maybe hundreds, of Hamas prisoners. Also, today was the quietest day since October 7 in terms of rockets fired at Israel from the enclave. Does this signal the beginning of the end? I do not believe that this is possible without Deif and certainly Sinwar being caught or killed.

We received an email today from people we have known for some years and whom we considered as friends. The wife, who wrote, expostulates on the horrible carnage perpetrated by the IDF in Gaza. We didn't get a word from her after October 7, nor since, about the Israelis massacred or taken hostage. In situations like this, many so-called friendships are put to the test and shown for what they are.

Friday, December 8

According to well-informed Israeli sources, President Biden wants the IDF to complete its operations by the end of the year. Secretary-General António Gutteres will use Article 99 of the UN Charter in a vote of the Security Council to put an end to the operations in the enclave before the "occurrence of a humanitarian catastrophe." The article has not been used since the Bangladesh war, fifty years ago.

The United States applied its veto, Great Britain abstained, and thirteen countries voted for the resolution. It shows that Israel is now fighting on borrowed time, until December 31.

Al Arabiya, the TV network of the UAE, showed an elderly Palestinian woman shouting that Hamas was stealing the humanitarian aid arriving in the enclave and hoarding it in its tunnels. "Shoot me if you want," she added. Apparently, as the fighting in Khan Yunis goes on, a new set of negotiations is being planned, with Egypt in the main mediating role: Hamas would release the women and children it is still holding as hostages in exchange for a given number of Palestinian prisoners. There is no doubt that the hostages are a major asset in the entire Hamas strategy.

Saturday, December 9/Sunday, December 10

Netanyahu will do everything to keep his hard-right coalition in power. He now plays the role of tough guy; he doesn't miss an opportunity of being photographed in uniform, with troops; he may reject Biden's deadline and show his "mettle" by pursuing the war in Gaza against the whole world, when the reasonable aim is not to eradicate Hamas but to make sure that it does not rule Gaza any more. He will do anything to push away the trial for corruption that awaits him. His son Yair has received a diplomatic passport . . .

It occurs to me that Netanyahu may wish to contribute to Biden's difficulties with the progressives and to Trump's electoral victory.

The US administration bypasses Congress and sells 14,000 rounds of tank ammunition to Israel in an emergency deal.

The war with Hezbollah is heating up. It seems that from the outset, Defense Minister Gallant has been intent to fight the Iranian-led organization with full force. Why? In the South, the suffering of the civilian population is not abating.

Monday, December 11

Today the details of Netanyahu's enormous strategic mistake regarding Hamas came to light in the *New York Times*. For years, the PM encouraged Qatari payments to Gaza to keep the enclave quiet and build up a counterweight to the Palestinian Authority in the West Bank: that is, to hinder the possibility of a Palestinian state. Of course, part of the money went to Hamas and financed its military preparations. Avigdor Lieberman, for a while defense minister in Netanyahu's government, saw and warned of the danger, and then resigned when no policy change occurred. The financing of Gaza went on, and at some stage money was simply transferred in Qatari suitcases, with Israeli encouragement. Indirectly, it continued to finance Hamas.

As Curd Jürgens is quoted at the beginning of this diary: "One cannot eat as much as one wishes to . . ." Revelation follows revelation, each more outrageous than the last, and the war goes on without an immediate end in sight. It may be time to conclude this text.

In the Guise of a Conclusion

I admit that the coming days are hidden from me in deep fog. Let me nonetheless attempt to say how I imagine a possible future. Hopefully, a better future. Of course, it could be that the war will end without the destruction of Hamas, as a result of American and other pressure on Israel, or simply because this kind of terrorist organization cannot be destroyed under existing conditions, be it to save the hostages, or because of the impossibility of eradicating the tunnels, or because of the conditions of warfare in such a densely populated environment, or as a result of all these factors. This would imply difficult times ahead for Israel, a sort of permanent state of alert that could last for years, due to what happened on October 7, notwithstanding all the international guarantees that could be given.

The other possibility looks as follows. The leadership of Hamas, ensconced underground up to now, will probably escape (or be allowed to escape) to some Islamic country. The major questions pertain to what comes afterward. When the fighting dies down, the main problems return to the fore.

As far as Israel is concerned, there is one most urgent question: where are the hostages? They have to be released immediately, maybe as a guarantee of safe escape for the leadership of Hamas. Then, and only then, can the other issues be discussed.

First among those, how will massive help be most urgently extended to the desperate Gaza civilians, and then what countries and agencies will take over the physical reconstruction of the enclave? Then, and for Israel this is a major issue, which form of governance and security control will ensure that Hamas won't be able to reappear in Gaza and become a threat once more?

The last question is of course the most difficult one. There will be debates about the composition of an international controlling force to be stationed in the enclave, about the width of a demilitarized zone between Israel and Gaza, etc. The main issue will be that of the long-term political future of the enclave, together with the West Bank. The answer will depend on the government of Israel existing at that time.

The present coalition will oppose any solution that includes, eventually, a Palestinian state, even if it means a clash with the United States. But the coalition may be doomed at the war's end. Netanyahu is held responsible for October 7 and many previous mistakes, and there is a good chance that he will be swept out of power. Last July, in my concluding note to the first part of this diary, I mentioned that a Gantz-Lapid coalition was not obvious, given the personal hostility between them, but now a Gantz-Eisenkot government could be on the cards. Whether a government like that would accept the idea of a Palestinian state is not certain either. It may possibly accept one as a long-term project. To my mind, as I have repeatedly stated here, this is the only long-term solution that has a chance to hold and to ensure peace and security for all.

Actually, I am only imagining the optimistic outcome. In this conflict, one cannot unfortunately avoid looking also at the other possibility. Even if (and this is a big "if ") a future Israel government were to accept the idea of a Palestinian state, one cannot exclude a refusal by the Palestinians to accept the presence of a Jewish state on their land. This was Moshe Dayan's vision of the future which, it will be remembered, he expressed in his speech at the tomb of a friend killed by Palestinian infiltrators from Gaza, in the early 1950s, and which he repeated to me in our conversation in 1966, as I mentioned in the first part of this diary. Over the years, the Palestinian "refusal front" has become militarily stronger, particularly with Iran's help, as we see at this very moment. Its aim is not a compromise around the two-state solution, but the eradication of the Jewish state. This feeds the extremists on the Israeli side and the endless cycle of violence. As things stand, because both sides hope to overcome the other in the end, the cycle may be endless indeed. In this scenario, only international pressure on both sides may ultimately lead to a compromise.

As you may see, I am pushed back (or push myself back) to some optimism, but then, to be safe I must admit my inability to dispel the fog I mentioned at the beginning of this conclusion and again paraphrase General de Gaulle: "I addressed the complicated Middle East with ideas that were (too) simple."

Acknowledgments

I wish to thank my friends and colleagues Carlo Ginzburg and Sanjay Subrahmanyam for having introduced me to Tom Hazeldine at Verso. I wish to thank Verso for agreeing to publish this book, notwithstanding our, hopefully small, differences of opinion. I wish to thank Amir Kenan, editor and writer in the School of Professional Studies at Columbia University, for his initial editing of my text. I also wish to thank my son David for his careful reading of the text and his remarks. Finally, I wish to express my gratitude to my wife, Orna Kenan, for her constant support throughout a work that often meant, for both of us as Israelis, dealing with painful news. This book is dedicated to her.